In Search of Politics

In Search of Politics

———

Zygmunt Bauman

Polity Press

First published in 1999 by Polity Press
in association with Blackwell Publishers Ltd.

Reprinted 2000

Editorial office:
Polity Press
65 Bridge Street
Cambridge CB2 1UR, UK

Marketing and production:
Blackwell Publishers Ltd
108 Cowley Road
Oxford OX4 1JF, UK

ISBN 0–7456–2171–6
ISBN 0–7456–2172–4 (pbk)

A catalogue record for this book is available from the British Library.

Typeset in 11 on 13 pt Sabon
by SetSystems, Saffron Walden, Essex
Printed in Great Britain by T. J. International, Padstow, Cornwall.

This book is printed on acid-free paper.

Contents

3 In Search of Vision   154

The second reformation and the emergence of modular man ·
Tribe, nation and republic · Liberal democracy and the
republic · A parting of the ways · The political economy of
uncertainty · The cause of equality in the uncertain world ·
The case for a basic income · Recalling universalism from
exile · Multiculturalism – or cultural polyvalence? · Living
together in the world of differences

Acknowledgements

It has been ten years since I first was offered the benefit of David Roberts's insightful, indefatigable and emphathetic editorial co-operation. I cannot refrain from using this occasion to thank him for all he has done to smooth up the communication between the author and his readers.

The author and publisher are grateful to The Guardian for permission to reprint extracts from articles by Decca Aitkenhead from *The Guardian* 23.1.98 and 24.4.98, both copyright © The Guardian 1998.

Introduction

Beliefs do not need to be coherent in order to be believed. Beliefs that tend to be believed these days – our beliefs – are no exception. Indeed, we consider the case of human freedom, at least in 'our part' of the world, to be open and shut, and (barring minor corrections here and there) resolved to the fullest conceivable satisfaction; at any rate, we do not feel the need (again barring occasional minor irritations) to take to the streets to claim and exact more freedom or better freedom than we feel we already have. But, on the other hand, we tend to believe equally firmly that there is little we can change – singly, severally, or all together – in the way the affairs of the world are running or are being run; and we believe too that, were we able to make a change, it would be futile, even unreasonable, to put our heads together to think of a different world from the one there is and to flex our muscles to bring it about if we consider it better than the one we are in. How these two beliefs can be held at the same time would be a mystery to any person trained in logical thinking. If freedom has been won, how does it come about that human ability to imagine a better world and to do something to make it better was not among the trophies of victory? And what sort of freedom is it that discourages imagination and tolerates the impotence of free people in matters which concern them all?

The two beliefs fit each other ill – but holding both of them is not a sign of our logical ineptitude. The two beliefs are by no means fanciful. There is more than enough in our shared experience to support each of the two. We are quite realistic and rational when believing what we do. And so it is important to know why the world we live in keeps sending us such evidently contradictory signals. And it is also important to know how we can live with that contradiction; and, moreover, why most of the time we do not notice it and are not particularly worried when we do.

Why is it important to know that? Would anything change for the better once we obtained this kind of knowledge? This, to be sure, is by no means certain. An insight into what makes things to be as they are may prompt us to throw in the towel just as much as it may spur us into action. The knowledge of how the complex and not readily visible social mechanisms which shape our condition work cuts notoriously both ways. Time and again, it prompts two quite distinct uses, which Pierre Bourdieu aptly called 'cynical' and 'clinical'. Knowledge may be used 'cynically': the world being what it is, let me think of a strategy which will allow me to exploit its rules to my best advantage; whether the world is fair or unjust, likeable or not, is neither here nor there. When it is used 'clinically', the same knowledge of how society works may help you and me to fight more effectively what we see as improper, harmful or offending our moral sense. By itself, knowledge does not determine which of the two uses we resort to. This is, ultimately, a matter of our own choice. But without that knowledge there would be no choice to start with. With knowledge, free men and women have at least some chance to exercise their freedom.

But what is there to know? It is with this question that this book tries to come to grips. The answer it comes up with is, roughly, that the growth of individual freedom may coincide with the growth of collective impotence in as far as the bridges between private and public life are dismantled or were never built to start with; or, to put it differently, in as far as there is no easy and obvious way to translate private worries into public issues and, conversely, to discern and pinpoint public issues in private troubles. And that in our kind of society the bridges are by and large absent and the art of translation seldom practised in public. In the absence of bridges, the sporadic communication between the private and public shores is maintained with the help of balloons which have the vexing habit of collapsing or exploding the moment they land – and, more often than not, before reaching their targets. While the art of translation is in its present sorry state, the sole grievances aired in public are sackfuls of private agonies and anxieties which, however, do not turn into public issues just for being on public display.

In the absence of strong and permanent bridges and with translating skills unpractised or altogether forgotten, private troubles and pains do not add up and can hardly condense into common causes. What, under the cicumstances, can bring us together? Sociality, so to speak, is free-floating, seeking in vain solid ground in which to anchor, a visible-to-all target on which to converge, companions with which to close ranks. There is a lot of it around – wandering, blundering, unfocused. Lacking in regular outlets, our sociality tends to be released in spectacular one-off explosions – short lived, as all explosions are.

Occasion for release is sometimes given by carnivals of compassion and charity; sometimes by outbursts of beefed-up aggression against a freshly discovered public enemy (that is, against someone whom most members of the public may recognize as their private enemy); at other times by an event most people feel strongly about at the same time and so synchronize their joy, as in the case of the national team winning the World Cup, or their sorrow, as in the case of the tragic death of Princess Diana. The trouble with all these occasions is, though, that they run out of steam quickly: once we return to our daily business things by and large come back, unscathed, to where they started. And when the dazzling flash of togetherness goes out, the loners wake up just as lonely as before, while the shared world, so brightly illuminated just a moment ago, seems if anything still darker than before. And after the explosive discharge there is little energy left for the limelights to be lit again.

The chance of changing this condition hangs on the *agora* – the space neither private nor public, but more exactly private and public at the same time. The space where private problems meet in a meaningful way – that is, not just to draw narcissistic pleasures or in search of some therapy through public display, but to seek collectively managed levers powerful enough to lift individuals from their privately suffered misery; the space where such ideas may be born and take shape as the 'public good', the

'just society' or 'shared values'. The trouble is, though, that little
has been left today of the old-style private/public spaces, whereas
new ones able to replace them are nowhere in sight. The old
agoras have been taken over by enterprising developers and
recycled into theme parks, while powerful forces conspire with
political apathy to refuse building permits for new ones.

The most conspicuous feature of contemporary politics, Cornelius Castoriadis told Daniel Mermet in November 1996, is its
insignificance, 'Politicians are impotent . . . They no more have a
programme. Their purpose is to stay in office.' Change of governments – of 'political camps' even – is no watershed; a ripple at
most on the surface of a stream flowing unstoppably, monoton-
ously, with dull determination, in its own direction, pulled by its
own momentum. A century ago the ruling political formula of
liberalism was a defiant and impudent ideology of the 'great leap
forward'. Nowadays, it is no more than a self-apology for surrender: 'This is not the best of imaginable worlds, but the only real
one. Besides, all alternatives are worse, must be worse and would
be shown to be worse if tried in practice.' Liberalism today boils
down to the simple 'no alternative' credo. If you wish to find out
what the roots of the growing political apathy are, you may as
well look no further. This politics lauds conformity and promotes
conformity. And conformity could as well be a do-it-yourself job;
does one need politics to conform? Why bother with politicians
who, whatever their hue, can promise nothing but more of the
same?

The art of politics, if it happens to be *democratic* politics, is
about dismantling the limits to citizens' freedom; but it is also
about self-limitation: about making citizens free in order to enable
them to set, individually and collectively, their own, individual
and collective, limits. That second point has been all but lost. All
limits are off-limits. Any attempt at self-limitation is taken to be
the first step on the road leading straight to the gulag, as if there
was nothing but the choice between the market's and the government's dictatorship over needs – as if there was no room for the
citizenship in other form than the consumerist one. It is this form
(and only this form) which financial and commodity markets
would tolerate. And it is this form which is promoted and
cultivated by the governments of the day. The sole grand narrative
left in the field is that of (to quote Castoriadis again) the accu-

mulation of junk and more junk. To that accumulation, there must be no limits (that is, all limits are seen as anathema and no limits would be tolerated). But it is that accumulation from which the self-limitation has to start, if it is to start at all.

But the aversion to self-limitation, generalized conformity and the resulting insignificance of politics have their price – a steep price, as it happens. The price is paid in the currency in which the price of wrong politics is usually paid – that of human sufferings. The sufferings come in many shapes and colours, but they may be traced to the same root. And these sufferings have a self-perpetuating quality. They are the kind of sufferings which stem from the malfeasance of politics, but also the kind which are the paramount obstacle to its sanity.

The most sinister and painful of contemporary troubles can be best collected under the rubric of *Unsicherheit* – the German term which blends together experiences which need three English terms – uncertainty, insecurity and unsafety – to be conveyed. The curious thing is that the nature of these troubles is itself a most powerful impediment to collective remedies: people feeling insecure, people wary of what the future might hold in store and fearing for their safety, are not truly free to take the risks which collective action demands. They lack the courage to dare and the time to imagine alternative ways of living together; and they are too preoccupied with tasks they cannot share to think of, let alone to devote their energy to, such tasks as can be undertaken only in common.

The extant political institutions, meant to assist them in the fight against insecurity, offer little help. In a fast globalizing world, where a large part of power, and the most seminal part, is taken out of politics, these institutions cannot do much to offer security or certainty. What they can do and what they more often than not are doing is to shift the scattered and diffuse anxiety to one ingredient of *Unsicherheit* alone – that of safety, the only field in which something can be done and seen to be done. The snag is, though, that while doing something effectively to cure or at least to mitigate insecurity and uncertainty calls for united action, most measures undertaken under the banner of safety are divisive; they sow mutual suspicion, set people apart, prompt them to sniff enemies and conspirators behind every contention or dissent, and in the end make the loners yet more lonely than before. Worst of all: while such measures come nowhere near hitting at the genuine source of anxiety, they use up all the energy these sources generate – energy which could be put to much more effective use if channelled into the effort of bringing power back into the politically managed public space.

This is one of the main reasons why there is such a meagre demand for private/public spaces; and why the few remaining ones are empty most of the time, and so the favourite target for downsizing, or better still phasing-out. Another reason for their shrinking and wilting is the blatant inconsequentiality of anything that may happen in them. Assuming for a moment that the extraordinary happened and private/public space was filled with citizens wishing to debate their values and discuss the laws which are there to guide them – where is the agency powerful enough to carry through their resolutions? The most powerful powers float or flow, and the most decisive decisions are taken in a space remote from the *agora* or even from the politically institutionalized public space; for the political institutions of the day, they are truly out of bounds and out of control. And so the self-propelling and self-reinforcing mechanism will go on self-propelling and self-reinforcing. The sources of *Unsicherheit* will not dry up, seeing to it that the daring and the resolve to challenge them would not be immaculately conceived; the real power will stay at a safe distance from politics and the politics will stay powerless to do what politics is expected to do: to demand from all and any form of human togetherness to justify itself in terms of human freedom to think and to act – and to ask them to leave the stage if they refuse or fail to do so.

A Gordian knot indeed – one that is too tangled and twisted to be neatly untied, and so can only be cut . . . The deregulation and privatization of insecurity, uncertainty and unsafety seem to hold the knot together and so to be the right spot to cut through, if one wants the rest of the loop to fall apart.

Easier said than done, to be frank. Attacking insecurity at its source is a daunting task, calling for nothing less than rethinking and renegotiating some of the most fundamental assumptions of the type of society currently in existence – assumptions holding all the faster for being tacit, invisible or unmentionable, beyond discussion or beyond dispute. As the late Cornelius Castoriadis put it – the trouble with our civilization is that it stopped questioning itself. No society which forgets the art of asking questions or allows this art to fall into disuse can count on finding answers to the problems that beset it – certainly not before it is too late and the answers, however correct, have become irrelevant. Fortunately for all of us, this need not happen – and being aware that it might happen is the warrant that it won't. This is where sociology enters the stage; it has a responsible role to play, and it would have no right to make excuses if it shed that responsibility.

The frame in which the entire argument of the book is inscribed is the idea that *individual liberty can be only a product of collective work* (can be only *collectively* secured and guaranteed). We move today though towards *privatization of the means to assure/insure/guarantee individual liberty* – and if this is a therapy for present ills, it is such a treatment which is bound to produce iatrogenic diseases of most sinister and atrocious kinds (mass poverty, social redundancy and ambient fear being most prominent among them). To make the present plight and the prospect of its repair more complex yet, we live also through a period of the privatization of utopia and of the models of the good (with the models of the 'good life' elbowing out, and cut off from, the model of the good society). The art of reforging private troubles into public issues is in danger of falling into disuse and being forgotten; private troubles tend to be defined in a way that renders exceedingly difficult their 'agglomeration', and thus their condensation into a political force. The argument of this book is an (admittedly inconclusive) struggle to make the translation possible again.

The changing meaning of politics is the topic of the first chapter; the troubles which beset the existing agencies of political action and the reasons for their falling effectiveness are discussed in the second; and the broad outlines of a vision which may guide the much-needed reform are sketched in the third. The prospects of ideology in a post-ideological world, of tradition in the post-traditional world, and of shared values in a society tormented by 'value crisis' are broached in separate sections.

Much of this book is contentious and meant to be such. The most controversial, though, are probably the issues discussed in the last chapter, and this for a double reason.

Visions born and floated in an autonomous society or a society aiming to become autonomous are and must be many and diverse, and so, were one to wish to avoid controversy, one would have to refrain from thinking of alternatives to the present – let alone alternatives arguably better than the present. (Evil, as we know, has its best friend in banality, while banality takes the routine for ultimate wisdom.) But what makes the chapter more controversial still, is that visions as such have nowadays fallen into disrepute. 'The end of history' is all the rage, and the most contentious issues that haunted our ancestors are commonly taken to have been settled, or treated as settled by not being noted (at any rate noticed *as problems*). We tend to be proud of what we perhaps should be ashamed of, of living in the 'post-ideological' or 'post-utopian' age, of not concerning ourselves with any coherent vision of the good society and of having traded off the worry about the public good for the freedom to pursue private satisfaction. And yet if we pause to think why that pursuit of happiness fails more often than not to bring about the results we hoped for, and why the bitter taste of insecurity makes the bliss less sweet than we had been told it would be – we won't get far without bringing back from exile ideas such as the public good, the good society, equity, justice and so on – such ideas that make no sense unless cared for and cultivated in company with others. Nor are we likely to get the fly of insecurity out of the ointment of individual freedom without resorting to politics, using the vehicle of political agency and charting the direction which that vehicle should follow.

Certain orientation points seem to be crucial when planning the itinerary. The third chapter focuses on three of them: the republican model of the state and of citizenship, a basic income as universal entitlement, and stretching the institutions of an autonomous society far enough to restore its enabling capacity – by catching up with powers that are at the moment exterritorial. All three points are discussed in order to provoke and foment deliberation, not to offer solutions – which in an autonomous society anyway can come only at the far end of, not at the beginning of, political action.

I happen to believe that questions are hardly ever wrong; it is the answers that might be so. I also believe, though, that refraining from questioning is the worst answer of all.

August 1998

1

In Search of Public Space

Commenting on the widely reported events triggered in three different towns of the West Country by the news that paedophile Sidney Cooke had been released from prison and returned home, Decca Aitkenhead,[1] a *Guardian* reporter blessed by a sociological sixth sense, of whose rich harvest we shall repeatedly avail ourselves here, observed:

> If there's one thing guaranteed to get people out on the streets today, it is the whispered arrival of a paedophile. The helpfulness of such protests is increasingly being questioned. What we haven't asked, however, is whether these protests actually have anything to do with paedophiles.

Aikenhead focused on one of these towns, Yeovil, where she found that the variegated crowd of grandmothers, teenagers, and businesswomen who had seldom, if ever, expressed any previous wish to engage in a public action had now laid protracted siege to the local police station, being not even sure that Cooke did indeed hide in the besieged building. Their ignorance concerning the facts of the matter took second place only to their determination to do something about them and to be seen to be doing it; and their determination gained enormously from the haziness of the facts. People who had all their lives steered clear of public protests now came, and stayed, and shouted 'Kill the bastard', and were prepared to keep vigil for as long as it took. Why? Were they after something other than the secure confinement of one public enemy whom they never saw and of whose whereabouts they were far from confident? Aitkenhead has an answer to that baffling question, and it is a convincing one.

> What Cooke offers, wherever he is, is a rare opportunity to really hate someone, loudly, publicly, and with absolute impunity. It is a matter of good and evil . . . and so a gesture against Cooke defines you as decent. There are very few groups of people you can respectably hate any more. Paedophiles are the very thing.

'At last I've found my cause', said the chief organizer of the protest, herself a woman with no previous experience of any public role. 'What Debra had probably found', comments Aitkenhead, 'is not "her cause", but common cause – the sensation of communal motivation.'

> Their demonstrations have shades of political rallies, religious ceremonies, union meetings – all those group experiences which used to define people's sense of selves, and which are no longer available to them. And so now [they] organise against paedophiles. In a few years, the cause will be something else.

A prowler around the house

Aitkenhead is right again: a shortage of new causes is a most unlikely prospect, and there will always be enough empty plots at the graveyard of old causes. But for the time being – for days, rather than years, allowing for the mind-boggling speed of the wear-and-tear of public scares and moral panics – the cause is Sidney Cooke. Indeed, he is an excellent cause to bring together people who seek an outlet for long-accumulated anxiety.

First, Cooke has a name attached to him: this makes him into a tangible target, which fishes him out of the pap of ambient fears and gives him a bodily reality few other fears possess; even if unseen, he still can be construed as a solid object that can be handled, tied down, locked up, neutered, even destroyed – unlike most threats, which tend to be disconcertingly diffuse, oozy, evasive, spilt all over the place, unpinpointable. Second, by a happy coincidence Cooke has been placed on a spot where private concerns and public issues meet; more precisely, his case is an alchemical crucible in which love for one's children – a daily experience, routine, yet private – can be miraculously transsubstantiated into a public spectacle of solidarity. Cooke has become a gangplank of sorts, however brittle and provisional, leading out of the prison of privacy. Last but not least, that gangplank is wide enough to allow a group, perhaps a massive one, escape; each lonely escapee is likely to be joined by other people escaping their own private prisons, and a community can be created just by using the same escape route and which will last as long as all feet are on the gangplank.

Politicians, people supposed to operate in the public space professionally (they have their offices there, or rather they call 'public' the space where their offices are), are hardly ever well prepared for the invasion by intruders; and inside the public space anyone without the right type of office, and who appears in the public space on anything other than an officially scripted, filed and stage-managed occasion and without invitation, is, by definition, an intruder. By these standards Sidney Cooke-bashers were, no doubt, intruders. Their presence inside the public space was from the start precarious. They therefore wished the legitimate inhabitants of the public space to acknowledge their presence and endorse its legitimacy.

Willie Horton had probably lost Michael Dukakis the American presidency. Before running for president, Dukakis served for ten years as governor of Massachusetts. He was one of the most vociferous opponents of the death penalty. He also thought prisons to be, predominantly, institutions of education and rehabilitation. He wished the penal system to restore to criminals their lost or forfeited humanity and prepare convicts for a 'return to the community': under his administration the inmates of state prisons were allowed home leaves. Willie Horton failed to return from one of those leaves. Instead, he raped a woman. This is what can be done to us all when the soft-hearted liberals are in charge, pointed out Dukakis's adversary, George Bush – a staunch advocate of capital punishment. The journalists pressed Dukakis: 'If Kitty, your wife, was raped, would you be in favour of capital punishment?' Dukakis insisted that he would not 'glorify violence'. He bade farewell to his presidency.

Victorious Bush went on to be defeated four years later by the governor of Arkansas, Bill Clinton. As governor, Clinton authorized the execution of a retarded man, Ricky Ray Rector. Some commentators think that just as Horton lost Dukakis his election, Rector won Clinton's. This is probably an exaggeration: Clinton did other things that also endeared him to 'middle America'. He promised to be tough on crime, to hire more policemen and to put more policemen on the beat, to increase the number of crimes punishable with death, to build more prisons and more secure prisons. Rector's contribution to Bill Clinton's success was merely to serve as the living (sorry: dead) proof that the future president meant business; with such a feather in Clinton's cap, 'middle America' could not but trust his words.

The duels at the top were replicated further down. Three candidates for the governorship of Texas used their allocated speech time at the party convention trying to outbid each other in their dedication to the death penalty. Mark White posed in front of the TV cameras surrounded by photographs of all the convicts who had been sent to the electric chair while he was governor. Not to be outdone, his competitor Jim Mattox reminded the electors that he personally supervised thirty-three executions. As it happened, both candidates found themselves outsmarted by a woman, Ann Richards, the vigour of whose pro-death-penalty rhetoric they obviously could not match, however strong their other credentials. In Florida the outgoing governor, Bob Martinez, made a spectacular come-back after a long period of losing steadily in popularity polls, once he reminded the electors that he had signed ninety decrees of execution. In California, the state which used to pride itself that it had not executed a single prisoner for a quarter of a century, Dianne Feinstein made her bid for office by declaring herself to be 'the only Democrat in favour of the death penalty'. In response the other competitor, John Van de Kamp, hastened to let it be known that though 'philosophically' he is against execution, which he considers 'barbaric', he would put his philosophy aside once elected governor. To prove the point, he had himself photographed at the opening of a state-of-the-art gas-chamber for future executions and announced that when in charge of the state Department of Justice he put forty-two criminals on Death Row. In the end the promise to betray his convictions did not help him. The electors (three-quarters of whom favoured the death penalty) preferred a believer – a convinced executioner.

For more than a decade now, promises to be tough on crime and to send more criminals to their death have figured matter-of-factly at the top of the electoral agenda, whatever the political denomination of the candidate. For current and aspiring politicians, the extension of the death penalty is the prize-winning ticket in the popularity lottery. Opposition to capital punishment means, on the contrary, a self-inflicted political death.

In Yeovil the vigilantes pressed for a meeting with their MP, Paddy Ashdown. He refused to give them the legitimation they sought. Being himself of an uncertain public-space position, and certainly not one of its appointed/elected managers, he could only embrace the protesters' cause at the expense of further jeopardizing his own public-space credentials. He chose to speak his mind, whatever he believed to be the word of truth, comparing the Cooke-bashers to 'lynch mobs' and resisting all pressures to endorse their actions and to put the stamp of a 'public issue' on their not quite clear private grievances.

Jack Straw, the Home Secretary, could not afford this sort of luxury. As one of the protest leaders declared, 'What we would like to do now is link up with other campaigns. There are lots of little voices in lots of areas around the country. If we can get a big voice things might move a bit quicker.' Such words portend an intention to settle in the public space for good; to claim a permanent voice in the way that space is administered. It must have sounded ominous to any politician currently in charge of the public space, though any seasoned politicians would know well that 'linking up campaigns' and 'connecting little voices' is neither easy to accomplish nor likely to happen; neither little (private) voices nor (local, one-issue) campaigns add up easily, and one could safely assume that this specific hope/intention to do so, like so many similar hopes and intentions before, would soon run its natural course, that is run aground, capsize, be abandoned and forgotten. Straw's problem boiled down to showing that the administrators of the public space do take the little voices seriously – that is, that they are willing to take measures which will make it unnecessary for the little voices to be voiced; and, hopefully, that they should be remembered for showing that willingness. And so Jack Straw, who in all probability shared privately Paddy Ashdown's publicly expressed opinion, said no more but that 'It is vital that people do not take the law into their own hands' (reminding us thereby that the law is meant to be handled by chosen hands only) and then went public, declaring that perhaps measures will be taken to 'keep dangerous criminals behind bars indefinitely'. It may be that Jack Straw hoped to be remembered as a caring/sharing, listening administrator of public space; the previously quoted protest leader, after all, passed her verdict on the non-cooperative Paddy Ashdown: 'I just hope that people don't have short memories when it comes to the election.'[2]

Perhaps (a big 'perhaps', given the vigilance of the European Court of Human Rights) the dangerous criminals (that is, whichever criminals happen to attract and focus upon themselves the public fears of danger) will be kept behind the bars 'indefinitely'; and yet getting them off the street and out of the headlines and the limelight will not make the fears, which made them the dangerous criminals they are in the first place, less indefinite and undefined as they are, as long as the reasons to be afraid persist and as long as the terrors they cause are suffered in solitude. Scared loners without a community will go on searching for a community without fears, and those in charge of the inhospitable public space will go on promising it. The snag is, though, that the only communities which the loners may hope to build and the managers of public space can seriously and responsibly offer are ones constructed of fear, suspicion and hate. Somewhere along the line, friendship and solidarity, once upon a time major community-building materials, became too flimsy, too rickety or too watery for the purpose.

Contemporary hardships and sufferings are fragmented, dispersed and scattered; and so is the dissent which they spawn. The dispersion of dissent, the difficulty of condensing it and anchoring it in a common cause and directing it against a common culprit, only makes the pains the more bitter. The contemporary world is a container full to the brim with free-floating fear and frustration desperately seeking outlets. Life is over-saturated with sombre apprehensions and sinister premonitions, all the more frightening for their non-specificity, blurred contours and hidden roots. As in the case of other over-saturated solutions, a speck of dust – a Sidney Cooke, for instance – is enough to trigger a violent condensation.

Twenty years ago (in *Double Business Bind*, Baltimore University Press, 1978) René Girard considered hypothetically what could have happened in equally hypothetical pre-social times when dissension was scattered throughout the population, and feud and violence, fed by the cut-throat competition for survival, tore communities apart or prevented their coming together. Trying to answer that question, Girard came forward with a self-consciously and deliberately mythological account of the 'birth of unity'. The decisive step, he ruminated, must have been the selection of a victim in whose killing, unlike other killings, *all* members of the population would take part, thereby becoming 'united in murder' by turning into helpers, accomplices or accessories after the fact. That spontaneous act of co-ordinated action had the potential of sedimenting the dispersed enmities and diffuse aggression as a clear division between propriety and impropriety, legitimate and illegitimate violence, innocence and guilt. It could bind the *solitary* (and frightened) beings into a *solidary* (and confident) community.

Girard's story is, let me repeat, a fable, an etiological myth, a story which does not pretend to historical truth, only to making sense of the unknown 'origins'. As Cornelius Castoriadis pointed out, the pre-social individual is, contrary to Aristotle, neither god nor beast, but a pure figment of philosophers' imaginations. Like other etiological myths, Girard's story does not tell us what actually did happen in the past; it is but an attempt to make sense out of the *current* presence of a phenomenon which is bizarre and difficult to comprehend, and to account for its continuous presence and rebirth. The true message of Girard's story is that whenever dissent is scattered and unfocused, and whenever mutual suspicion and hostility rule, the only way forward or back to communal solidarity, to a secure – because solidary – habitat, is to pick a joint enemy and to unite forces in an act of joint atrocity aimed at a common target. It is solely the community of accomplices which provides (as long as it lasts) a guarantee against the crime being named a crime and being punished accordingly. What the community will therefore not suffer lightly are such people as refuse to join the hue and cry, who by their refusal cast doubt on the righteousness of the act.

The cauldron of *Unsicherheit*

Exactly seventy years ago Sigmund Freud wrote *Das Unbehagen in der Kultur*, translated into English, somewhat awkwardly, under the title *Civilization and its Discontents*. In that seminal book Freud suggested that 'civilization' (what he meant, of course, was our, Western, *modern* civilization; seventy years ago the term 'civilization' seldom appeared in the plural – and it was only the Western type of existence that gave itself the name of 'civilization') is a trade-off: one cherished value is sacrificed for another, equally imperative and close to heart. We read in the English translation that the gift that civilization brings is security – security from the many dangers which come from nature, one's own body and other people. In other words, civilization offers freedom from fear, or at least makes the fears less awesome and intense than they would otherwise be. In exchange, however, civilization puts constraints – sometimes severe, as a rule oppressive, always irksome – on individual liberty. Not everything that their hearts desire are human beings allowed to pursue, and almost nothing can be pursued to the fullness of one's heart's desire. Instincts are kept within bounds or suppressed altogether, an unhappy condition – pregnant with psychic discomfort, neuroses and rebellion. The most common discontents and types of order-threatening behaviour stem, Freud implies, from sacrificing a lot of individual freedom for whatever we have gained, all together and each one of us, in terms of individual security.

I have suggested in my *Postmodernity and its Discontents* (Polity Press, 1997) that, were Freud writing his book seventy years later, he would probably need to reverse his diagnosis: the most common present-day human troubles and discontents are, like their predecessors, products of a trade-off, but this time it is security which is sacrificed day by day on the altar of ever-expanding individual freedom. On the way to whatever passes for greater individual liberty of choice and self-expression we have lost a good deal of that security which modern civilization supplied, and even more of the security it promised to supply; worse still, we have almost stopped hearing promises that the supply will be resumed, and instead hear more and more often that security goes against the grain of human dignity, that it is much too treacherous to be desired and much too dependency-breeding, addictive and altogether quagmire-ish to be cherished.

But what is it actually that we are told not to bewail, but which we miss nevertheless and the missing of which makes us anxious, fearful and irate? In the German original Freud writes of *Sicherheit*, and that German concept is in fact considerably more inclusive than the 'security' of the English translation. In the case of *Sicherheit* the German language is uncharacteristically frugal; it manages to squeeze into a single term complex phenomena for which English needs at least three terms – security, certainty and safety – to convey.

Security. Whatever has been won and gained will stay in our possession; whatever has been achieved will retain its value as the source of pride or respect; the world is steady and reliable, and so are its standards of propriety, the learned habits to act effectively as well as the learned skills needed to stand up to life's challenges.

Certainty. Knowing the difference between reasonable and silly, trustworthy and treacherous, useful and useless, proper and improper, profitable and harmful, and all the rest of the distinctions which guide our daily choices and help us take decisions we – hopefully – will not regret; and knowing the symptoms, the omens and the warning signs which allow us to guess what to expect and to tell a good move from a bad one.

Safety. Providing one behaves in the right manner, no terminal dangers – no dangers one cannot fight back against – threaten one's body and its extensions, that is one's property, home and neighbourhood, as well as the space in which all such elements of a 'greater self' are inscribed, like one's home ground and its environment.

All three ingredients of *Sicherheit* are conditions of self-confidence and self-reliance on which the ability to think and act rationally depends. The absence or dearth of any of the three ingredients has much the same effect: the dissipation of self-assurance, the loss of trust in one's own ability and the other people's intentions, growing incapacitation, anxiety, cageyness, the tendency to fault-seeking and fault-finding, to scapegoating and aggression. All such tendencies are the symptoms of *gnawing existential mistrust*: the now broken and unreliable daily routine, which if followed unselfconsciously should have saved the actor the agony of incessant choice, forces itself under apprehensive scrutiny, revealing the risks it entails; worse still, time and again the learned responses lose their validity too quickly to condense into habits and freeze into routine behaviour. The likelihood of undesirable consequences flowing from each choice and the awareness that those consequences cannot be precisely calculated prompt less the urge to better control the results of one's actions (this becoming a hardly realistic prospect) than the desire to insure oneself against the risks involved in all actions and to shed responsibility for the results.

The effects of weakened security, certainty and safety are remarkably similar, and so the reasons of troublesome experience are seldom self-evident, but notoriously easy to displace. The symptoms being virtually indistinguishable, it is not clear whether the ambient fear derives from the inadequate security, the absence of certainty, or threats to safety; anxiety is unspecific, and the resulting fear may be easily blamed on wrong causes and may prompt actions glaringly irrelevant to the genuine cause; genuine reasons for agitation being difficult to locate and even less easy to control if discovered, there is a powerful temptation to construe and name putative, yet credible culprits against whom one can wage a sensible defensive (or, better still, offensive) action. One would then perhaps be barking up the wrong tree, but at least one would be barking and would neither be reproached nor feel the need for self-deprecation for taking the blows hands down.

All three ingredients of *Sicherheit* nowadays suffer continuous and intense blows; and the awareness is spreading that – unlike in the case of the uncertainties of yore – the shakiness of life road-signs and the elusiveness of existential orientation-points can no longer be seen as a temporary nuisance likely to be cured if more information is discovered and more effective tools are invented; it becomes increasingly obvious that present-day uncertainties are, in Anthony Giddens's apt expression, *manufactured* – and so living in uncertainty is revealed as a way of life, the only way there is of the only life available.

Insecure security

One in three employees in the United States of America have spent in their current jobs in their current companies less than one year. Two in three have been in their present occupation less than five years.

Twenty years ago in Britain 80 per cent of jobs were – in principle, if not in fact – of the '40/40' kind (a forty-hour-long working week for forty years of life), and of a kind protected by a dense network of union, pension and compensation rights. Now no more than 30 per cent of jobs come into that category, and the proportion continues to fall fast.

A noted French economist, Jean-Paul Fitoussi, points out that the global quantity of available work is shrinking – this being, though, not a 'macro-economic', but a *structural* problem, related directly to the passing of control over crucial economic factors from the representative institutions of government to the free play of market forces. There is, therefore, little that the orthodox expansionist strategy of the state may do to combat it. If finance ministers are still a 'necessary evil', the ministers of the economy are increasingly things of the past[3] – or merely a form of lip-service rendered to a nostalgia for a once steadfast, now rapidly vanishing state sovereignty. In his recent study of the coming 'informatics society' Manuel Castells suggests that while capital is flowing freely, politics stays hopelessly local. The speed of movement makes the real power exterritorial. We may say that, with extant political institutions no longer able to slow down the speed of capital movements,[4] power is increasingly removed from politics – a circumstance which accounts simultaneously for growing political apathy, the progressive disinterestedness of the electorate in everything 'political' except the juicy scandals perpetrated by top people in the limelight, and the waning of expectations that salvation may come from government buildings, whoever their current or future occupants may be. What is done and may be done in government buildings bears less and less consequence for the issues with which individuals struggle in their daily lives.

Hans Peter Martin and Harald Schumann, economic experts of *Der Spiegel*, calculate that if the present trend continues unabated, 20 per cent of the global (potential) workforce will suffice 'to keep the economy going' (whatever that means), which will make the other 80 per cent of the able-bodied population of the world *economically* redundant.⁵ One can think (and many do) of the ways to reverse, arrest or at least slow down the trend, but the major issue today is no longer *what is to be done*, but *who has the power and the resolve to do it*. Behind the expanding insecurity of the millions dependent on selling their labour, lurks the absence of a potent and effective agency which could, with will and resolve, make their plight less insecure. Fifty years ago, in the Bretton Woods era (now ancient history), when they thought of the way global affairs were going, people in the know spoke of *universal rules* and their *universal enforcement* – of something we ought to do and will do eventually; today they speak of *globalization* – something that *happens to us* for reasons about which we may surmise, even get to know, but can hardly control.

Present-day insecurity is akin to the feeling the passengers of a plane may experience when they discover that the pilot's cabin is empty – that the friendly captain's voice was merely a replay of an old recorded message.

Insecurity of livelihood, compounded with the absence of a trustworthy and reliable agency capable of making it less insecure or at least serving as an address for the demands of greater security, strikes a severe blow at the heart of life-politics. Jean-Paul Sartre's advice to put together and then to follow *le projet* sounds hollow, neither wise nor particularly attractive. Not only does the drudgery of identity-construction look limitless and never likely to end, but it must now entail, as a crucial building norm, the product's capacity for self-effacement or the builders' capacity for recycling it into something other than originally intended. Most certainly, the labour of self-identification neither is nor should advisedly be a cumulative process: it looks more like a string of new beginnings and is guided on its way by the faculty of forgetting more than by learning and the ability to memorize. Whatever has been acquired or put together, is until further notice. It is not that there is a shortage of rules and guidelines bidding for our trust (on the contrary, the insecure world is the site of a counselling boom and a greenhouse of ever more numerous and variegated ranks of 'how-to-do-it' experts); it is, rather, that to invest trust unreservedly in any one rule or guideline no longer seems reasonable; sooner rather than later it may prove downright disastrous given the apparently endemic volatility of all the rules and guidelines on offer.

'The composition of the workplace is in continuous flux', is how Kenneth J. Gergen sums up the situation. He dubs that aspect of contemporary living 'plasticity'; moving from one workplace to another, or just watching the workplace changing under her or his eyes, often beyond recognition, 'the individual is challenged with an increasingly variegated array of behavioural demands'. In this sort of environment

> there is little need for the inner-directed, one-style-for-all individual. Such a person is narrow, parochial, inflexible . . . We now celebrate protean being . . . One must keep moving, the network is vast, commitments are many, expectations are endless, opportunities abound, and time is a scarce commodity.[6]

Gergen expands on the topic elsewhere:

> It becomes increasingly difficult to recall precisely to what core essence one must remain true. The ideal of authenticity frays about the edges; the meaning of sincerity slowly lapses into indeterminacy . . .
>
> The pastiche personality is a social chameleon, constantly borrowing bits and pieces of identity from whatever sources are available and constructing them as useful or desirable in a given situation . . . Life becomes a candy store for one's developing appetites.[7]

Let us observe that even in a life shaped after the pattern of a candy store, not the sweet taste of candies but the feeling of acute, insomnia-pregnant insecurity would be the main effect of the 'plasticity' Gergen so vividly portrays. Few people would name a candy store – a pleasant place to visit once in a while – when asked about their ideal permanent abode. Life filled by picking, sucking and swallowing candies is likely to be punctuated by fits of nausea and stomach pains for those who got inside the store, even if they forget (and forget they hardly can, however keenly they try) another life – a life filled with anger and self-deprecation – lived by those others who, due to empty pockets, avidly eye the customers from the other side of the store-window. After all, it is just the rotating door, and the rotating contents of the wallet, which separate the first group from the second.

Niklas Luhmann proposed, memorably, that, given the multiplicity of the roles we play and the settings in which we play them, each of us everywhere is 'partly displaced'. We may say that, due to the multiplicity of competing and mutually cancelling opportunities and the cacophony of voices calling to go after them, we are all – everywhere and always – 'partly deprived'. Only the scale, not the presence, of deprivation depends on the side of the store-window we currently happen to be. Whichever side we happen to be on at the moment ('identity', says Harvie Ferguson, 'is a transitory selfhood',[8] and life, we may add, is a graveyard of killed or deceased identities), we look deprived, whenever our condition is measured (as it must so be measured, if only because alternative yardsticks are missing) by the apparent infinity of obtrusive, and intrusive, tempting, seductive and – above all – untried, possibilities.

John Seel suggests that two propositions – 'The self is indeterminate; any self is possible' and 'The process of self-creation is never finished' – are among the major axioms traceable in all studies of postmodern identity problems. Daily life supplies a lot of evidence to encourage the view that these propositions do not indeed require further proof and could be accepted as axioms.

> One observes its [the identity concern's – Z. B.] logic in the ways self-understanding is pursued and self-expression manifested: in the teenage walking-billboards who advertise the latest designer label or rock group; in the proliferation of cosmetic surgery, tattoos, and body piercing; in the rise of gender politics; in the popularity of virtual chat rooms and cybersex; in the mega-status afforded fashion models; in the necessity of impression management in business and politics; and in the ubiquitous talkshow experts on daytime TV. Issues of sexuality, personhood, and the body are all transformed by the galvanizing effect of these emerging conceptions of self.[9]

The image conveyed by the above (certainly incomplete) list of symptoms is one of the piling-up and never slackening pressures to discard the old ways and embrace new and untried ones; of an identity forever chased but never caught; of the identity-chasers avidly clinging to little tokens of publicly recognizable self-expression, only to be prompted/cajoled/forced by the mind-boggling speed of their public devaluation to abandon and replace them; of men and women ever searching, hardly ever finding, and never certain that what they have found was what they were seeking, while being almost sure that, whether what they find was what they wished for or not, the fact of finding it will not long absolve them from further search. The lasting value of anything already gained cannot be taken for granted; the value of anything one is incited to acquire or applauded for acquiring cannot – should not – be taken for granted either. When one is told and shown that everything is up for grabs, endemic insecurity is the only non-perishable catch.

To cut a long story short: at the heart of life-politics lies a profound and unquenchable desire for security; while acting on that desire rebounds in more insecurity and ever deeper insecurity.

In trying to escape insecurity, one can no longer deploy the age-old stratagem of conformity to *vox populi*, since one can no longer count on the irrevocability of its pronouncements, and since there is hardly a single one of its verdicts which has not been questioned and contested the moment it has been voiced. But, as for the other traditional escape route, leading into the company of like-minded, sharing and caring others, ready to stay solidary through thick and thin, come what may – that route as well has been all but severed.

The insecure life is lived in the company of insecure people. It is not just me who is uncertain about how durable is my present self and for how long the others around me will be willing to go on endorsing it. I have every reason to suspect that those others around me are in a pretty similar predicament and feel as insecure as I do. Listlessness and irritation tend to be shared, but sharing irritation does not make lonely sufferers into a community. Our kind of insecurity is not the stuff of which joint causes, united stands and solidary ranks are moulded. Blows as much as opportunities seem to select their victims or beneficiaries at random, and so rule-enforced regularity may well be disadvantageous when it comes to seizing the opportunity and of little consequence when avoiding the blow.

Were individuals indeed eager to follow the precepts of rational choice, as some theorists suggest they do, they would under such circumstances be prompted to steer clear of companies and partnerships without a free exit. They would develop vested interests in 'flexible settings', in bonds no more durable than their usefulness. Their rationality would advise them against following the desire for a secure and lasting community. Their rational choices would therefore make them unwilling and unsuspecting accomplices in the manufacturing of the self-same insecurity of the lived world which makes the avoidance of secure anchorings a matter of rational choice. Insecurity has reached the point where it can boast the rational faculties of calculating individuals among its faithful and reliable servants.

Uncertain certainty

The two things we tend to be certain of nowadays more than of anything else is that there is little hope that the pains of our present uncertainties will be assuaged; and that yet more uncertainty looms ahead.

On the occasion of the acceptance of a common currency by the first eleven of the sixteen European Union member-states, the economic page of the *International Herald Tribune* announced the impending 'golden opportunity for corporate efficiency gains'. It spelled out a few paragraphs later what that golden opportunity, when taken up, would mean for the non-corporate remainder of Europe: it 'will result in more corporate downsizing and, initially, more unemployment'. (Let us observe that in the quoted phrase 'more downsizing' is a well-informed prediction, while 'initially' has the status of a doctrinaire belief). Alan Friedman, the *IHT* 'global economics' correspondent, goes on to quote Kim Schoenholtz, the chief economist at Salomon Smith Barney in London, and 'many other private sector economists'' opinion that, for the Common European Currency to bring the predicted 'efficiency gains', 'deep structural changes are needed'. Friedman leaves his readers in no doubt about what sort of structural changes constitute 'the missing ingredient which politicians still need to add'. Structural change, he explains, is 'the code word for making hiring and firing easier, for reducing public spending on pension and other welfare state benefits, and for lowering continental Europe's high employer contributions and social charges . . .'[10]

A few days previously the same paper had noted, though only on the 'opinion' page, that, in response to the profound economic crisis which had struck East Asian societies, the International Monetary Fund 'stepped in with its standard prescription [previously tried, with quite unprepossessing results, in Mexico – Z. B.]: layoffs, higher interest rates and the opening of local economies to international investors'. It goes without saying that the advice was fortified by sanctions: any financial rescue package had been made dependent on compliance with the prescription. According to Jeffrey Sachs of Harvard University, as a result of that stance 'a wave of bankruptcies is sweeping Korea, and a massive rise in unemployment seems to hit all three of the [East Asian – Z. B.] economies'. The author of the 'opinion' feature, Søren Ambrose, out of character with the usual tone of the *IHT* economic column, concludes that 'it is time to face up to the damage that has been wreaked by the IMF' and quotes, approvingly, a group of United States church leaders to the effect that the IMF's activities might require the 'sacrifice of generation'.[11] And who but God himself can look further than that?

In an interview accorded to Babette Stern of *Le Monde*, the director-general of the IMF, Michel Camdessus, confirms the intentions ascribed by economic opinion to the institution he leads; he presents them as a matter of pride. 'Methodical liberalization of capital movements', he says, 'must become the new mission of the IMF.' The prospects arising from the mission successfully accomplished are breathtaking: new chances of development will be brought about thanks to 'the pooling of the totality of world savings, which would make possible a better allocation of resources', though one must admit the associated risk of 'marginalizing the poorest countries' (the possible effects on the livelihood of the poorest sections of the 'wealthier countries' are not mentioned at all). The chances outweigh the risks: on balance, Camdessus is proud of the achievement thus far and even more of the triumphs still to come: 'Indeed, we have changed the century', he concludes.[12]

Yes, the century has changed or has been changed, and it keeps changing. Neither Camdessus nor the rest of the advocates and eulogists of the world-wide 'liberalization of capital movements' promise more certainty as a result; the catchword is instead 'transparency' (meaning a world holding no secrets and barring nothing from market operators) and 'flexibility' (meaning that nothing except the consideration of anticipated 'economic effects' – that is, of next year's benefits for the shareholders – may put limits on the market operators' freedom of decision). Transparency and flexibility can hardly add to the sum total of certainty; they would, as a matter of fact, *redistribute* the certainties which accompany actions, and in that seems to lie their main attraction for the spokesmen of the global liberty of finances.

Transparency and flexibility augur more certainty for some (for the globals-by-choice), portend more uncertainty for others (for the locals-by-default). The advocates and warriors of transparency are not the ideologists of the glass pane, but of one-way mirrors: on the one side a paradise for voyeurs; on the other a chance to watch and contemplate their own growing misery for those whose defences, sorely inadequate as they already are, have been laid bare for all present and future trespassers. The advocates and warriors of flexibility are not pursuing freedom of movement for all, but the exhilarating lightness of being for some, rebounding as an unbearable oppressiveness of fate for the rest; the right to avoid the consequences for some, the duty to bear the consequences for the others. The postulates of transparency and flexibility are, in the last account, about control exercised by the resourceful on the conditions under which the others, less self-reliant, are bound to choose between the humble set of options left, or be forced to submit to the fate visited upon them when no choice remains. The postulates demand that nothing may (is allowed to, or can survive the disregard for the prohibition) reduce the speed at which those on the transparent side or the one-way mirror may move. The 'flexibility' of the world for those on the move bears an uncanny resemblance to a rock-hard, indomitable reality from the viewpoint of those who have been forced to stay.

The postulates, and the pressures which they simultaneously reflect and reinforce, turn increasingly into the major factors of a new inter-societal and intra-societal polarization.[13] Scope and speed of movement make all the difference between being in control and being controlled; between shaping the conditions of interaction and being shaped by them; between acting 'in order to' and behaving 'because of'; between pursuing goals with near-certainty of success or defensive actions undertaken in a situation composed entirely of unknown variables that change without warning.

The point is, though, that whenever individual existence is plotted between an alluring and a repulsive pole and the position allocated on the continuum is neither fixed nor adequately insured, none of the positions offers a degree of certainty sufficient for spiritual comfort. The joy of 'having travelled to the top' cannot but be poisoned by the awareness of the horrors at the bottom, which are difficult to suppress at the happiest of moments; while hardly any moment can be lived through as pure, unalloyed bliss of ultimate arrival – of 'having done it, once and for all'.

These are, indeed, the conditions under which all people plotted on the continuum nowadays labour; in these days of global deregulation perhaps more than at any other time. Their plight may differ as to the degree of self-confidence or resignation, sanguinity or despair, trust or mistrust, elation or cynicism, high or low spirits which it may spawn and reasonably sustain, but the differences are fluid. In their moments of sobriety all but the most carefree among our contemporaries are painfully aware of that. The uncertainty about the outcome of actions and the duration of their effects, incumbent (though in varying measure) upon every position from the top to the bottom, is therefore exacerbated (again from top to bottom) by 'meta-uncertainty' – uncertainty as to the degree of certainty one can sensibly claim as one's own, and particularly as one's secure possession.

Living and being obliged to act under conditions of uncertainty is not, of course, a novelty. Modern history was, however, punctuated by determined (and, from time to time, successful) efforts to fix the value of a growing number of unknown variables in the life equation. As if following the rule spelled out by Michel Crozier in his classic study of *The Bureaucratic Phenomenon*, groups and categories of people cast on the side of particularly vicious uncertainty did their best to tie the hands of those in a better position in order to be able to calculate the effects of their moves – while simultaneously trying hard to untie their own hands and thus to become sources of uncertainty for their adversaries. As Crozier convincingly argued, domination and control over situations belong to those whose freedom of manoeuvre generates more uncertainty for others than the others, because they are relatively more constrained in their choices, are able to generate for them. All organized groups throughout the modern era behaved as if aware of Crozier's principle. One may even surmise that the chance of following that principle was the prime motive for 'getting organized'; that the methodical application of that principle was the deepest meaning of 'being organized'.

A genuine novelty is not the necessity to act under conditions of partial or even total uncertainty, but the systematic pressure to dismantle the painstakingly constructed defences – to abolish the institutions meant to limit the degree of uncertainty and the extent of damage the untamed uncertainty has caused and to prevent or stifle the efforts to design new collective measures aimed at keeping uncertainty in bounds. Instead of joining ranks in the war against uncertainty, virtually all effective institutionalized agencies of collective action join the neo-liberal chorus singing the praise of unbound 'market forces' and free trade, the prime sources of existential uncertainty, as the 'natural state of mankind'; and unite in hammering home the message that letting capital and finances free and giving up all attempts to slow down or regulate their erratic movements, is not one political choice among many, but a verdict of reason as well as a political necessity.

Indeed, Pierre Bourdieu has recently defined the neo-liberal theories and practices as, in their essence, a programme to destroy the collective structures capable of resisting the logic of the 'pure market'.[14] By now, as Bourdieu points out, the neo-liberal discourse has acquired all the features of Ervin Goffman's 'strong discourse', a type which is almost impossible to combat and whose 'realism' is difficult to question because – far from being but an exhortation to take certain steps instead of others – it represents the co-ordinated actions of all forces which count, all forces which combine in giving reality the shape it has; the 'strong discourse' of neo-liberalism has passed the 'reality test' by 'orienting economic choices of all those who dominate economic relations and adding its own, properly symbolic, force to the relation of forces emerging in the result'.

The neo-liberal discourse becomes ever more 'strong' as the deregulation proceeds, disempowering political institutions which could in principle make a stand against free-floating of capital and finances. Another seminal step on the road to its almost uncontested rule has been taken with the recent signature of the Multilateral Agreement on Investments, which for all practical purposes ties the hands of national governments and unties the hands of exterritorial companies. One by one, all the actual and potential obstacles to free movement of capital are being dismantled:

> nation-states, whose margin of manoeuvre shrinks non-stop; working groups, in view, for instance, of the individualization of salaries and careers relative to individual competences resulting in the atomization of the employees; collective defences of the rights of the workers, the trade unions, associations, co-operatives; even the family – which, in the wake of the restructuration of the markets according to age classes has lost a good part of control over consumption.

The joint outcome of disparate but converging assaults on the defensive lines is the 'absolute rule of flexibility' aimed at the 'precarization', and thus disablement, of people placed at the potential bridgeheads of resistance. The deepest socio-psychological impact of flexibility consists in making precarious the position of those affected and keeping it precarious. Such measures as the replacement of permanent and legally protected contracts by fixed-term or temporary task-related jobs allowing instant dismissal, rolling contracts and the kind of employment that undermines the principle of accretion of entitlements through continuous evaluation of performance, making the remuneration of each individual employee dependent on current individual results, inducement of competition between sectors and branches of the same enterprise which deprives the employees' united stand of all rationality – all such measures together produce a situation of endemic and permanent uncertainty. In the Darwinian world of universal struggle it is in that overwhelming feeling of paralysing uncertainty, in the fear, stress and anxiety born of uncertainty, that obedient service to the tasks set by the companies is to be rooted. And, as the ultimate weapon, there is the permanent threat, at all levels of hierarchy, of dismissal – and of the loss of livelihood, social entitlements, place in society and human dignity which goes with it: 'The ultimate foundation of all economic regimes placed under the sign of liberty is therefore *the structural violence* of unemployment, of precariousness of jobs and of the threat of dismissal which they imply.'

Solidarity (or, rather, the dense network of solidarities – big and small, overlapping and criss-crossing) served in all societies as (however imperfect) a shelter and a guarantee of certainty, and thus of trust, self-confidence and the courage without which the exercise of freedom and the willingness to experiment are unthinkable. It is that solidarity which has fallen prime victim of neo-liberal theory and practice. 'There is no such thing as society', went Margaret Thatcher's ill-famed declaration of the neo-liberal creed. There are, she said, men and women as individuals, and there are families.[15]

The invocation of the families emerges in this context, to be sure, as a gratuitous gesture; families are now expected, like all other collectivities, to operate strictly within the limits set by the market, and to follow internally as well as externally the rules of market rationality. In the face of that expectation the concept of the family becomes deeply contradictory. After all, the most prominent and, in a sense, 'foundational' act of the market is – as Stuart Hall put it – that 'it dissolves the bonds of sociality and reciprocity. It undermines in a very profound way the nature of social obligation itself.' But the spinning, servicing and keeping in good shape of the bonds of sociality and reciprocity, nurturing the very impulse of social obligation, is the life-blood of the family; it is this activity in which the family comes into being and which keeps it alive. The constitutive principle of rampant individualism permeating the neo-liberal 'non-society' from the top to the bottom can hardly leave the family unaffected. 'The new managerialism', Hall points out, was to do with 'how these ideas were driven through one institutional sector after another.' All sectors had to be, and had been indeed, 'transformed in the image of the market. Not by "marketizing" or privatizing only, but by making [them] mimic the market, by making it seem as if there is only one kind of questions which you can ask about this. These are the questions set by market forces.'[16]

This is why the neo-liberal calls to close the ranks of the families sound hollow, if not downright duplicitous. If seriously meant to soften or counterbalance the blows of 'rugged individualism', to offer the victims of cut-throat competition a cushion in case they stumble and fall, they just document the ignorance of the preachers and practitioners of the neo-liberal faith as to the contradiction running through the heart of the idea of society's vanishing act – in other words, of a society getting rid of itself in order to give free rein to non-social individuals; of a body tearing itself in shreds so that each of its cells, or at least the liveliest among them, can live better on their own.

Contrary to what the metaphysical prop of the 'invisible hand' suggests, the market is not after certainty, nor can it conjure it up, let alone make it secure. The market thrives on uncertainty (variously called competitiveness, deregulation, flexibility etc.), itself reproducing uncertainty in ever-growing volumes as its principal nourishment. Far from being a bane of market-type rationality, uncertainty is its necessary condition and inescapable product. The sole equality which the market promotes is an equal or near-equal plight of existential uncertainty, shared by the victors (always, by definition, the 'until-further-notice' victors) and the defeated alike.

Unsafe safety

No one's presence in the world is *safe* any more. But why 'any more'? After all, the precariousness of human existence is hardly news. Since humans, as one living species among zillions, acquired the ability of articulated thought, certain awkward questions have appeared among creatures of language to make that precariousness evident – and since it is evident, also frightening.

The greatest discovery made by the human species, a discovery which rendered it so special and its peace of mind, its feeling of safety, so difficult to obtain, was the fact of mortality: of universal, unavoidable, intractable death awaiting every single member of the species. Humans are the only living creatures who know that they are going to die and that there is no escape from death. Not all of them must necessarily 'live toward death', as Heidegger asserted, but all live their lives in the shadow of death. Humans are the only living creatures to know of their own transience; and since they know that they are but *temporary*, they also can – must – imagine *eternity*, a perpetual existence, which, unlike their own, has no beginning or end. And once eternity has been imagined, it becomes obvious that the two kinds of existence have meeting points, but no hinges or rivets.

There is but a contingent, loose and friable connection between the two, always vulnerable, ready to be broken at any moment. Their link is as vulnerable as the single, temporary life itself. The second, the eternal, time-free existence, seems callously indifferent to whatever happens in the individual's life and stays majestically out of bounds for whatever may be done within the first, the individual 'presence in the world'. The two are, for all one may know, incommensurable. Whatever secure links or permanent bridges might exist between the two kinds of existence must still be discovered or built, perpetually guarded and regularly serviced. Hence the questions 'Where do I come from?', 'What should I do with my life?' and 'What happens to me at death?' are, as John Carroll put it in his most recent exploration of the human condition,[17] 'age-old' and 'fundamental'. We may say that they are fundamental in a literal, non-metaphorical, primary sense, that of being 'foundational' – constitutive of the specifically human life, setting the human fashion of 'being in the world' apart from any other variety of similarly temporary and transient organic existence.

Indeed, culture – that ongoing activity of drawing boundaries or building bridges, separating or joining, making distinctions or connections which 'nature' (that is, the rest of the world that does not contain thinking and acting humans as its factor) – always was and forever will be about securing credible answers to the above three questions, which condense into one big mystery: since my visit to the world is but temporary, why am I here – and for what purpose, if any? It was that puzzle which spurred all known varieties of humans into the frantic, often frenzied action which by the late eighteenth century, retrospectively, have been given the name of culture; and it was that enigma which made culture, with its dense network of explaining/consoling stories, into the foremost value – indeed, a *sine qua non* value for creatures aware of their mortality.

There were a number of strategies which human cultural inventiveness deployed, intermittently or concomitantly, while struggling to crack the enigma or to give the impression that the enigma had been cracked and thus make life in the shadow of death liveable.

The most obvious strategy was, to use Cornelius Castoriadis's favourite terminology, blatantly *heteronomous*. It presented the world of passing time as a mere temporary blip in the endless duration of eternity; a half-way inn, in which one stays overnight to prepare for the real thing, which is eternal life. Neither the time of arrival nor the moment of departure are of the traveller's choice; each one has been sent into that world down here not of his or her own choice, and will leave when the time comes, again by no choice of his or her own. The timetable of arrivals and departures is not of the travellers' making, and there is nothing they can do to change it; and the order of things in which the passengers, the pilgrims-through-life, have no say in making the timetables is not of human making either. The crux of the matter, though, is that life, however transient, is of great consequence for that eternal existence which comes *after* death. This and that in life may seem odd, odious, or downright repulsive – but things are not necessarily what they seem to be to those whose sight and mind are enclosed in their earthly labours; happiness here may be paid for by eternal suffering, while misery in the transient world may be repaid with eternal bliss. One should follow the verdicts without trying to fathom what they decree or striving to penetrate the intentions which caused them to be what they are.

The heteronomous strategy had a number of important advantages. This is perhaps why it prevailed among human life-forms. After all, it 'plays on the essential components of human psychique'.[18] First, it takes the poison out of the sting: death is not the dying person's fault, just as birth was not that person's merit. For neither the beginning nor the end does one bear personal responsibility, and thus need not torment oneself for neglecting it. Second, it replaces the onerous injunction to choose with the less nerve-breaking commandment of rule-following. Third, being by definition impermeable to all tests and experiments, the heteronomous solution cannot be proven false or misleading – and thus its precepts discourage in advance all closer examination, stave off or qualm future doubts and absolve from the guilt of taking things on trust. More than any other conceivable alternative, the heteronomous strategy fortifies itself against all bluff-calling and whistle-blowing; it alone can come close to being virtually fool-proof and immune to criticism.

Another strategy combines heteronomy with autonomy; somewhat awkwardly, it can be described as a heteronomous/autonomous strategy. Its time has come with the advent of modernity, when the assurances offered by the purely heteronomous strategy, in most cases institutionalized in the religious form, started to jar, ever more stridently, with the experience of living a volatile, mobile life in a volatile, mobile world. An appeal to the indomitable powers up on high and their no-appeal-permitted verdicts, to a one-off act of creation and the one-off grace of revelation, derived much of its persuasive strength from an apparently stagnant, repetitive and monotonous existence; such a kind of life experience squared well with the idea of a preordained order of things which the stormy and unstable modern world (that is, a constantly 'modernizing' world – a-changing, dismantling the tracks behind while laying the new stretches ahead) could hardly make credible. Inherited or learned rules alike ceased to suffice, and the widening gap between revealed or any other variety of extant wisdom on the one hand, and the complexity of unprecedented and uncharted situations on the other, could be filled only by human choices – hazardous, even gambling moves, decisions made with incomplete knowledge and with anything but complete certainty about the outcomes.

Such were the conditions which made the passage from a heteronomous to a heteronomous/autonomous strategy almost a foregone conclusion. The new strategy, though, proved to be much less monolithic and cohesive than its predecessor.

The new, modern, strategy was heteronomous: like its premodern predecessor it dwelled on the predetermined inclusion of each transient individual life into a chain of being which originated before it had begun and was destined to survive its termination. Such larger and longer-lasting totalities of modern times were seldom able to claim a divine, superhuman sanction; this, however, did not matter much, as far as the vexing enigma of entry and exit from the world was concerned, since the production of a sensible solution to the mystery, giving meaning to individual life, still did not depend on those who might have been troubled by such questions and cut down considerably the limits of their individual choices and thus of their responsibilities. As in the case of the pre-modern, purely heteronomous strategy, not much more was left to the individual than to embrace and accept the fate and follow a transient life which in its essential outlines was, in fact, preordained by the membership in a durable totality. And yet the modern strategy was, simultaneously, autonomous – since it also made salient the human origin of the totalities in question; and since, moreover, it brought into sharp relief the mutual dependence between the life itinerary chosen by each member of the long-lasting totality and the duration of the latter. The unchosen destiny cancelled out the senseless brevity of individual life and linked it to eternity; but it was the conscious and eager acceptance of that destiny by each and every individual, and subsequently the individual will and zeal in following its consequences, which sustained that link and made the transcendence of individual death effective.

With all its residual heteronomy, the new strategy posited the individual as an agency, and a crucial agency at that. The membership of a durable totality, the circumstance not of one's choice, was cast as giving sense to otherwise brief and meaningless individual life, though the determination was incomplete without due effort from the individuals themselves; but it was now the task of the individual to give her or his life a trajectory which made the totality truly durable and so capable of performing its sense-endowing function. The importance attached to the individual's actions, to the following of a preordained itinerary and to conformity to the rules of life it set, was thereby radically enhanced; no longer was it merely an issue of posthumous reward or punishment, condemnation or redemption, but the condition of availing oneself of the chance of transcendence otherwise denied, the warrant of meaningful and fulfilling, against senseless and empty, life.

Among the totalities which fit that strategy well, two stood out: nation and the family.

As few other modern inventions, the imagery of the nation neatly dovetailed necessity and choice, being and doing, immortality and mortal life, duration and transience. As the most outspoken preachers of modern nationalism, like Fichte or Barrès, insisted, the life of a German derives its meaning from his Germanness, just as the life of a Frenchman is meaningful thanks to his Frenchness. Meaning is the pre-given chance of everyone born German or French, but it still needs to be gratefully embraced, cherished, celebrated and lovingly cultivated, as it draws its life-juices, vitality and resilience from being massively and repeatedly, generation after generation, embraced, cherished and cultivated. *Being* a German means *becoming* German and *acting* as it is in the nature of Germanhood; being a Frenchman means becoming a Frenchman and behaving the French way. Transience and duration thereby merge. The absurdity of individual mortality does not haunt any more thanks to the immortality of the nation to which all mortal lives contribute. The inherited immortality of nationhood endows mortal life with meaning, but perpetuation of that immortality gives mortal acts an added value of transcendence. It is nationhood which offers mortal beings their chance of surviving their individual death and entering eternity, but there is no other way to take up that chance than to dedicate one's life to the survival and well-being of the nation.

We may surmise that the nation-building spurt, the effort to melt and blend locally based and directly accessible communities and traditions into supra-local and remote, imagined entities which marked modern times, had the urgent need of replacing the now jaded and impotent, pre-modern variety of heteronomous strategy with a new one, more adequate to modern conditions and more resonant with the modern spirit, among its most potent causes. As abstract – imagined – totalities, nations fit the bill well: their image hovered high above the world of immediate, face-to-face and personal experience and so there could be little doubt as to their supra-individual nature. Against the mortality of its individual members the imagery of the nations could deploy the timeless perpetuity of symbols.

As a preventive cure for the psychical devastation which the awareness of mortality was bound to perpetrate, nationhood had an important advantage of being available to all and any individual; no special talents, extraordinary efforts, breadth of vision or power of mind were required – the most ordinary resources available matter-of-factly to any human being would do well enough. Immortality-through-nationhood was cut to the measure of common folk, not of heroes or otherwise exceptional, outstanding, unlike-all-the-rest and towering-above-the-rest personalities. To be effective, that medicine needed conformity, not daring; abiding by standards, not breaking them; observing the limits, not blazing new trails. This was, therefore, a popular and populist medicine, for common, repeated and continuous use. The same advantage privileged another focal totality of the modern heteronomous/autonomous strategy – the family.

The family displays yet more clearly than the nation ever

managed the typically modern dialectics between transience and duration, individual mortality and collective immortality. It is in the institution of the family that all the hauntingly contradictory aspects of human existence – mortal and immortal, doing and suffering, determining and being determined, being created and creating – most vividly meet and enter their never-ending game of mutual sustenance and reinvigoration. Everyone is born of a family, and everyone can (should, is called to) partake in giving birth to a family. The family of which one is a product and the family which one would produce are the links in a long chain of kinship/affinity which precedes the birth and will survive the demise of every individual it has contained and will contain; but to endure, it needs every individual's zestful contribution. In the family, the drama of immortality put together by the deeds of mortals is put on display, for everybody to watch and to act in the spectacle.

The common explanation of the modern attention to parenthood, offspring and family continuity in terms of economic considerations and particularly by inheritance concerns seems wide of the mark – or, at any rate, it is just a part of the story. If anything, the opposite is true: it was mostly in the pre-modern and pre-capitalist society that wealth, and the privileges and entitlements which came with it were primarily a matter of the family and of the right to inheritance. Tracing pedigrees, paying acute attention to kinship connection and guarding the standards of entered affinities was then the preoccupation of the aristocracy and the upper crust of the merchant class – the only categories which linked their own transcendence of time to family-based heredity. With the advent of modernity, the centrality of the family in individual life had been, so to speak, democratized; it turned into a cultural precept addressed to each and every individual, regardless of the presence or absence of a family fortune to be passed to future generations. Economic concerns could not be of much significance in that seminal shift, since a parallel democratization of family wealth never took place.

It must have been something else that explains the new importance of the family and particularly the spreading to all classes of modern society of the cultural constructs of marital loyalty, paternal and maternal love, and child care (and childhood itself as a particularly vulnerable and care-demanding stage of life).

This something else was, in all probability, the new role which had fallen upon the family to play, in view of the all-too-obvious bankruptcy of the pre-modern means of investing mortal life with immortal significance. With other bridges leading to eternity now falling into disrepair and no longer usable, it was the turn of the family to bear a load which it had never before been expected to carry. It was now primarily through 'starting a family' that the individuals who came into the world thanks to some others who had before them made a similar decision, could seriously contemplate leaving a durable trace on the world which would survive their own departure.

Both the nation and family are *collective* solutions to the torments of *individual* mortality. They both spell a similar message: my life, however short, was not in vain nor devoid of meaning, if in its own small way it has contributed to the durability of an entity larger than myself (or than any other individual like me, for that matter) and one that precedes and will outlast the span of my own life, however long I may live; it is that contribution which bestows an immortal role upon mortal life. Once the message has come across, the question 'What happens after *my* death?' sounds less sinister: I will die, but my nation, my family, will last – and it will last partly because I have done my share. Instead of taking the predicament of my mortality hands down, I have done something (and not just something, but something that truly counts) to rise above it. I have made of my own individual mortality a tool of collective immortality. When I die, I will leave something behind, and this something will be the survival (who knows? – perhaps even a genuinely eternal duration) of something greater and more important than my own fleeting existence.

The heteronomous/autonomous strategy has defused the potentially devastating effects of the awareness of one's own mortality by shifting the sense of life to hopefully immortal collectivities, and by weaving the mortal lives of the individual into the collective labour of immortality-production. The individual was spared the agony of coping with the absurdity of endemically vulnerable life-towards-death. The awesome truth of incurably fragile, unsafe personal existence had been dimmed if not denied, and the damage it could cause had been limited, if not eliminated entirely, by the compensatory preoccupation with the safety of the group. The fears generated by the awareness of personal death were channelled, at least in part, to the concerns with the existential safety of larger totalities, from which the meaning of individual life, brief and fragile as it was, was derived – but which, unlike any of the mortal individuals, stood a genuine chance of defeating death.

It is now these wholes, though, which gradually and relentlessly fall apart, which seem everything but safe, let alone bound for immortality; and so lose much, perhaps all, of their sense-giving potency.

At its birth, modernity deprived death of its transcendental (and heteronomous) meaning. On its way to its present stage, however, it denied also its communal meaning (and so sapped the viability of the heteronomous/autonomous strategy). Durkheim suggested that God was from the beginning not much more than the community in disguise; but now the community – large or small, imagined or tangible – is too weak to play God. Itself vulnerable, erratic and blatantly short-lived, it cannot claim its eternity with any degree of credibility. It is only now that death is on the way to becoming fully and truly meaningless. As Robert Johnson commented, death is regarded simply as the end of individual life as we know it. Some religious leaders acknowledge this quite bluntly: 'Dead is dead,' Rabbi Terry Bard, director of pastoral services at Boston's Beth Israel Hospital, has stated.[19] Albert Camus's *Stranger* had a premonition of that plight and all that follows. He knew that ultimately each of us is alone in this world and that life – the whole of life without any residue – ends with death; nothing stands now between the mortal individual and the 'benign indifference of the universe'.[20] The collectively built bridges between transience and eternity have fallen into disrepair and the individual has been left face to face with his or her own, unmitigated and unalloyed, existential unsafety. He or she is now expected to cope with the consequences on his or her own.

There is no point in looking to the 'wholes larger than the sums of their parts' for support and succour – the once rock-hard totalities now look as unsafe and death-bound as individual lives. They come and go, and as long as they stay in sight they never seem to be securely settled; they are unsure of themselves, uncertain about the merits of their condition, ignorant about their future and lacking in confidence. They seem to count their time in days rather than years, and to have 'use by' dates and 'unsuitable for home freezing' warnings glued on top. Most certainly, they are not the things from which one would extrapolate the idea of eternal being . . .

Nations are no longer secure in the shelter of the states' political sovereignty, which once was taken for a guarantee of perpetual life. That sovereignty is no longer what it used to be; the legs of economic, military and cultural self-sufficiency and near autarchy on which it once rested have been one by one and all together broken; sovereignty walks on crutches – lame and wobbly, staggering from one failed fitness test to another. The state authorities do not even pretend that they are capable, and willing, to guarantee the safety of those in their charge; politicians of all shades make it clear that given the stark demands of competitiveness, efficiency and flexibility 'we cannot afford' collective safety nets any more. Politicians promise to modernize the worldly frames of their subjects' lives, but the promises forebode more uncertainty, deeper insecurity and less insurance against the vagaries of fate.

As Eric Hobsbawm recently summed up the overall results of the uneven and unsynchronized processes of globalization, 'the basic structure of the global economy is increasingly separate from, and cuts across the borders of, the world's political structure'. The repercussions for the identity-building potential of nation-states are overwhelming: '[U]nlike the state with its territory and power, other elements of "the nation" can be and easily are overridden by the globalism of the economy. Ethnicity and language are two obvious ones. Take away state power and coercive force, and their relative insignificance is clear.'[21]

The more legless is the state, the more its spokesmen spell out the need for, the duty of, its self-reliance, of counting on one's own resources alone, of making one's own balances of gains and losses – in short, of standing of one's own, individual, legs. As Bernard Cassen, commenting on Pierre-André Taguieff's ideas, put it, the brutal tearing up of social solidarities, and with them of the 'structures of eternity' which stretch 'beyond individual life' has left 'the individual isolated in his fear of his own ineluctable disappearance'.[22] Somewhere on the way to global free trade the sense-giving function of the national community has gone by the board, and individuals have been left to lick their wounds and exorcize their fears in solitude and seclusion.

The family nowadays finds itself in no better state; it brings to mind anything except a safe haven of duration where one can cast the anchor of one's own vulnerable and admittedly transient existence. As easy to end as it is to start and as easy to dismantle as it is to put together, the family can no more be counted on lasting longer than those who bring it into the world. That bridge into eternity is as brittle and friable as the people who walk across it – perhaps even more short-lived than their passage. Emancipated from its reproductive function, sexual union looks less like the nature-provided gateway to perpetuity, a building tool in the construction of community and a way out of solitude, and more like another pleasurable but brief sensation meant to be instantly consumed alongside other sensations in the successive episodes into which the life of the solitary sensations-gatherer is sliced. From early childhood on, individuals learn from widely shared experience that the odds are against the family outliving their own life-spans. A family anticipated to last as long as (and no longer than) the satisfaction of both marriage partners can hardly be treated seriously as the stratagem to outwit the awesome and cruel might of individual mortality.

It is not that the late-modern or postmodern loners-by-choice have lost their enthusiasm for anything longer lasting than individual satisfaction; it is rather that the late-modern or postmodern loners-by-fate can find in the world they explore few if any exhibits which would render their passion realistic and their effort credible; and few if any secure shelters where the trust in longevity could be stored for safekeeping. But whether of choice or an unchosen and unasked-for predicament, the effects for the life strategy of late-modern or postmodern individuals are largely the same. As John Carroll has recently put it, referring to Jung's famous dictum that once killed, gods tend to be reborn as diseases,

individuals without belief, in order to give sense to what they do and how they live, will find themselves trapped in self-absorbed compulsions, depressions, anxieties – psychopathology as the modern form of illness. Indeed, the very term 'psycho-pathology' means suffering of the soul in the original Greek, but in the modern usage soul has been dropped in favour of personality, in effect ego.

Let us observe that if 'ego' carries a different meaning from the one once connoted by 'soul', this is for the blunt and stout refusal of the 'ego' to be plotted in a frame wider than the span of an individual life – a decision which the 'soul' sometimes successfully resisted. The 'soul' has fallen out of use precisely because it stubbornly clung to the vestiges of its age-long link with eternity, and despite all secularizing recycling could not be really freed from its past associations. Unlike the 'soul', the 'ego' was meant from the beginning to fit the modern condition, in which no heteronomy was admitted unless conjured up by autonomous – that is, choice-making humans' – means. As the souls of the pious have fallen into disuse, followed, in fits and starts, by the souls of the patriots and those of the *patri familiae*, only the ego, abandoned and lonely, has been left on the battlefield, now obliged to deploy its own meagre weapons, sorely inadequate for the purpose of the ongoing fight with the absurdity of transient life in an eternal universe. The result, to quote Carroll once more, is 'the rancorous edge', 'restless insecure selfishness'; 'if we cannot have the food we truly crave, spiritual food, then we shall accumulate the goods of this world on a vast scale.'[23]

I propose that the current obsessive preoccupation with the body, with its fitness, its defence capacity, its *safety* – preoccupations closely intertwined with equally obsessive vigilance against genuine or putative malevolent threats or conspiratorial plots aimed against that safety – reflect the retreat of the two formerly dominant strategies of coping with the all-too-human awareness of mortality (the heteronomous and the heteronomous/ autonomous strategies) and the advance of the sole strategy left (that is, the purely autonomous one). 'Autonomous' means in this case self-contained and self-centred, one that does not engage resources other than those in the ego's actual or potential possession and under the ego's actual or potential control, nor sets it objectives beyond the confines of the ego, of its immediate *Lebensraum* and of its life-span.

As the prospects of building a truly lasting and extra-temporal community fade and look increasingly nebulous, the now unused supplies of restless energy generated by the endemic unsafety of human existence are shifted to the space-and-time-bound realm of the self. Unlike its alternatives, the autonomous strategy is not really about immortality, unless it is the 'imortality experience' (in tune with the publicity fliers of theme parks), meant for on-the-spot, instant and one-off consumption. It is rather about elbowing-out the concerns with immortality altogether from the territory of life-politics, and consequently exorcizing its spectre from the realm of right and proper worries. This strategy is not aimed at transcending the mortality limits of the self, nor building bridges between mortal life and the eternal universe. It is about getting that awesome and worrisome task off one's chest, so that all material resources and mental energy can be deployed in the effort of making the ego's life-span more capacious: not through stretching its time limits, but through packing it more densely with chattels, gadgets, trinkets and curios.

One hopes, though (albeit implicitly rather than explicitly), to strike out the inevitability of death from the agenda of life. As Theodor Adorno observed, '[terror] before the abyss of the self is removed by the consciousness of being concerned with nothing so very different from arthritis or sinus trouble.'[24] Busy as one is with fighting or keeping at a distance the ever growing variety of poisonous food, fattening substances, carcinogenic fumes, unhealthy life regimes and the multitude of afflictions threatening the fitness of the body, there is little time left (hopefully none at all) to brood and sulk over the futility of it all. Doctors proclaim with pride that ever fewer people 'die of natural causes': at the horizon of the autonomous strategy looms the vision of such a life as may come to an end only because of the self's neglect of duty, so that the self-contained and self-centred life-policy with the care of the body firmly placed at its centre could truly become an adequate and sufficient source of life-meaning. When there are so many means to attend to, who would waste time in examining the ends?

Decca Aitkenhead informs us that 'there are 6000 Weight Watchers meetings each week in Britain, and thousands more at other clubs'. Having discovered that according to the spirit of our time a 'modest weight gain is the most important thing to ever happen to anyone' (the *Titanic* star, Kate Winslet, was offered to the attention of British tabloid readers not so much for the brilliance of her film performance, as for the unforgivable lapse of self-care which resulted in 'piling on the pounds'), Aitkenhead resolved to see for herself what the crowds of Weight Watchers do when they meet. This is what she found out:

> Our leader tells her story. That picture of the mildly chubby woman on the notice board, we discover, was her! Incredible! And we can all do it. One woman keeps coming each week, battling to lose the last two pounds, never mind that she's lost 23 already, she's still fighting! Our Leader is lost in admiration. She knows what it's like. There will be a lot of 'soul searching', but we will 'live for the scales', and getting up on them will be 'heaven'. . . . [Among the weight watchers, with capital letters or not] few are significantly overweight, yet they are tyrannising otherwise interesting lives with the exhausting fantasy of weighing four pounds less.

Gloomily, Aitkenhead concludes:

> While the media's New Feminists are rejoicing on the 'right' to look lovely, church halls and primary schools all over the country are full of women whose principal sense of self is located in a contest they will never believe they have won.

And then Aitkenhead observes: 'What none of them demand is a simple solution – that we stop worrying about it.'[25] This observation comes as a surprise; having given so much perceptive thought to the issue, Aitkenhead should have realized that 'to stop worrying' is everything but a 'simple solution': the whole point of preoccupation with ounces and inches is that worry we must . . . We must have *something* to worry about, and not *any kind* of something, but a pinpointable, tangible something – something which we might at least imagine to be within our reach and power, something 'we can do something about'.

In its pure and unprocessed form the existential fear that makes us anxious and worried is unmanageable, intractable and therefore incapacitating. The only way to suppress that horrifying truth is to slice the great, overwhelming fear into smaller and manageable bits – recast the big issue we can do nothing about into a set of little 'practical' tasks we can hope to be able to fulfil. Nothing calms better the dread one cannot eradicate than worrying and 'doing something' about the trouble one can fight. Considering such need, fat seems less like a collective craze, and more like a God-sent gift. Self-delusion it might be (self-delusion it is: no amount of inches and ounces dropped will ever fill the abyss), but as long as one can go on deluding oneself one can at least go on living – and living with a purpose, and thus living a meaningful life.

Fat is but one issue of the large family of 'practical tasks' which the orphaned self may set itself just to sink and drown the horror of loneliness in the sea of small but time-consuming and mind-absorbing worries. But it is a well-chosen specimen, bringing into relief all the most important features of the whole family. It focuses on the body; though not exactly on the target, at least it stays close to the target; it is after all the mortality of the *body*, its relentless and unstoppable descent into nothingness, that breeds the existential horror which lies at the foundation of all obsessive worries about personal safety. Concern with the integrity and fitness of the body is the sole common denominator of all such obsessions, however diverse they might otherwise seem. That concern casts the world, including the people who inhabit it, as the source of vague and often unspeakable, yet ubiquitous dangers. The main danger being the ultimate death and thus beyond reach, it is salutary to condense the ambient fear in an easily recognizable, named and localized part of the world or category of persons. The snag is that hitting any of the substitute or displaced targets brings at best only a temporary relief. None can truly measure up to the magnitude of the principal cause of horror, and as a rule the blows aimed at surrogate targets land wide of the mark as far as the genuine cause of terror is concerned. There is therefore inexhaustible demand for ever new, as yet not discredited because untried, surrogate worries. All of them must be, however, related to the 'defence of the body'.

In every war one fights the enemy outside and the enemy agents implanted or parachuted behind the frontline. Fat belongs to that second category. Fat is to the embattled individual what the fifth column of spies, subversives, fellow-travellers or saboteurs were to embattled nations: an essentially alien body, working inside the besieged fortress at the behest of and for the benefit of the enemy beyond the walls. Fat is *in but not of* the body; like the enemy aliens, it has to be vigilantly spied out in order to be rounded up and deported, squeezed out of the body ('lipo-sucked'), or famished to extinction.

The inborn and incurable mortality of the body being the truth which one wants (needs?) to keep secret, the dangers which one fears and fights tend on the whole to be mapped outside the body. They are at their most credible, though, when located at the interface between the body and the rest of the world – particularly around the orifices of the body, where the most intense but, alas, unavoidable border traffic and exchange take place. One should beware of everything that goes inside the body, of what one eats, drinks, inhales. The moribund destination of all metabolism (again an issue too big to handle) is thereby spread thinly over a variety of ingested substances and blamed each time on another selection of foods on offer. Since no diet saves its practitioners from dying, one selection of forbidden ingredients or their combinations must be sooner rather than later replaced by another – not necessarily better, but different. (The formula 'new and improved' is, psychologically speaking, pleonastic; 'new' and 'improved' are synonyms.) The emotionally gratifying, assuaging effect of avoiding the intake of the stuff on which one's fears are condensed at a given moment wears off quickly, hence the room for further diet-scripting is unlikely ever to become scarce. The same applies to the prescriptions for the right and proper bodily regime, aimed at getting the wrong kind of substances 'out of one's system'. The body is seen as infested with a lot of unnecessary, unwanted and downright harmful stuff; all that stuff must share the fate of the fat – be destroyed or expelled. Again, since no edict of deportation can bring the ultimate goal any nearer, the accusing finger never rests for long, seeking ever new culprits.

The case of fat illuminates as well other distinctive features of the obsessive preoccupation with the body into which the terrors, generated by privatization of existential unsafety, have been redirected.

The Weight Watchers assembly bears an uncanny resemblance to a community; members seek eagerly each other's company, travel regularly for their gatherings, go together through weekly rituals, and synchronize their life pursuits between meetings, dedicating them concertedly to the implementation of whatever they have been advised or indoctrinated to do. They all embrace willingly and keenly the same set of behavioural norms, and all, though with a varying degree of zeal and success, attempt to follow them to the letter. But here the similarity with the model community as described (or postulated) by sociologists ends. The 'community' of Weight Watchers is reduced to just one function – to the repetition in many voices of the concerns which by their nature can be only voiced singly and can only be singly handled. That community is not 'greater than the sum of its parts'. It does little more than bring together, within ear-and-eye reach of each other, a number of lonely 'problem-solvers' who shed nothing of their loneliness by being brought together. If anything, they emerge from their meetings with the awareness of their loneliness reinforced; even more convinced than before that whatever troubles them is of their own making and whatever can be improved in their sorry plight can only be accomplished by them alone. The sole change made in their plight by the weekly ritual incantations of the common gospel is that they now know that they are not alone in their loneliness, that there are other 'people like them' doomed to fight similar lonely battles and bound to rely solely on their own will, stamina and wit. What the case of fat shows is that once the task of coping with human existential unsafety has been privatized and left to individual resources, individually experienced fears can only be 'head-counted', but not shared or melted into a common cause and the new quality of joint action. The privatization of fears has a self-perpetuating capacity. There is no obvious way leading from privatized terrors to common causes which can benefit by being confronted and tackled together.

The only form of togetherness conceivable under such circumstances is a formation which could fittingly be called a 'peg-style community': a group coming together through finding a peg on which the fears of many individuals could be simultaneously hanged. Fat is such a peg. From time to time there crop up other pegs, which (unlike the 'fat issue', outspokenly sincere about the private nature of trouble which brought the concerned people together) create a visibility of a cause common in a stronger sense, that is such a cause as may actually gain if all those afraid of individual harm join forces and stand fast arm in arm; the awareness of 'strength in numbers' may lead in its turn to the perception of the cause in question as concerning *public* welfare, rather than being an aggregate of private worries seeking a joint outlet – a vent more reliable and reassuring precisely for being used by so many others. Among such pegs (disguised as buckles, and for that reason more likely to cloud the real troubles, worries and psychological shifts and transfers which make them attractive and to mislead an analyst) one can find cases as diverse as a prospect of recycling poisonous substances in the immediate neighbourhood or the release of an acknowledged paedophile from prison, leniency towards the perpetrators of passive smoking and the news that a plot of unused land nearby has been allocated to a travellers' camp. The true springs of action in such cases may be more difficult to disclose, but they do not differ in substance from those operative in other, more straightforward kinds of 'peg-style communities'. Like them, they draw their strength from providing outlets for the pent-up fear and anger which are only obliquely, at best, related to the 'issue in question'. As in those more straightforward cases, due to their misplacement and glaring inadequacy, the 'issues in question' may generate only fleeting, ephemeral, ultimately dissatisfying and frustrating formations, hardly reminiscent of whatever could be conceived as a 'genuine community'.

Privatized unsafety wears many masks, but hardly ever shows its true face, which – like that of Medusa – can be looked at only at the peril of paralysis.

Fears on the move

Unreliable and ultimately frustrating as the common translations of fears into individual actions might be in the case of privatized *unsafety*, they are still superior to all and any translations conceivable in the case of *uncertainty* or *insecurity*. Indeed, there seems to be little the individuals, singly or severally, can do to fight back, let alone defeat, the threats to the security of their social standing or to the certainty of their future prospects. The exact locations of those threats are elusive and difficult to chart; such locations as can be eventually guessed stay as a rule far beyond the reach of real or imagined individual powers. Attempts to find them, if undertaken at all, lead more often than not to a resigned or despaired conclusion of the 'there is nothing I can do about it' type.

Such a conclusion is hardly unwarranted. There is nothing much that the employees of whatever rank can do if the company which employed them has decided at short notice or without any notice at all to move its business elsewhere or to start off another round of 'rationalization' through downsizing, slimming down its labour force, cutting administrative costs or selling off or winding up the non-profitable parts of the business. There is even less the individuals can do to prevent the devaluation of their hard-won know-how or the drying-up of the market demand for their kinds of abilities. The idea of manipulating the deeper causes of all such blows of fate – such as the notoriously obscure 'market forces', inscrutable 'laws of competition', erratic and apparently unmotivated convulsions of stock exchanges or the mysterious 'pressures of globalization' – look altogether fantastic to the overwhelming majority of affected individuals. Seeking guidance in astrology, fortune-telling and occult practices, much as seeking a secure future through the purchase of lottery tickets, does not seem too irrational by comparison with other forms of individually undertaken preventative or remedial actions.

There is a story of a drunken man who searched for a lost banknote under a lamp-post – not because he lost it there, but because the part of the pavement underneath was better lit. Transferring anxiety from global insecurity and uncertainty, its genuine causes, into the field of private safety, follows roughly the same logic. Threats to safety, real and imputed, have the advantage of being fleshy, visible and tangible; this advantage is topped and reinforced by another – that of the relative facility of confronting them and perhaps even defeating them. No wonder that the transfer is so common; no wonder either that as a result the popular concerns about safety, nicknamed 'law and order', dwarf the popular interest in the productive mechanisms of insecurity and uncertainty and the popular willingness to arrest or at least slow down their operation.

What we are witnessing today, in consequence, is something like 'safety overload'. The usual impulse of survival and self-defence has now been burdened with emotions which far exceed its carrying power. That impulse is now doomed to ingest, recycle and discharge psychologically poisonous detritus of the lost battles for certainty and security. Moreover, with the collectively maintained scrap heaps and waste-recycling plants by and large dismantled, the labour of waste-disposal falls fairly and squarely upon individual shoulders. Once collectivities cease to erect and service the city walls and moats, each single resident of the city must attend karate courses. The overall result was vividly described by Ronald Hitzler:

> Cutting oneself off, locking oneself in, hiding – these are today's most common ways of reacting to the fear of the things happening 'out there' which seem to threaten us in a variety of masks. Deadbolts on the door, entrance locks, multiple security systems, alarms and surveillance cameras have spread from upper-class villas to middle-class areas. Living behind a wall of mechanical locks and electronic walls, whistles, pepper sprays, tear-gas guns or tazer guns is part of individual urban survival orientation.[26]

The mechanisms standing behind the manufacture of uncertainty and insecurity are largely global, and so remain beyond the reach of extant political institutions; notably beyond the reach of elected state authorities. As Manuel Castells recently suggested,[27] the world today is kept together as a set of overlapping networks: of stock exchanges, television channels, computers, or states. Networks are sites of 'flow' – of power, capital, information – a process essentially no longer subject to spatial and temporal constraints. The Internet-user's experience serves this description as the essential cognitive frame. We live, says Castells, in a class society without classes, in a 'global electronic casino' in which capital and power escape into the hyperspace of pure circulation and are no longer embodied in the 'capitalist' or 'ruling' classes. Politics, on the other hand, remains as before an essentially local affair, and since the language of politics is the only one in which we can speak of cures and medicines for shared miseries and worries, there is a natural tendency among the political class to seek explanations and remedies in an area close to the home ground of daily experience.

There is thus a well-understandable inclination of political elites to divert the deepest cause of anxiety – that is, the experience of individual insecurity and uncertainty – to the popular concern with (already misplaced) threats to safety. There is quite a convincing pragmatic reason for such diversion to be politically (to wit, electorally) attractive. Since the roots of insecurity are thrust in anonymous, remote or inaccessible places, it is not immediately clear what the local, visible powers could do to rectify the present afflictions. If one gives more than a passing thought to the politicians' electoral promises of pursuing a better life for everybody through greater flexibility of labour markets, freer trade, more attractive conditions for foreign capitals etc., one can glean, if anything, the portents of more insecurity and more uncertainty to come. But there seems to be an obvious, straightforward answer to the other trouble, that related to the *collective* safety. Local state powers may still be deployed to close the borders to migrants, to tighten the asylum laws, to round up and deport unwelcome aliens whom one suspects of invidious and condemnable inclinations. They may flex their muscle fighting the criminals, be 'tough on crime', build more prisons, put more policemen on the beat, make the pardoning of convicts more difficult and even, catering to popular sentiments, follow the 'once a criminal, forever a criminal' rule.[28]

To cut a long story short, governments cannot honestly promise their citizens a secure existence and a certain future; but they may for the time being unload at least a part of the accumulated anxiety (and even profit from it electorally) by demonstrating their energy and determination in the war against foreign job-seekers and other alien gate-crashers, intruders into once clean and quiet, orderly and familiar, native backyards. Doing so may be richly satisfying; perhaps modest and short-lived, yet nevertheless a compensation for the humiliating feeling of helplessness in the face of an unsympathetic or coldly indifferent world.

In his perceptive study of xenophobia among young Londoners, Phil Cohen found one of his respondents named John seeking desperately, yet with exemplary determination, a definition of 'Britishness' which would include himself but exclude a sizeable category of coloured people whose exclusion from the locality seemed at least a feasible, and thus attractive, goal. Cohen explains the determination by the fact that 'the construct makes John feel part of something vastly bigger than himself and also immensely strong'.[29] Strength was one quality John, and many others in his situation of a young person without much chance of meaningful life in an unwelcoming and impenetrable world, missed most – as they craved for at least a glimmer of hope to make their vulnerable existence just a bit less precarious and a whit more secure.

In the language of vote-seeking politicians closely following opinion poll statistics, the widespread and complex sentiments of *Unsicherheit* are reduced to much simpler concerns with law and order (that is, with bodily safety and the safety of private homes and possessions), while the problem of law and order tends to be, in its turn, blended time and again with the problematic presence of ethnic, race or religious minorities – and, more generally, of alien styles of life, of everything deviant or merely 'abnormal'.

The trouble, though, as Antoine Garapon points out, is that the diffuse yet pervasive ambience of insecurity and vulnerability emanating from the polyphonic, opaque and unpredictable world, makes the unambiguous mapping of experience and the voicing of confident judgements all but impossible; and so it saps the very notion of deviant behaviour. But 'when the deviant becomes normal, all normality is suspect of deviancy'. As things look at the moment, one may well adumbrate that 'the destination of postmodern penal law is the reinstitutionalization of the ancient dialectics of pollution/purification, with its attendant sacrificial mechanisms'. Today, crime is no longer stigmatized and resented for being a breach of the norm, but as a threat to safety. 'Excessive speed, smoking in public [*tabagisme*] and sexual delinquency are all treated in the same fashion, that is in terms of the policy of public safety.' One can see the universal tendency to 'shift all public affairs toward penal justice'[30] – to criminalize all social problems, and particularly such problems as are deemed, or can be construed as, affecting the safety of the person, of its body and possessions.

Remoulding the intractable and incurable worries about *individual security* into the urge to fight actual or potential crime and thus to defend *public safety* is an effective political stratagem and may bring handsome electoral rewards. To take but one example, a state television survey conducted in October 1997 showed that more Danes were concerned with the presence of foreigners than with growing unemployment, a damaged environment or any other trouble.[31] And as the *International Herald Tribune* of 17 November 1997 reported, that majority view found resonance in the resented foreigners' sentiments: 22-year-old Suzanne Lazare, settled in Copenhagen from Trinidad twelve years earlier, told the *IHT* correspondent that she was thinking of leaving Denmark. 'Their eyes have changed,' she said of her hosts. 'The Danes look down on you now. People are becoming very cold.' And then came a shrewd, insightful afterthought: 'Funny thing, it's toward themselves, too.'

The cooling-off of the human planet

A perceptive comment that was indeed. That coldness against 'foreigners in our midst', the aliens becoming neighbours and the neighbours cast as aliens, signals a fall of temperature in all human relations, all over the place. Cold are the people who have long forgotten how warm human togetherness may be; how much consolation, comfort, encouragement and just ordinary pleasure one may derive from sharing one's own lot and one's hopes with others – 'others like me', or more exactly others who are 'like me' precisely for the reason of *sharing* my plight, my misery and my dream of happiness; and even more so for the fact of my concern with their plight, their misery and their dreams of happiness.

In his novel *L'identité*, Milan Kundera ponders the historical fate of human friendship. Once upon a time, Kundera's hero muses, being friends meant to stand shoulder to shoulder in battle; to be ready to sacrifice one's welfare, one's life if need be, for a cause which can be defended only *as* common and *in* common. Life was fragile and full of dangers; friendship could make it a little more solid and a little safer. The threats to any one of the friends could be averted, the dangers could be made somewhat less terminal, if all the friends joined hands and resisted the adversity in unison. Now, however, neither threats or dangers are likely to be cured or even made less painful by the friends' united stand. They are, purely or simply, *threats and dangers of a different kind* – as if meant to hit each of its victims separately, each one in his or her own time, destined to be suffered alone. Present-day individual miseries are not synchronized; to each door catastrophe knocks selectively, on different days, at different hours. The visits are apparently unconnected. And the disasters are not the misdeeds of an enemy whom the victims can name, point at with their fingers, unite against, stand up to and together fight back against. The blows of fate are perpetrated by mysterious forces without a fixed address, hiding under such curious and baffling names as financial markets, global terms of trade, competitiveness, supply and demand. Of what possible use can friends be when one loses one's job in another 'downsizing' exercise, when one wakes up to the obsoleteness of hard-won skills, to the neighbourhood or the family or the partnership suddenly falling apart?

To the kind of disasters which used to befall people, Kundera suggests, other people may nowadays react in two ways only. Some may join the hue-and-cry, add their voices to the chorus blaming the victims, ridicule and deride the good-for-nothings who brought the bad luck upon themselves; such people the hapless victim may justly view as enemies. Others may show compassion and abstain from rubbing salt into the wound; they pretend that nothing has happened and go on as before, yet all the same do nothing to undo the damage – openly or obliquely admitting their impotence, or afraid of adding insult to injury. Those of this other kind – the restrained and subtle, gentle and polite people – come as close as possible to the idea of friends as it can be realistically conceived nowadays. The choice is now between malice and indifference. Friendship in the old 'One for all, all for one' style has been all but squeezed out of the realm of the possible. No wonder people are getting cold . . .

It is not that we have lost the humanity, the charm and the warmth that came easy to our ancestors; it is rather that our hardships are of a kind which on rare occasions only can be cured or mollified by sharing even the warmest of sentiments. The sufferings which we tend to experience most of the time do not add up and so do not unite their victims. Our sufferings divide and isolate: our miseries set us apart, tearing up the delicate tissue of human solidarities.

Let me repeat what has been already said in the beginning. Contemporary hardships and sufferings are dispersed and scattered; and so is the dissent which they spawn. The dispersion of dissent, the impossibility of condensing it and anchoring it in a common cause and unloading against a common culprit, only makes the pains yet more bitter. Individuality, the 'authenticity of the self', was a sweet dream and a tocsin rousing to heroic pursuits at a time when obtrusive and ubiquitous communal surveillance and pressure to conform all but stifled individual expression. It became bitter once the dreams came true and the individual – whether in his triumph or his humiliation – was left alone on the battlefield. Victories and defeats alike became equally bitter, abhorring and offputting once bound to be celebrated or bewailed on one's own.

The contemporary world is a container full to the brim with free-floating fear and frustration desperately seeking a kind of outlet which one sufferer could reasonably hope to share with others. The craving for this type of outlet, as Ulrich Beck reminds us, 'does not contradict individualization, but is in fact a product of individualization gone pathological'.[32] Individual life is super-saturated with sombre apprehensions and sinister premonitions, all suffered alone and all the more frightening for that reason, as well as for the reason of being elusive and more often than not unspecific. As in the case of other supersaturated solutions, a speck of dust is enough to trigger a violent condensation.

Remember René Girard's updated version of the 'original sin' that stands at the cradle of the human community? It goes some way (but most certainly not all the way) towards 'making sense' of the resurgence of tribal hostility which otherwise seems puzzling, considering the genuine causes of current anxiety and fears. One should beware, however, of going further than the story is capable of leading, and to assume that its evident sense-making capacity renders it the only scenario which these anxieties and fears make feasible and likely to be followed. We will be well advised to remember that none of the responses and ensuing itineraries is a predetermined choice, that they are merely plausible scenarios, and that the choice between them and the way they are staged depends each time not only on the actors who play the leading characters but also on the crowds of anonymous extras and stage-hands.

As to these extras and stage-hands, neither group can be relied upon for the unambiguous selection of lines. Things falling out of joint, decayed timber and rusty nails spied out in the ostensibly stiff and solid frames, allegedly rock-hard foundations melting like shifting sands – all that tends to instil fear. But it may also inspire laughter, that – in the ultimate account – noisy sigh of relief that the adversities are not as mighty as they seemed, and the turn of events is not exactly the fate which leaves the victims no choice but to obey. As Milan Kundera put it in his inimitable way,

Things deprived suddenly of their supposed meaning, of the place assigned to them in the so-called order of things ... make us laugh. Laughter has something malicious about it (things suddenly turning out different from what they pretended to be), but to some extent also a beneficent relief (things are less weighty than they appeared to be, letting us live more freely, no longer oppressing us with their austere seriousness).[33]

There is a measure of that ambivalence in all laughter: bad, that things are not as stable and reliable as they pretend to be; good, that they are not as tough and suffocating as they look. It is good to be freer than one thought one was; it is bad having been told over and over again that free people have no one and nothing to blame for their plight but themselves. In fact, one would say, fear and laughter do not oppose each other. They are branches growing out of the same stem. And there are faint echoes of fear in all laughter. Hopefully, there is also a seedling of laughter in every outburst of horror.

As if to make the situation yet more complex and confusing, Kundera points out that there are, as a matter of fact, two kinds of laughter, but that it is awfully difficult to tell one from the other. The angel, he says ('angels are partisans not of Good but of divine creation', while the devil 'is the one who refuses to grant any rational meaning to that divinely created world'), hearing the devil laughing, 'knew that he must react swiftly somehow, but felt weak and defenceless. Unable to come up with anything of his own, he aped his adversary.' And so the angels and the devil went on emitting strikingly similar sounds – yet sounds given opposite meanings and expressing quite opposite thoughts: 'whereas the devil's laughter denoted the absurdity of things, the angel on the contrary meant to rejoice over how well ordered, wisely conceived, good, and meaningful everything here below was.'

The result of all that?

[T]he angels have gained something from it. They have tricked us into a semantic imposture. Their imitation of laughter and (the devil's) original laughter are both called by the same name. Nowadays we don't even realize that the same external display serves two absolutely opposed internal attitudes. There are two laughters, and we have no word to tell one from the other.

Let me add that there is a devil and an angel sitting in each one of us. As a matter of fact, we have imagined the devil and the angels to account for two feelings so different that we find it hard to believe that they come from the same heart and respond to the same experience. One would hear both laughters when we laugh, were one listening attentively – but we seldom do. This is why the 'semantic imposture', in most cases, works so well.

2

In Search of Agency

In his perceptive study of Mikhail Bakhtin's idea of the carnival, Ken Hirschkop illuminates the close link which Bakhtin postulated between fear and power. Bakhtin spied out the fear at the cradle of power. What he found there, at the birth place of power, was *cosmic fear* – akin to Rudolph Otto's 'tremendous' and partly to Kant's 'sublime' fear:

> fear in the face of the immeasurably great and immeasurably powerful: in the face of the starry heavens, the material mass of the mountains, the sea, and the fear of cosmic upheavals and elemental disasters in ancient mythologies, worldviews, systems of images, in languages themselves and the forms of thinking bound up with them . . . This cosmic fear, fundamentally not mystical in the strict sense (being a fear in the face of the materially great and the materially indefinable power), is used by all religious systems for the suppression of the person and his consciousness.[1]

That cosmic – sublime – fear was, in Bakhtin's view, the prototype of mundane, earthly power, which, however, remoulded its primeval prototype into *official fear*, the fear of the human yet not fully human power, man-made but exceeding human capacity to resist.

We may add that, unlike the cosmic prototype, the official fear had to be, and indeed was, *manufactured* – designed, 'made to measure'; it needed human-made replicas of starry heavens and mountain masses; like them it was distant and inaccessible, but unlike them it sent a clear and unambiguous message to the mortals. In the laws which Moses brought to the people of Israel, the echoes of thunders high up on the top of Mount Sinai reverberated. But the laws spelled out light and clear what the thunders only darkly insinuated. The laws offered answers so that the questions might cease to be asked. Out of the unknown threat the demand of obedience to the known commandments had been conjured. The mundane power reforged primeval fear into the horror of deviation from the rule.

In its official avatar, the cosmic fear had been now *mediated*. It did not abate – it had only been tamed and domesticated. Once hovering freely and ominously high above the vale of tears, it now settled among its dwellers. It obtained an earthly address, though that did not make it more accessible: its new residence could be on a hilltop rather than in heaven, but access to it was closely guarded.

Fear and laughter

Unlike the cosmic powers, their earthly replicas *spoke* – and spoke in order to be *heard* and *obeyed*. That was, in a way, reassuring: the mortals now knew, or believed they knew, how to placate the powers' wrath and so how to put their own fear to rest. The deal was on offer: a trade-off easy to comprehend – quiet nights in exchange for compliant and obeisant days. One could now move around the stage, repeating whatever lines the life drama entailed; as long as one followed the script to the letter, one could trust the fearsome powers to doze peacefully in the wings.

The 'constitutive moment' of all earthly power is, says Bakhtin, 'violence, suppression, falsehood, trepidation and fear of the subjected'. This is, in his view, 'the suprajuridical crime of all power'. On which Hirschkop comments: the 'essence of political fear is the sense of one's utter vulnerability to the other, rather than worry over a specific threat of danger'. In this respect as well, official fear is the replica of its prototype, cosmic fear. And yet what the cosmic parent attains matter-of-factly must be

carefully worked out in the case of its official offspring: vulnerability must be *manufactured*. It is not enough to spell out the
rules which ought to be obeyed. What is needed in addition is the
terror of punishment that follows disobedience to the rules –
whatever the disobeyed rule might be like. One can argue the
wisdom of every rule; conformity to whatever may be the rule, to
the rule as such, is not, though, the matter of argument. The fear
which guards conformity must be of the cosmic kind. It must bear
more than casual resemblance to the pristine horror of that
ineluctable and ineradicable existential unsafety that is reborn
daily from the inexorable memory of ultimate vulnerability – of
death.

And yet, however hard they may try to shelter behind the
cosmic forces, their earthly spokesmen are nevertheless – look,
sound, smell – hopelessly human and thus, like all humans,
mortal. Cosmic fear would not flow into the mould of official
fear unless poured through the funnel of law, but human finger-
prints are hard to wipe off the tables of divine commandments.
In law, the imperturbable might of immortal cosmic forces and
the fragility of its mortal objects meet and mix. Like its objects,
law is vulnerable, only perhaps somewhat less so. Just how
vulnerable it is, is a matter of experiment and test. Bakhtin's
laughter is the way of recalling that this is, indeed, the case. It is
also the way to act out the chances which the recalling throws
open.

Of Enlightenment Lessing said that it emancipated us from the
myths of creation, revelation and eternal condemnation. Once
that happened, official fear lost a portion of its cosmic sanction –
just large enough to enable the experimenting and testing to start.
From the early Renaissance on, says Bakhtin, a struggle between
official fear and unofficial, popular laughter is waged, with mixed
fortune and the outcome far from determined. Laughter – confined at first spatially and temporally in the enclave of the annual
carnival feast – 'provided a completely different, emphatically
unofficial, extra-ecclesiastical and extra-governmental aspect of
the world' – the world of 'the person in human relations'. As a
matter of fact carnival laughter set up another, festive, world,
sharply opposed to the official seriousness of dull quotidianity.
That alternative world was visited on the occasion of the grip of
the first, official and serious, world being loosened for a time or

suspended. Visits to that other world, the world of laughter, 'freed people from fear, brought the world closer to the person'. From now on, there were to be two worlds instead of one, and human life was to alternate between fear and laughter, just as human cohabitation was to alternate between conformity to law and the never-fully-tamed, admittedly unbridlable exuberance of human togetherness.

The two worlds – how do they relate to each other? No single answer to this question seems right on its own. The mutual relation of the two worlds is probably much too complex to allow for a straight answer; or, rather, it is multi-faceted enough to sustain a number of different answers. One answer is war – a regular and continuous trench war, a war split between periodical campaigns and intervals of calm or a war sliced, guerrilla-style, into a multitude of scattered skirmishes and duels. Another answer is the division of labour, catering for the disparate and contradictory needs of the *homo* irredeemably *duplex*, forever torn between other-worldly tremor and this-worldly carousal. Yet another is complementarity – with the laughter making the fear bearable and the fear keeping the laughter within bounds; with laughter providing the respite necessary to recuperate from the fears of yesterday and gather the strength needed to face up to the fears of tomorrow; *Kraft durch Freude* as the necessary supplement of torture chambers and concentration camps; town-square dances, fairs and festivities as the indispensable addendum to mass terror. And there is also the safety valve effect – laughter as the dumping ground for the fear-production waste, a safeguard against the consequences of the natural tendency of all power to the over-production of official fear. A satisfactory answer, were it ever to be found, would probably be a mixture of all these, and more.

Modernity is an endemically 'transgressive' formation. It broke many a hard-and-fast borderline. Among other dividing lines broken, blurred or effaced in the times of modernity was that between fear and laughter. It is as if dark, fear-saturated quotidianity and bright, laughter-infested carnivals were crammed in a mortar and thoroughly crushed so that one ingredient of the compound can no more be told from the other – not with any degree of certainty. Like clouds lined with silver, fears tend to be lined with laughter; while the echoes of distant fears are faintly audible in most outbursts of laughter. What used to be confined to carnival venues and dates is now spilled all over the time/space of life. But so is the fear – with no more special enclaves from which it is barred entry.

One wonders, though, whether it makes sense to go on repeating after Bakhtin that laughter is the power of the powerless, and the limit set to what the official fears manufactured by the powers-that-be can reach when breaking the resistance of their subjects. It seems rather that modern power has found a way to harness laughter, its ancient enemy, to its chariot – to enlist it in its service. No longer is fear deployed to stifle and silence laughter. It is as if power has picked laughter as its most secure shelter; as if fear wants more laughter so that it will have more room to hide in and so that resistance to fear-wielding power could be paralysed before it started, and if it did explode, it would leave the fearsome intact. Like the phoenix from the ashes, or the ageing witch from the bathtub full of virgin blood, power arises from laughter reborn and rejuvenated.

The profound change in the mutual relation of fear and laughter runs parallel with another seminal departure, noted by Theodor W. Adorno: the reversal of directional tendency in the essence/appearance relationship. The genuine or craved-for essence is no longer sited in the authenticity or irreducible uniqueness of the self (the concept grasped in John Carroll's idea of the 'soul'), rather it 'passes into what lies concealed beneath the facade of immediacy, of the supposed facts, and which makes the facts what they are'. Such essence 'is the fatal mischief of a world arranged so as to degrade men to means of their *sese conservare*, a world that curtails and threatens their life by reproducing it and making them believe that it has this character so as to satisfy their needs.'[2]

To say that the essence moved onto the side of appearances so that all effort to reach the essence leads into the thicket of appearances, and to say that laughter is the sound through which fear makes itself audible, is to speak of one and the same process. Laughter no longer portends rebellion; rather, it signifies reconciliation with fear, submission to fear and recognition of its invincibility, resolution to take it lightly, intention to domesticate it and exploit it for the self's benefit; an intention which by a ruse of privatized life turns into an insurance policy of existential fear.

Men and women can no longer laugh without admitting the right of fear to be; as Adorno puts it, 'the individual is now scarcely capable of any impulse that he could not classify as an example of this or that publicly recognized constellation'.[3]

The official, power-manufactured fear mediated once for its cosmic prototype and ancestor. We live now through mediation mark two. The condensed official fear with an address fixed somewhere in the closely guarded streets of the governmental quarters has been taken apart and pulverized, and the dust arising from the demolition site has been sprinkled all over the vast expanse of individual life. The turn has come for the manufactured fear, itself a mediation, to be mediated – by countless individual terrors subsumed under the rubrics of uncertainty, insecurity and unsafety, all proclaiming (though in various degrees and with various measures of frankness) the inhuman might of the human-made fate.

The individual has been set free to construe her or his own fears, to baptize them with privately chosen names and to cope with them on her or his own. The big fear has been parcelled out into little units and then *privatized* – and so has laughter. Neither of the two has been given the opportunity, or at least a faintly viable prospect, to coalesce back into the grand oppression or grandiose rebellion. Fear and laughter left the street and settled in private homes. Private fears seldom meet other private fears, and when they do they do not easily recognize each other. That difficulty to concur and converge, to combine and be combined, to join and be joined, has come to be called individual freedom.

How free is freedom?

To be an individual does not necessarily mean to be free. The form of individuality on offer in late-modern or postmodern society, and indeed most common in this kind of society – *privatized* individuality – means, essentially, *unfreedom*.

In his perceptive study of the avenues available to contemporary individuals who struggle to escape the uncertainties that haunt them, Alain Ehrenberg selects an October 1983 Wednesday evening as the breakthrough moment. On that evening, Viviane and Michel, an ordinary and on the whole unremarkable couple easily lost in the city crowd, appeared in front of French TV cameras (and so on millions of TV screens) so that Viviane could say of Michel: 'My husband suffers from premature ejaculation', and complain that when with him, she 'never experienced pleasure'. Well, this was a breakthrough date for France (similar break-throughs occurred in other countries on different dates): an important taboo had been broken once and for all; words unspeakable in public had been made speakable, experiences meant to be confided only to one's nearest and dearest had been made fit for public confession. As Jacques Pradel put it ten years after the event,[4] 'we break with everything we have learned thus far: that emotions are signs of weakness, that it is wrong and ugly to cry. We break the taboos, we explore the personal territory, we traverse the no-man's-land of intimacy.' All this has also begun on that memorable Wednesday evening: permission to brandish emotions in public and parade the most intimate secrets of partnership – the secrets which, for being secret, used to make partnership intimate or make intimacy into a partnership.

By a curious reversal, that private sphere which stood out for its *right to secrecy*, has been redefined in one fell swoop as a sphere with the *right to publicity*. Expropriation came in the disguise of endowment. The break-in occurred while wearing the mask of emancipation.

But more things, and more important things than those mentioned already, happened on that fateful evening. To start with, not just the status of affairs previously confined to the private sphere changed; it could not be transformed, anyway, without a parallel change in the meaning of the 'public'. The latter concept used to be reserved for things and events by their nature 'collective', things or events no one could claim to be her or his private affair, let alone an exclusive possession, but in which everyone could demand to have a say on the ground that such things and events affect their private interests and possessions. Now the definition of the public has been also reversed. It has become a territory where private affairs and exclusive possessions are put on display, and the fact that no one can reasonably claim that they affect their own private interests or well-being has been declared irrelevant to the question of such display. True, display has been pronounced to be 'in the public interest' – but by the same token the meaning of 'interest' has also undergone a seminal shift, now being reduced to that of curiosity and the 'interest' in satisfying that curiosity. Making public whatever aroused or could arouse curiosity has become now the hub of the idea of 'being in the public interest'. And seeing to it that whatever is made public is put on display in a form attractive enough to arouse curiosity has become the main measure of 'serving public interests well'.

The 'public' has been emptied of its own separate contents; it has been left with no agenda of its own – it is now but an agglomeration of private troubles, worries and problems. It is patched together of the individual cravings for assistance in making sense of private, as yet inarticulate, emotions and states of mind, for instruction how to talk about such emotions in a language which others would comprehend, and for advice about how to deal with the flow of experience which the individuals find so difficult to cope with. The list of 'public issues' is no different from that of 'private affairs'; neither is that particular list richer than 'the sum of its items'.

At their best, the innumerable 'talk-shows' of the type triggered in France by Viviane's and Michel's public confessions perform a legitimizing function. Using the authority of numbers ('Everyone goes through it'; 'It may happen to everybody'; and so 'There is no shame in admitting, let alone going through, this sort of experience') they put a stamp of public acceptability (more than that: publicly affirmed desirability) on certain emotions. They offer words to express them and the cognitive frame in which to interpret their meaning. Having supplied the words and the keys of interpretation, they encourage individuals to seek similar emotions, to expect them to be experienced, to wonder why they are slow to arrive and less intense than promised when they come. Talk-shows, therefore, endorse the expression and simultaneously imply/induce/implant the genuine or putative, suffered or craved-for experience that is supposed to be clamouring to be expressed.

But here the public assistance stops. Nothing more can it offer, and among the items most conspicuously missing from the list of offers is the prospect of collective means to be collectively used in handling/solving individual problems. The public – the gathering of other individuals – can only applaud or whistle, praise or condemn, admire or deride, abet or deter, nudge or nag, incite or dampen; it would never promise to do something that the individual could not do herself or himself, to tackle the problem *for* the complaining individual (being but an aggregate of individual agents, the listening/commenting public is not an agency in its own right), to take the responsibility off the individual's shoulders.

Individuals come to the talk-shows alone with their troubles and when they leave they are sunk yet deeper in their loneliness. What they have learned – if they did not know it before, that is – is that the next move, and the move after that, and all the important and truly decisive moves in the future are and will be for them to make, that they can count solely on their own stamina and guts. Others may advise – may suggest the best steps to be taken – but it is up to the individual to take up the counsel or to desist, and it will fall upon the individual to bear with the consequences, whatever they might be. One lesson hammered home with particular strength and most likely to be absorbed is that in the case of the moves missing the target and failing to achieve their purpose the individuals will have only themselves to blame. The viewers learn in advance, well before entering the battlefield, that defeat – if suffered – will be due to his or her own mistakes, neglect or sloth. In the talk-show-style surrogate of public forum, objectivity serves the sole aim of endorsing the individuals in their monadic subjectivity. And 'subjectivity' comes to mean the self, left to its own muscles and cunning in its desperate struggle to navigate life between turbulent currents and treacherous reefs, while avoiding the mistakes which caused the *Titanic* to sink.

It was, though, the outspoken or inarticulate desire to escape from the monadic seclusion which brought the monads to the screens in the first place. The monads look and listen avidly because they find the monadic condition unpleasant, perhaps downright unendurable, and want to be monads no more. Individuals have become monads because they felt that the networks which linked them to other people and made them a part of 'larger totalities' have been one by one falling apart or were about to come apart.

Whatever has remained of the once dense and numerous safety nets no longer feels tight and reliable; one sees the nets being laboriously woven together only to decompose, be lacerated or torn apart altogether at short notice or without notice, with little or no effort. It has become all too evident that one cannot expect, as one expected in the past, that once woven according to the rules, the nets will stay firm and solid, needing only occasional repair. Quite a new type of skill is required now to keep them in good order; the habitual meticulous and laborious, 'once and for all' weaving techniques need to be replaced with ad-hoc, instant and flexible expedients of crisis-management. The monads have their eyes glued to the screen in the hope that they may learn such new techniques from other monads' experience. The talk-shows tell them how to do just that; ostensibly, they offer them knowledge about the means of escape from the monadic condition. But they also tell them that the feat can only be accomplished by pulling themselves out of the misery by their own bootstraps, counting on no one else's resources but their own.

The new know-how on offer is made to the measure of commercial contracts. These are tit-for-tat contracts: 'I'll deliver if you do.' And they are fixed-term contracts, up for renewal conditional on satisfactory reassessment, or altogether open-ended, liable to be terminated by either partner if a third person promises to deliver more attractive goods or deliver the goods for a lower price. They are also the type of contracts which assume a floating optimal point for compromise between interests which cannot be made fully compatible. (If they were, they would converge naturally and the contract would not be needed.) Where exactly that point is to be plotted depends on the balance of forces; the point may move following another shift in that balance and the best that a signed contract may achieve is to make the following of shifts too quickly somewhat less attractive to the partners. Finally, to extract the best possible benefits from a contract one needs above all the negotiating skills and experience in self-presentation; one needs to know 'how to sell' oneself and one's real or implied assets, and how to avoid selling either of the two too cheaply.

In short, the way of re-entering the togetherness which the monads seek tends to be modelled after bargaining/negotiating/ compromising procedure. The new nets are to be sewn in the fashion in which a temporary contiguity of not-fully-overlapping interests is achieved on the political stage, which itself becomes ever more closely modelled after the commodity market. This is, roughly, what is understood by the philosophy of 'life politics'

cultivated and spread by the talk-show culture. As Alain Ehrenberg puts it,[5] 'the family, like contemporary couples, tends to rest
on negotiated compromise: private life is publicized while being
modelled after the procedure of deliberation, negotiation and
compromise of political space.' It is indeed for that very reason
that the viewers feel that the spectacles address their own experience, or at any rate the interpretations which they themselves
have put on things that happened to them; it is for that very
reason that the messages conveyed are telling to their ears, look
credible and apparently trustworthy. The 'reality' in the form
given to it by 'reality shows', is – as Ehrenberg points out –
exactly what the viewers expected it to be. That picture 'confirms
the spirit of the time, recycles the dominant representations'. This
is an exercise not so much in realism as in rendering the imaginary
realistic. The spectacle is a look-alike of reality, but such a
convincing one that reality has to emulate it if it is to be
recognized for the reality it is.

In that imaginary-turned-reality the individual is set free; really
and truly free, that is free to use her or his resources at her or his
heart's pleasure and no longer dependent on any other resources.
The Enlightenment's promise that there is nothing which the
human species left alone and on its own cannot accomplish, if
only it is given enough time for the accumulation of necessary
knowledge, has been, as have so many other things, privatized.
The freedom of mankind has been translated as the freedom of
every one of its individual members. The big banknote has been
exchanged for a barrelful of coppers, so that all individuals may
carry some coins in their pockets. And they would be wise to do
so and to dig, if needed, into their own pockets – since the large-
denomination bill once kept in the collective trust of the species
and guaranteeing the solvency of each one and all together is no
longer in the safe. Privatization, let us remember, is not just about
the endowment of private persons, but also (and in the long run
most poignantly) about closing down the public treasury and
revoking its obligations to make the lot of private persons easier
to cope with. As Peter Drucker famously put it, 'No more
salvation by society.' And as Margaret Thatcher even more
famously phrased it, making the imaginary into reality, 'There is
no such thing as society.'

But imagining society was throughout modern times the primary ground on which the trust in the omnipotence of the human species rested. And imagining society was made plausible and feasible by the dense networks of duties and obligations in which all society's members were gradually, but relentlessly, entangled as they grew up into their adult rights. It was what each man and woman was expected to do or had to do in life and with life (the very fact that there was something indubitable and unquestionable that was to be done) that sustained the belief in some superior logic and purpose represented by society as a whole; a kind of society which was powerful, self-reliant and resourceful enough to absolve the individual from asking vexing questions she or he won't be able anyway to answer on her or his own. Such a trust is difficult to sustain by the experience of late-modern or postmodern life; by society which has lost much, perhaps all of its fleshy substance and muscular solidity since it neither demands much nor has much to offer in exchange; society evaporating from individual life together with the commandments once voiced in its name and the safety nets bearing its factory labels. As John Carroll observes,

> Today there is little practical welcome into the two main areas of life, love and work. On the one hand, the belief in marriage and family as central to well-being has weakened, and with it the rituals of entry and tissues of community support. On the other, high rates of youth unemployment and increasing insecurity of work tenure serve to accentuate the sense that your society neither needs nor wants you. If the only home they can foresee is the one they grew up in, then they are trapped between two alternatives, eternal childhood and death. And Punk may become the archetypal music of their time, addressed to those trying to live without belief in the future.

With the fast globalizing, and so increasingly exterritorial, knowledge elite at the top – a kind of elite which Jonathan Friedman succinctly described as 'modernists without modernism' (i.e. without any vision of a global state of affairs essentially better than the one in existence or any determination to help that better world into being) – spiritual leadership is becoming obsolete. It ceases to play its traditional role in societal integration; the relish with which a large section of the learned classes embraced the neoliberal vision of 'no society' testifies, in Carroll's opinion, to the 'diminishing social responsibility in the key elite institutions' and shows the potential but early-retired suppliers of societal meanings and values to be 'demoralized' and 'selfish'. This is, at any rate, how the rest of society views it. No wonder, therefore, that so many concur, some with joy but most with a varying degree of gloomy resignation, with Peter Drucker's blunt verdict.

Without belief in the collective destiny and purpose of the social whole, it is the individuals, each one on her or his own, who must give meaning to the life-pursuits. Not an easy task at the best of times, but truly daunting when no meaning can count on secure endorsement – secure enough to outlive the effort which its implantation takes.

No help can be reasonably expected from societal leaders. Even if they had enough power to give their preachings the air of durable, trustworthy solidity, they would not be of much assistance; they have stopped being preachers since they ran out of topics for homilies – except one, most persistently hammered, that of returning the buck to the former members of the congregation which they now have declared all but disbanded. With nothing to look for on high, one can only look around. And this is exactly what most people do, for the lack of better directions. According to Carroll, 'we learn by example, and there remains the need for exemplars, for heroes and morality tales about ambition, striving, success and failure.'[6] Indeed, the need for exemplars, for other lonely individuals like me, of others who, like me, have only their own ambitions and stamina to separate success from failure and who, like me, knew (or learned the hard way) that whatever is to be achieved in life, may be attained only *in spite of*, not *thanks to*, society. Learning by example is the lot of the monads and the way to internalize the demands and to master the routines of monadic existence. This is what talk-shows, together with the 'human-side stories' of celebrities currently in the limelight, are mainly about: about gnashing the teeth and tightening the fists, about cunning and avoiding the traps, about making the right impression and outsmarting those immune to impression-making.

Thomas Mathiesen has suggested[7] that as modernity has passed its phase of *Sturm und Drang* and moved into its late stage, Panopticon, the major tool of keeping people together in what has come to be known as 'society', has been gradually replaced with Synopticon: instead of the few watching the many, it is the many who nowadays watch the few. The many have no other choice but to watch; with the sources of instruction in public virtues all but missing, they may seek motives for life efforts solely in the available examples of private prowess and its rewards. And so they watch willingly, with gusto, and they demand loud and clear that there should be more of the like stuff to watch. Hiding private life from the public gaze is no longer 'in public interest'. The great and famous (great *because* famous) no longer aspire to pastoral power and thus no longer offer instruction in public virtues; the last service they may render to their former flock is to put their own lives on display for others to admire, but also to wish to and to hope to imitate. If Panopticon stood for the war of attrition waged against the private, for the effort to dissolve the private in the public or at least sweep under the carpet all particles of the private which would resist being put in a publicly acceptable shape, Synopticon reflects the disappearing act of the public, the invasion of the public sphere by the private; its conquest, occupation and piecemeal but relentless colonization. The pressures exerted on the borderline dividing/connecting the public and the private have been reversed.

Is this really the kind of freedom promised at the beginning?

Originally it was an active freedom, the freedom to make things and remake them so that they are more fit for human existence, that was promised by the thinkers of advancing modernity. What they had in mind was the *freedom of humankind*. Such freedom as included as its primal constituent the ability to bring things into such a shape that the members of the human species will no more be thwarted in their urge to act according to the most human of their natural endowments: the power to pass rational judgement and behave according to the precepts of reason. It was in the species' capacity to act, in the human collective ability to repair mistakes and neglectful actions of nature and their own past mistakes and neglectful actions, that the individual freedom – the freedom to follow the road of reason – was hoped to find its unshakeable foundation. Only inside the all-powerful human collectivity could the individual be really free – that is, not a slave to his pre-human and inhuman passions and lusts.

Much has been said about that idea, its benign and sinister sides, and its destructive potential fully revealed in the communist and fascist leaps to freedom so understood. There is no need to repeat it all now. What needs to be said, however, is that by now the idea has lost most of its credibility, that the promise to implement it has been withdrawn, and that the freedom which has been declared to arrive bears but a faint resemblance to the freedom which had been promised.

That freedom which has been declared to arrive is the aspect of the human condition to which Isaiah Berlin gave the philosophical name of 'negative freedom'; an aspect which in popular use has been spelled out as freedom to choose, and in its populist version as 'Less state, more money in the pocket' (as Margaret Thatcher unforgettably expressed it, the liberty 'to go to a doctor of my choice at a time of my choice'). The really existing freedom is explained as the absence of restraints imposed by a *political authority*. Neo-liberal philosophy and laissez-faireist practice of freedom does not wage war against all 'dictatorship over needs' (as Agnes Heller, Ferenc Feher and György Markus described that 'modernity running amuck', which was the communist experiment with total regulation); it only declared a war of attrition against *political* dictatorship over needs.

Assuming for a moment that 'negative freedom', freedom from constraints imposed by coercive limitation of individual choice, is indeed the sole libertarian aspect of the human condition that can be hoped for, are the excessive legislating/regulating ambitions of political power its sole, or at least its principal, enemy? Is the rolling back of the political legislative interference with human choices, nicknamed 'deregulation', a gateway to the genuine expansion of 'negative freedom'?

The deconstruction of politics

Individual choices are in all circumstances confined by two sets of constraints. One set is determined by the *agenda of choice*: the range of alternatives which are actually on offer. All choice means 'choosing among', and seldom is the set of items to be chosen from a matter for the chooser to decide. Another set of constraints is determined by the *code of choosing*: the rules that tell the individual on what ground the preference should be given to some items rather than others and when to consider the choice as proper and when as inappropriate. Both sets of constraints co-operate in setting the frame within which individual freedom of choice operates.

Throughout the classical phase of modernity the principal tool of setting the agenda of choice was *legislation*. From the point of view of the individual as chooser, legislation is first and foremost a power of preselection. The legislators make their choices before the time comes for the individuals to make theirs. The legislators cut down the range of choices open to the individuals: some choices, possible *in abstracto*, are excluded from the range of practical possibilities, or associated with punitive sanctions severe enough to make them exceedingly costly and thereby unlikely to be viewed by the ordinary chooser as feasible, let alone alluring. Legislation, in other words, separates the realm of practical availability from the range of abstract possibilities; the first is given a shape different from (above all, narrower than) the second.

The principal modern tool of setting the code of choosing was *education*. Education is an institutionalized effort to instruct and train individuals in the art of using their freedom of choice within the legislatively set agenda. Education is to supply the choosers with orientation points, the rules of conduct, but above all with the choice-guiding *values*, that is with the ability to tell the right reasons for according preference from the wrong reasons, and the inclination to follow the first while avoiding the second. Education is aimed at inducing individuals to internalize the norms which are henceforth to guide their practice. If the legislation sets the agenda by dividing the abstractly possible choices into such as are allowed to be made and other which are prohibited and punishable – education performs its code-setting function by further dividing the set of available/permitted choices into such as are desirable/advisable/proper and such as are unwelcome/inadvisable/inappropriate.

Explicitly or implicitly, the extant political institutions are nowadays in the process of abandoning or trimming down their role in agenda- and code-setting. This does not, however, mean – at any rate it does not mean necessarily – that by the same token the sphere of negative freedom is extended, or that individuals' freedom of choice is expanding. It only means that the function of agenda- and code-setting is being, to a consistently growing extent, ceded to forces other than political (that is, elected and in principle controlled) institutions. 'Deregulation' means curbing *the state's regulating role*, not necessarily the decline of, let alone the demise of, *regulation*. The retreat or self-limitation of the state has as its most salient effect a greater exposure of choosers to both the coercive (agenda-setting) and the indoctrinating (code-setting) impact of essentially non-political forces – primarily those associated with financial and commodity markets.

The agenda for most important choices can hardly under present conditions be politically constructed. A marked tendency of our times is the ongoing *separation of power from politics*: true power, able to determine the extent of practical choices, *flows*; thanks to its ever less constrained mobility it is virtually global – or, rather, exterritorial. All extant political (electable, representative) institutions remain so far stoutly local, virtually *glaebae adscripti*. Were not the agenda-setting task abandoned by territorial state authorities, it would anyway be ineffective; the hub of the present-day crisis of political process is not so much the absence of values or confusion caused by their plurality, as the absence of an agency effective enough to legitimate, promote, install and service any set of values or any consistent and cohesive agenda of choices.

The traditional agenda-setting role of the political state is presently focusing ever more narrowly on the 'direct rule' over certain social categories which only by a stretch of fantasy rather than imagination could be exposed and sensitized to market pressures and could therefore be hoped to move within the agenda set and maintained by those pressures (from the point of view of political authorities – to become 'self-regulated'). These categories entail, most notably, the postmodern poor recast as 'flawed consumers', and more generally all dangerous (potentially crimi-nal) classes which, having failed to get entry to the market-set agenda, are suspected of being eager to resort to alternatives which that agenda left off-limits. As for the rest of the population, an ever wider range of alternative choices is declared (explicitly or by default) *politically* 'adiaphoric', that is of no concern to political authorities.

If one follows the habitual mapping of the main modern battlegrounds of freedom, that latter tendency might be well read out as pointing towards the demise of coercive agenda-setting as such. The problem, however, is that an agenda of choice is still set, and that is does not tend to become less stiff and coercive for the reason of not being set *politically*. The agenda is set as before, only a new, non-political operating agent has elbowed out its political predecessor or at least comes now ever more often to play the first instead of the second fiddle. As principal agenda-setters, market pressures are replacing political legislation. In the field of consumer choices – however wide and varied the choices might appear – everybody *must*, as Adorno and Horkheimer observed, 'behave (as if spontaneously) in accordance with . . . previously determined and indexed level, and choose the category of mass product turned out for his type . . . What connoisseurs discuss as good or bad points serve only to perpetuate the semblance of competiton and range of choice.'[8]

Unlike in the case of the political operators, though, the present agenda crystallizes as an after-effect or side-effect of market operations: it does not precede them as a motive, even less as a deliberate intention or articulated objective. It has all the markings of a 'natural product' – and of a contingent, neither planned nor even anticipated, and so an unchosen product. The criteria of reason and rationality of action, adopted in the past to guide the agenda-setting activity of modern political institutions, do not apply therefore to the agenda emerging out of the play of market forces. This agenda is neither rational nor irrational, neither resonant with the precepts of reason nor militating against them. It just *is*, the way mountain ranges and oceans are – the appearance frequently endorsed in the politicians' favourite phrase, 'no alternative'. Indeed, the 'purposeful action' element in the final product is all but covered up, and so it is not immediately clear what kind of openly purposeful action could cause the agenda to be transformed.

Much the same observations apply to the present state of the code of choosing. Like the agenda of choices, that code is shaped and reshaped primarily by market pressures. Even if other institutions (including the educational/training ones) mediate in setting it up, the code they promote tends to be formed after the likeness of the model conduct which the individuals, were they responsive to market pressures, would need to adopt. Indeed, were the present-day code of choosing ever to reach the level of a declared, lucidly spelled-out and cohesively articulated objective, it would in all probability put that *responsiveness*, sensitivity to market suggestions and seductions, as its supreme target. This code prompts one to treat the world as primarily a container of potential objects of consumption; following the principle of consumption, it encourages the search for satisfaction; and following the principle of the consumer society, it induces individuals to view the arousal of desires clamouring to be satisfied as the guiding rule of the chooser's life and a criterion of a worthy and successful life.

Among the values toward which the choosers are trained to orient their choices, the entertainment potential of objects and events is assigned a superior place. As Pierre Bourdieu pointed out nearly twenty years ago, the manufacture of new desires is now doing the job once accomplished by normative regulation, so that publicity and commercial advertising may take the place once occupied by policing. It is the promise of pleasurable and previously untried sensation that triggers the desire; the offer of sensation-rich objects precedes as a rule the appearance of desire, so the latter is from the beginning object-directed. The current code of choosing therefore generates an agent whose skills consist primarily in the ability to spot the promise of pleasurable sensation and then to follow the hints and clues which mark the road toward its appropriation.

The effects by which the successful application of the code is assessed are, however, the experiences lived by the agents themselves; in their object-directed activities agents act as self-centred, self-preoccupied individuals, little interested in the repercussions their choices might have on anything other than their own sensations. Neither are such agents unduly preoccupied with the long-term effects of the choices. The pleasurable sensations they seek are as a rule short-lived, in many cases instant – instantly born yet instantly vanishing; few desires survive their satisfaction and ever new desires or new objects of desire are needed to keep the agents motivated to act.

Within the life-strategy serviced by the now prevalent code of choosing, human collectivities acquire value mostly as collections of such self-oriented agents; their own value is primarily that of the settings in which the sensation-seeking efforts may gain an added value through being replicated by similar agents and so in a way reinforced by the power of numbers. That repetition/

replication does not, however, assign to the collectivity of shared desires a quality distinct from (let alone superior to) the traits of its individuals that form it. Sensations which the agents jointly *seek* may only be *experienced* by each one of them individually; the pleasures are deeply private *Erlebnisse*, even if experienced in the company of other, similar or identical, pleasure-seekers. The most the company may offer is the endorsement of the desirability of desiring and the reassuring conviction that the object of desire has been rightly chosen.

The resulting decomposition of community finds its correlate in the fragmentation of life of each one of its constituting units. The life-process of every agent tends to split up into a series of episodes, each episode being in principle self-confined and self-sustained. Leaving the site cleared and ready for another sen-sation-seeking episode is perhaps the only self-limiting consideration which the code recommends. The pursuit of no desire should undermine, let alone pre-empt, the pursuits of future desires. Adorno and Horkheimer expressed this state of affairs rather sharply: 'Individuals are reduced to a mere sequence of instantaneous experiences which leave no trace, or rather whose trace is hated as irrational, superfluous, and "overtaken" in the literal sense of the word.'[9]

This fateful shift in the code – from the accretion and cumula-tion of achievements to the episodicity of experiences – has been exemplified in the gradual displacement of the value of health by that of fitness. As a value, health suggests a purpose-directed activity aimed at reaching and retaining a pattern; fitness, on the other hand, is open-ended and has no specific target nor an ideal pattern which, once attained, would justify the end of the effort. While health suggests a steady-state ideal to be worked out by systematic, consistent and monotonous effort, the ideal of fitness amounts, on the contrary, to a readiness for the new, the unknown and the unexpected. Health suggests equilibrium and continuity; fitness – rupture and discontinuity. Health assumes sameness; fitness emphasizes difference. The vision of health makes connections and suggests the unity of the life-process, while the vision of fitness dissociates that process into a sequence of one-off events best represented metaphorically by a string of beads.

The shift from health to fitness parallels a yet more seminal change in the treatment of time. Stretches of time used to acquire their meaning from the anticipation of further sections of the time-continuum still to follow; they are now expected to derive their sense from, so to speak, inside – to justify themselves without reference, or with only perfunctory reference, to the future. Time-spans are plotted beside each other, rather than in a logical progression; there is no preordained logic in their succession; they may easily, without violating any hard and fast rule, change places – sectors of time-continuum are in principle *interchangeable*. Each moment must present its own legitimation and offer the fullest satisfaction possible. And, obversely, the bliss, the peaking of desire and pleasurable sensation, may occur at any moment with equal likelihood. As locations of gratifying experience, moments do not differ. Hemingway's famous adage 'There is time for fishing and the time of drying the nets' was the product of a typically modern, not postmodern, code.

What follows from the above argument is that the passage to the late-modern or postmodern condition has not brought more individual freedom – not in the sense of more say in the composition of the agenda of choices or more capacity for negotiating the code of choosing. It only transformed the individual from political citizen into market consumer. If the losses in the three ingredients of *Sicherheit* are quite genuine, no less genuine than the loss of freedom was inside the 'classic' stage of modernity – the gain in freedom allegedly obtained in exchange in the late-modern or postmodern phase is to a large extent illusory. The illusion is, however, safely protected from unmasking in a context in which the processes of agenda- and code-setting are more or less invisible and in which the products of such processes reach the individual in the form of an 'offer one cannot refuse' rather than a commandment. Obedience to the code is disguised as self-propelled conduct; the poison of oppression has been squeezed out of the sting of unfreedom.

Where the private and the public meet

Unfreedom becomes oppression once agents are forced to act against their will and so suffer for not being able to behave according to their wishes and finding themselves doing what they would not do of their own will. Not all unfreedom, however, is experienced and lived through as oppressive; quite often the following of rules and commands which the actors neither composed nor chose feels neither distressing nor deplorable. There is a considerable element of compulsion, i.e. unfreedom, in every routine conduct; but routine, far from being perceived as tyrannical, underlies the feelings of safety and homeliness which on the whole are deeply gratifying. The state of unfreedom is endemically ambivalent. This makes that much easier the task of all powers, the task of eliciting discipline and obedience to its commands: the bossiness of pastoral power always hovers on the brink of oppression, but all too often tends to be gratefully received, perhaps even eagerly sought, by the flock – as the reliable warrant of safe and secure daily routine. Socialization, as most textbooks tell first-year sociology students, consists in inducing people to do willingly what do they must.

Yet whether it feels oppressive and repulsive or benign and comforting, all unfreedom means *heteronomy*, that is the state in which one follows rules and commands of someone else's; an *agentic* state, that is a state in which the acting person is an agent of somebody else's will. Persons may resent that alien will and watch for the occasion to deceive or rebel; they may accept – grudgingly – the uselessness of all resistance; they may be glad that someone else took the responsibility for their actions and freed them from the noxious need to choose and decide; they may even fail to notice that what they do and go on doing is done under compulsion, and never imagine a different way of going about their daily business. The fact remains that in all such cases the agents are *not autonomous*: they do not compose the rules which guide their behaviour nor do they set the range of alternatives they are likely to scan and ponder when making their big or small choices.

In his last speech, delivered on 22 March 1997, shortly before his death, Cornelius Castoriadis, one of the greatest political philosophers of our time, suggested that the decisive step towards autonomy had been taken once the ancient Greeks started to precede their laws with the preamble *edoxe te boule hai to demo* – 'it seems good to the council and to the people'.[10] 'It *seems* good', Castoriadis points out, *not* 'It *is* good'. The realm of autonomy begins where the realm of certainty ends.

Humans can be autonomous or self-confident – hardly both at the same time.

What was so unusual, indeed revolutionary, about the Greek formula was that all other societies before and most societies since would rather say of the rules they proclaimed and enforced that they *are* good and ought be obeyed for that very reason. Those other societies – almost all known societies with but few Hellenic and modern exceptions – were *heteronomous* societies, that is the kind of societies

> which certainly create their own institutions and significations, but they also occult this self-creation by imputing it to an extrasocial source – in any case, one that is external to the effective activity of the effectively existing collectivity: the ancestors, the heroes, the gods, God, the laws of history or those of the market. In these heteronomous societies, the institution of society takes place within a closure of meaning. All questions the society under consideration is capable of formulating can find a response within its imaginary significations, and those that cannot be formulated are not so much forbidden as mentally and psychically impossible for the members of that society.[11]

Let us note: whether they know it or not and whether they are ready to live with that knowledge or not, all societies are autonomous (all societies do create their institutions, and at any rate keep them alive, operative and effective), but only some, indeed very few, openly admit it and make a point out of it. Perhaps it is better not to divide societies into heteronomous and autonomous (while speaking of 'heteronomous' society, one obliquely endorses the cover-up operation which most societies perform by design or by default), but into autonomous *an sich* and autonomous *für sich*. The difference between the two kinds of society is one between the presence or absence of the *awareness* of autonomy and the degree to which that awareness has been *institutionalized* in the day-to-day operation of society.

It is the discovery and explicit admission of the inescapably human origin of human institutions, and hence the taking of collective responsibility for their merits and deficiencies, that makes society autonomous *für sich*. (Just as the admission of one's own responsibility for the virtues and vices of one's deeds makes the individual genuinely autonomous, i.e. autonomous in the *für sich* sense.) The consequence of being autonomous – that is, *self-consciously* autonomous – is the awareness that the institutions of society could be different, perhaps better, than they are, and thus no one of the extant institutions, however ancient or otherwise venerable, may claim immunity from scrutiny, re-examination, critique and re-evaluation.

Being autonomous *für sich* means being aware of society's historicity, but above all of its on-going, continuing, and *perpetual* historicity. It means refutation of the myth of closure, but also the stout refusal to be closed, now or ever after, either by the sacred and thus untouchable legacy of past resolutions or by an ideal pattern of a perfect society which, when reached, would have justified – indeed, impelled – the end to self-scrutiny and self-reformation. A truly autonomous society cannot exist in any other form but that of its own project: that is, as a society which admits an ever expanding freedom of self-examination, critique and reform, rather than a pre-given pattern of happiness, as its only purpose and *raison d'être*.

We may observe that an autonomous society so understood is an endemicably vulnerable form of human cohabitation. This vulnerability, however, chimes well with similarly endemic and, in addition, unavoidable vulnerability of the human existential condition. The autonomous society openly admits the in-built mortality of all its creations and attempts to derive from that unchosen fragility the chance of perpetual self-transformation, perhaps also self-improvement. Autonomy is a joint, concerted effort to reforge mortality from a curse into a blessing . . . Or, if you wish, the audacious attempt to deploy the mortality of human institutions in the bid for perpetual viability of human society.

A few months before his death Hans Jonas, one of the greatest ethical philosophers of our time, noted that the idea of 'personal' immortality is inherently paradoxical and self-defeating.[12] Personal immortality, were it at all thinkable, would make everything truly worth while in human life impossible to achieve as well as imagine; it is personal mortality which stands behind the possibility of transcendence and so of all value. This incontestable fact makes mortality into a blessing. 'To each of us, the knowledge that we are here but briefly and a nonnegotiable limit is set to our expected time may even be necessary as the incentive to *number our days and make them count*' [my italics – Z. B.]. It is thanks to that knowledge that each of our days counts and that one day is not – cannot be, cannot be allowed to be – the same as the days before and the days after. Fertility, creation, imagination – they all have sense only in the context of mortality; it is that context which makes life worth living. And 'life' here is not just the personal life of the human individual, but the duration of the human species and each collectivity that endures in its midst. Jonas takes his own life experience as a ground for the verdict:

> a native sensibility for visual and poetic art persists, not much dulled, in my old age; I can still be moved by the works I have learned to love and have grown with. But the art of our own time is alien to me, I don't understand its language, and in that respect I feel already a stranger in the world.

It is because the rejuvenation of individuals is no more than a topic for fairy tales and science fiction stories, and because 'starting anew' (let alone 'returning to the starting point') is but a dream hardly ever surviving the moment of wakening, that human societies may retain their youthfulness in an unending series of new beginnings. Mortality as a 'natural complement' of birth is the constant source of that marvel which is the perpetually renewed and refreshed face of the world; the youth and creative power of humanity persists, immune to the ageing of each and every human.

> The term evolution itself already reveals the creative role of individual finitude, which has decreed that whatever lives must also die . . . The ever-renewed beginning, which can only be had at the price of ever-renewed ending, is mankind's safeguard against lapsing into boredom and routine, its chance of retaining the spontaneity of life.

It is not despite, but thanks to mortality that societies may keep their options forever open. Keeping the options open means welcoming accidents and hazards. It also means accepting that no solutions, however ingenious and however perfect they may seem at the time, are likely to persist forever nor that it should be desired that they do. The perpetuity of society is built of transient and mortal ingredients. And a viable society, resistant to senile lethargy, paralysis, stupor and rigor mortis is possible only in as far as there is no confusion between the duration of society and the eternity of any of the forms it assumes and abandons in its history.

In Castoriadis's succinct expression, 'the test [*l'épreuve*: a semantically complex word, also meaning, among other things, trial and hardship] of freedom is undetachable from the test of mortality . . . No being – neither an individual nor a society – can be autonomous without accepting mortality.'[13] And accepting mortality means perpetual questioning, re-examining all judgements and verdicts, also the grounds on which judgements rest and the premisses that led to the verdicts. To put it differently (as Castoriadis did himself in another context), accepting mortality means denying any lasting grounds and immortal/eternal/extemporal foundations to *de facto* validity of institutions and significations; that validity which is but a sediment of past autonomous choices, but tries nevertheless, in the false hope of greater solidity, to 'heteronomize' the autonomy of its own nature.

De facto validity is the product of institutional inertia which sets itself against the incisiveness of reason; *de facto* validity is a premonition and prodromal symptom of death – or life which takes death for its pattern. It is only *de jure* validity – validity that is a product of reflection and deliberation and knows that it is this and nothing else – which a society bent on endurance may honour. If *de facto* validity is *given*, *de jure* validity is always *a task*, something yet to be established, something sought and never found 'absolutely', once and for all times. *De facto* validity is moribund precisely for the original sin of denying (or forgetting about) its own transcience and mortality. *De jure* validity is forever viable and exuberant thanks to having accepted its own temporality and impermanence.

The search for *de jure* validity calls therefore for critical reflection and refrains from exempting anything, itself including, from it. It is the only human faculty which can confidently shake off the charge of 'infinite regression', that favourite argument of all advocates of absolute and ultimate foundations. Infinite regression – using the foundations already built in the job of dismantling and clearing the site for other, no less temporary, foundations – is but one manifestation of the paradox of duration put together from, and by, transient beings. It is the other side of the infinite progression. Critical reflection is one human activity that – very much like life itself – does not have foundations but does not need them either, and so feels no need to justify itself, let alone apologize, when asked questions from utility or instrumentality – questions like 'On what authority?', 'What for?' or 'For the sake of what?'

Critical reflection is guided by the need to scrutinize the *de jure* validity of human institutions and significations, but as much as it is devoid of foundations other than its own impetus it also lacks a point of destination. It is not foreclosed (it refuses to be foreclosed) by either a preceding brief or a *telos* given before the take-off point. It builds and dismantles its own foundations and targets as it goes.

Critical reflection is the essence of all genuine *politics* (as distinct from the merely 'political' – that is, related to the exercise of power). Politics is an effective and practical effort to subject institutions that boast *de facto* validity to the test of *de jure* validity. And democracy is a site of critical reflection, which derives its distinctive identity from that reflection. Or, to quote Castoriadis once more, we can define politics as

> explicit and lucid activity that concerns the instauration of desirable institutions and democracy as the regime of explicit and lucid self-institution as far as is possible, of the social institutions that depend on explicit collective activity.
>
> It is hardly necessary to add that this self-institution is a movement that does not stop, that it does not aim at a 'perfect society' (a perfectly meaningless expression) but, rather, at a society that is as free and as just as possible. It is the movement that I call the project of an autonomous society, and that, if it is to succeed, has to establish a democratic society.[14]

The above is, of course, an articulation of the *ideal type* of politics and democracy, not the description of a 'really existing' politics and democracy nor the characteristics of societies which are called by their spokesmen 'democratic' and of governmental processes commonly presented as politics. Really existing politics and democracy are as distant from their ideal types as contemporary societies are remote from the model of an autonomous society. The latter is present in contemporary practice at best as a *project*, and as all projects it has a powerful adversary in the realities it is meant to transform. The 'explicitness and lucidity' which Castoriadis names as the foremost characteristics of politics made to the measure of societal autonomy are continually thwarted and compromised by the fact that all thinking and the activity which follows it can be conducted only in the cognitive framework supplied by 'tradition' – and 'tradition means that the question of the legitimacy of tradition cannot be posed.'[15]

Yet the autonomic thinking and conduct that gestates within tradition and has no other place to be born and take shape cannot proceed without such questioning. Opposing the natural inclination of human – never confident enough – reason to seek foundations outside itself and to exempt them from the list of its legitimate targets, autonomous thinking derives its resolve from the refusal to leave any thought-construct, including its own explicit or tacit presumptions, outside its critical brief. So comprehensive a task must be daunting. Autonomous reason is cast in the situation of permanent creation, and there are no signposts nor recipes which it could trust and consider once for all tested and having their reliability certified. It is a *conditio sine qua non* of all genuine autonomy that 'no problem is resolved in advance. We have to create the good, under imperfectly known and uncertain conditions. The project of autonomy is end and guide, it does not resolve for us effectively actual situations.'[16]

One thing that autonomous reason stubbornly refuses to offer (and cannot offer as long as it remains what it is) is an advance assurance of a happy ending – of a good resolution. Uncertainty, moreover, does not cease once a resolution has been taken. Autonomous reason, unlike its heteronomous cousin, makes no clear distinction betwen past and future; the past is as uncertain, unfinished, incomplete and open to re-examination (bound to be re-examined, sooner or later, and shown to be different from its currently imputed identity) as the future consequences of the present actions. Uncertainty, and worse still a boundless uncertainty, uncertainty of the projects and the grounds alike, is a permanent condition of autonomous reason.

The strength and the weakness of autonomous reason stem from the same root. That reason flouts the desperate human desire for reassurance. This is why it is so often and so widely resented. Its weaknesses strengthen the hand of its heteronomous adversary; the thirst for absolute foundations and codes of practice cannot be easily quenched, and more often than not can only grow more intense – with every mouthful of the freedom-cum-uncertainty cocktail served by autonomous reason.

The chances of autonomous reason depend on the existential condition of its prospective users. But the nature of this dependence appears to be the reverse of what common sociological wisdom would suggest. Contrary to that wisdom, the chances that the call of autonomous reason will be heeded and the ranks of its users/practitioners will expand does not grow in proportion to the degree of adequacy of the autonomous reason's message to the experience of its addressees. There is little hope that people will listen more eagerly to the clarion call of autonomy the better it corresponds to the realities of their daily life. It seems more likely that the deeper their feeling of insecurity, the more keenly they will turn their ears in the opposite direction – to the promises of the new heteronomy. It is the people who feel secure and in control of their lives who will probably find the 'autonomy project' most attractive, and the vision of acting without the *a priori* certainty of the results most palatable. It is therefore unlikely that the message of autonomy may reach people who need it most merely through an effort of enlightenment, education or propaganda. Some deeper-reaching reform of the existential plight is required. The key to autonomy is not in the hands of philosophers. Its fate is, by and large, the matter of politics.

The *agora* under attack: the two invasions

The 'autonomy project' is double-edged, and cannot be otherwise: society, to be autonomous, needs autonomous individuals, and individuals can be autonomous only in an autonomous society. This circumstance casts doubt on the preoccupation of political theory in general, and the theory of democracy in particular, with the *separation* between the public and the private domains and their mutual *independence*. It is rather the *link*, the mutual *dependency*, the *communication* between the two domains which should lie in the centre of both theories. The boundary between the public and the private which these theories are so keen on drawing should be seen as an *interface*, rather than viewed after the model of the closely guarded inter-state border meant primarily to slow down and limit the cross-border traffic and to sift out illegal travellers.

The distinction between private and public spheres is of ancient origin; it goes back to the Greek *oikos*, the household, and *ecclesia*, the site of politics, where matters affecting all members of the *polis* are tackled and settled. But between *oikos* and *ecclesia* the Greeks situated one more sphere, that of *communication* between the two; the sphere whose major role was not keeping the private and the public apart and guarding the territorial integrity of each, but assuring a smooth and constant traffic between them. That third and intermediate sphere, the *agora* (the private/public sphere, as Castoriadis puts it), bound the two extremes and held them together. Its role was crucial for the maintenance of a truly autonomous *polis* resting on the true autonomy of its members. Without it, neither the *polis* nor its members could gain, let alone retain, their freedom to decide the meaning of their common good and what was to be done to attain it. But the private/public sphere, like any ambivalent setting or any no-man's land (or, rather, a land of too many owners and disputed ownership), is a territory of constant tension and tug-of-war as much as it is the site of dialogue, co-operation or compromise.

There are two ways in which the *agora* may be attacked, its integrity endangered and its role distorted or altogether undermined with the effect of folding back the autonomy of society and of its individual members alike. One is the totalitarian tendency, deeply entrenched in the 'modern project', but one that has become particularly salient in the gory history of the century now coming to its close. The memory of two gigantic totalitarian experiments and the multitude of their paler yet no less ugly copies is still fresh in the turn-of-the-century generation. No wonder it hangs over political imagination of our times and like any other historical memory is a blessing and a curse at the same time. Most current models of 'civil society', allegedly the contemporary equivalent of the *agora*, acquired their shape in the shadow of that memory. While alerting against one mortal danger hovering over the present-day *agora*, it prompts the playing down of the other dangers, whose true nature and, above all, true consequences for the human condition are yet to be unpacked in full.

The totalitarian tendency, in Hannah Arendt's epigrammatically concise definition, is the tendency to 'make human beings superfluous': redundant, disposable as individuals, as separate beings with their own motives, thoughts, preferences and dreams, as 'private' beings in the sense of eluding any classificatory exercise oblivious to the irreducible idiosyncrasy and uniqueness of each human creature.

> [C]ertain peculiar qualities of secret police are general qualities of totalitarian society rather than peculiarities of the totalitarian secret police. The category of the suspect thus embraces under totalitarian conditions the total population; every thought that deviates from the officially prescribed and permanently changing line is already suspect, no matter in which field of human activity it occurs. Simply because of their capacity to think, human beings are suspect by definition, and this suspicion cannot be diverted by exemplary behaviour, for the human capacity to think is also a capacity to change one's mind.

The totalitarian tendency aims at the total annihilation of the private sphere, of the realm of individual self-constitution and self-determination – at the ultimate, irreversible dissolution of the private in the public. The aim is not so much to stop individuals from thinking – since that would be impossible even by the most fanatical of standards; but to make that thinking impotent, irrelevant and of no consequence for the success or failure of power. At the far end of the totalitarian tendency communication channels between public power and whatever has remained of private individuals are sealed. There is no need for dialogue, since there is nothing to talk about: the subjects have nothing to say which could possibly be of value to the business of power, and the powers-that-be have no further need to convince, convert or indoctrinate their subjects. Even the *monologue* of power fades and gradually falls silent. Only snappy commands and 'orders for the day' are issued, the rest having been entrusted to the now thoughtless obedience to the routine. The logic of the routine takes over from ideology; it was logic, after all, unanchored and free-floating logic, a self-centred and self-referential logic, a logic no more hampered by the resistance of the matter and immune to all reality-tests, which was the principal attraction of totalitarian thinking as it caught the imagination of all modern dreamers of the 'perfect order'. Arendt quotes Stalin's admission that it was not the idea nor the oratory, but

> irresistible force of logic [that] thoroughly overpowerd [Lenin's] audience . . . [That logic] like a mighty tentacle seizes you on all sides as in a vice and from whose grip you are powerless to tear yourself away; you must either surrender or make up your mind to utter defeat.

And comments:

> [I]n perfect accordance with 'ice-cold reasoning' and the 'irresistible force of logic', the workers lost under Bolshevik rule even those rights they had been granted under tsarist oppression and the German people suffered a kind of warfare which did not pay the slightest regard to the minimum requirements for survival of the German nation.[17]

The totalitarian tendency needs ideology as a ladder, but the ladder was of no more use once, having climbed to the top, the tendency turned into state power. That distant ideal, which like a powerful star pulls the totalitarian tendency out of the magma of insecure and confused existence, is not a vision of an ideology-dominated society, but of a society which neither will have a need for, nor will have made room for, ideology – since it will have put paid to argument, the struggle of opinions and interest clashes. In such a society, logic would replace argument, and deduction would suffice where laborious and painstaking processes of induction, experimenting, testing and monitoring were required in the really existing, messy, impudent and uncompliant society. Such an ideology-free society is not a wild dream nor an ideal hatched in a demented mind; the totalitarian tendency shared that ideal with the modern, all-too-modern pilgrimage to the land of certainty. The totalitarian tendency was dormant, sometimes fully awake, in every modernist project.

Many modernist intellectuals – avant-garde architects, artists, novelists and poets – radicalized the modern dream of order. They shared in that dream and were furious that it took such a long time to come true. They saw no reason to waste more time; they were impatient and itching to act and to act *now*, as is the desire of all zealots, including the zealots of modernity. Unbound by the pragmatic concerns of the politicians, who must, willingly or not, practise 'the art of the possible', the architects and the urban designers, and even more so the architects and designers of words, could set their imagination free, at least on their writing desks and drawing boards, if not in the street. But thanks to that freedom they could express the spirit of modernity more fully and vividly than any politician confronted with the messy and confused realities of order-keeping. By the same token, however, the seeds of rift and discord between thought and practice had been sown. The modernist artists' courage was the politicans' impracticality; the artists' consistency was the politicians' levity and irresponsibility.

Hence the bizarre and puzzling – ambivalent, convoluted, schizophrenic, *Haßliebe* kind – relationship between modernist arts (and, more generally, modernist ideas) on the one hand, and modern powers on the other. Enthusiasm for and fascination with force, with power and particularly with the power of enforcement, alternating with long periods of disenchantment and resentment of all powers-that-be; an incongruous mixture of attraction and repulsion – love of the high-and-mighty never free of suspicion, and hatred never devoid of fascination. Love was destined to stay unrequited, but hatred bore all the symptoms of the agonies of the lover betrayed, though no less besotted for the beloved's treachery. And there was more than one reason for that unresolvable ambivalence to engrave itself on the history of modernist arts.

The majority of modern thinkers, modernist artists prominent among them, laid the guilt at the door of those many who stuck to the ways and means already left behind: people with outdated taste (that is, in modernist language, tasteless people), unable or unwilling to catch up with the insights of the avant-garde. They blended such atrocious and contemptible people into a collective image of the *bourgeois*, labelled them philistines, decried them as vulgar, coarse, uncultured or dilettantish. They refused the so-construed enemy the right to artistic judgement and particularly the ability to pass sound judgements. Coming from such an enemy – powerful in numbers, base and mediocre in spirit – any judgement could be nothing but backward and obsolete; no more than an expression of the past which had forfeited its right to exist, not to mention the right to speak with an authority able to bind the present. And they blamed the indolent, toothless, meek democracies, together with their ideas of equality, freedom and equality in freedom (which in their view could result only in the rule of mediocrity) for legitimizing and reinforcing the pretences of the vulgar and the ignorant. It was the fault of democratic regimes that, as Ortega y Gasset spelled out and many repeated after him, 'commonplace mind, knowing itself to be commonplace, has the assurance to proclaim the rights of the commonplace and to impose them wherever it will . . . Anybody who is not like everybody, who does not think like everybody, runs the risk of being eliminated.'[18]

Of the early twentieth-century intellectuals, Edward Timms remarked that their characteristic was the 'unprecedented concern to change the world, not merely to interpret it'; they knew that – to change – the world power is needed; and not just any power, but a huge, confident and resolute one. But they had less and less hope that the liberal-democratic politics cut to the measure of the circumspect and cowardly bourgeois will ever muster that kind of determination. No wonder that many modernist thinkers and avant-garde artists 'began to see themselves as agents of social protest and cultural transformation'; no wonder either that they looked feverishly for political forces radical and impatient like themselves and like themselves disgusted by the sluggish pace of change, but also promising a genuine and thorough overhaul of all social realities. The Bolshevik Revolution and Mussolini's March on Rome 'exerted a remarkable fascination on leading European writers of this period . . . [M]any of the finest minds were drawn towards ideologies which promised more radical solutions . . . [T]hese new systems seemed glamorous and dynamic, offering visions of fraternal solidarity and collective action.'[19]

Few modernists followed Jules Benda's call to non-partisanship, political detachment and neutrality. But even fewer found palatable the moderate centre of the political spectrum. Most felt truly at home among revolutionary slogans; they welcomed calls to violence. In her bitter indictment of the modernist rebellion against reality and the 'bourgeois politics' that defended it, Hannah Arendt recalls Ernst Jünger, who greeted the slaughter of the World War battlefields hoping that the whole texture of life might go down in its 'storms of steel'; as well as the 'carefully chosen' words of Thomas Mann, who described the war as 'chastisement' and 'purification', and pointed out that 'war in itself, rather than victories, inspired the poet'. Arendt warns the reader:

> Simply to brand as outbursts of nihilism this violent dissatisfaction with the prewar age and subsequent attempts at restoring it (from Nietzsche and Sorel to Pareto, from Rimbaud and T. E. Lawrence to Jünger, Brecht and Malraux, from Bakunin and Nechayev to Aleksander Blok) is to overlook how justified disgust can be in a society wholly permeated with the ideological outlook and moral standards of the bourgeoisie. Yet it is also true that the 'front generation', in marked contrast to their own chosen spiritual fathers, were completely absorbed by their desire to see the ruin of this whole world of fake security, fake culture and fake life. This desire was so great that it outweighed in impact and articulateness all earlier attempts at a 'transformation of values', such as Nietzsche had attempted, or a reorganization of political life as indicated in Sorel's writings, or a revival of human authenticity in Bakunin, or a passionate love of life in the purity of exotic adventures in Rimbaud. Destruction without mitigation, chaos and ruin as such assumed the dignity of supreme values.[20]

The modernist souls breathed freely in the 'proto-totalitarian atmosphere' of inter-war Europe of rapidly shrinking centre and increasingly powerful radical wings. Some artists – like Gottfried Benn, Ezra Pound, Marinetti and Céline – opted for the fascist right with its gospel of blood-letting, destruction and the 'great purification'. Like Spengler, they waxed lyrical about war and violence 'as the superior form of human existence'; Jünger believed that only war was capable of expressing 'life in all its might'. Jünger proposed replacing the petty and trivial squabbles of liberal democracy with the 'heroic landscape of dream' drafted by arms. The long line of nationalist thinkers, which included names as illustrious as those of Arthur Moeller van der Bruck (the author of a book the title of which Hitler's state adopted as its name), Werner Sombart, Othmar Spann and Carl Schmidt, were never far behind in their fascination with the resolute and merciless force.[21] Some other (admittedly more, if one believes the history of intellectuals written mostly by the victors as long as they remained the victors) members of avant-garde movements and schools felt more at home in the communist camp with its promise to bring forth the long-awaited demise of corrupt and rotten bourgeois society and free men from the shackles of historical necessity (as the unplanned, contingent and blundering course of history, repulsive to the very spirit of modern intellectual endeavour, was dubbed). But whether they opted for the right-wing or the left-wing variety of radical politics, they were all drawn, seduced and enthused by the prospect of doing away in one fell swoop with cowardice, poverty of imagination, false consciousness and everything else that refused to obey the milder methods of persuasion and so frustrate the effort to combat the infuriating stupor, inertia, resilience and inflexibility of social realities. The modernists sought powers mighty enough to match the size of their own ambitions; only the political extremes seemed to meet the bill. No parliamentary democracy seemed to be able or willing to throw open the gates to whatever was dear to modernist hearts.

According to Renato Poggioli, the Futurism of Philippo Tommaso Marinetti displayed from the outset 'the activism and the agonism' which were the constitutive features of all avant-garde movements.[22] The Futurists were bedazzled by the 'multicoloured, polyphonic tides of revolution in modern capitals', that 'perpetual becoming', which – as they thought – offered the desperately needed setting for that 'complete renewal of human sensibility' which was to be accomplished by the artists with the modernist ideas close to their hearts. They found the 'Machine-Man' a right and proper foundation for the rejection of the mawkish and maudlin sentimentalizing about nature and the lyrical obsession with the 'I' – the two major obstacles on the road to the 'new sensibility'. All this prompted them to welcome the street marches of the Black Shirts with the orchestrated incantations as the only sounds to be heard, the disbanding of parliamentary 'talking shops' and the promise to wash off the weaknesses of the 'I' in the mighty, powerful, but silent and obeisant tides of the masses.

Ideologists and their ideologies assist the totalitarian tendency in climbing the ladder of power. Ideologists are the most outspoken and vociferous inhabitants of the modern *agora*, that social space where private worries struggle to lift themselves to the rank of public issues and where the *pronunciamentos* of current or would-be power-holders battle to represent themselves as public solutions to private troubles. The ideologists most useful, perhaps indispensable for the progress of the totalitarian tendency, are those which use the *agora* to charge it with the crime of being what it is – that is a noisy, unruly and rowdy market-place of complaints and demands. In their ideologies, the *agora* is blamed for the selfsame afflictions whose victims came to it in search of a cure and redress. It is, in addition, accused of standing in the way of resolute and effective action, while the abolition of the *agora* is praised as the radical way to exterminate the troubles which brought the complainants to it in the first place.

Such ideologies must sound sweet and soothing to ears eager to catch a hint of hope – and they sound all the more sweet and soothing for the *agora*'s frequent failure to relate the private – and divisive – worries to the public – and uniting – issues. 'Nothing proved easier', Hannah Arendt observed, 'to destroy than the privacy and private morality of people who thought of nothing but safeguarding their private lives.' Intellectual detractors and scoffers of the *agora* prepared the ground for that destruction through depriving people of their only chance to think of something other than their private lives; and above all of that something which – as time would show – was the sole trustworthy safeguard of all privacy and all morality.

All offers of unconditional love and good behaviour becoming of faithful fellow-travellers remained, though, unanswered, if not downright repulsed by black, brown or red shirts alike – as in the case of Gottfried Benn in Germany with his gut-hatred of 'random processes' and unalloyed enthusiasm for the *Zucht*, or the modernist poets and painters and architects of Bolshevik Russia with their celebration of the 'Scythians and New Barbarians', hoped to feel no pity for whatever outlived its right to exist. Everywhere the loving advances were repelled for the same reason. There were good reasons for the romance to remain one-sided and the love unreciprocated. As Raymond Williams put it, all their internal squabbles notwithstanding, the diverse modernist movements were alike in that they

> were pioneering new methods and purposes in writing, art and thought. It is then a sober fact that, for this very reason, they were so often rejected by mainstream political forces. The Nazis were to lump left, right and centre modernists together as *Kulturbolshevis-*

mus. From the middle and late 1920s, the Bolsheviks in power in the Soviet Union rejected virtually the same range.[23]

'The mainstream political forces' in question were, to be sure, the totalitarian outposts of the aggressive and arrogant modernity, the sections of modern forces which cut themselves loose from all constraints – above all, the constraints of the *agora* – and run amuck. There was something morbidly attractive in that madness for the modernist soul disenchanted with broken or stubbornly unfulfilled promises, exasperated by the tedious banality of modern life's daily routines, and impatient with the tedious and apparently aimless bargaining, log-rolling, compromise and wishy-washy or 'second-best' solutions. The bait was, however, deadly; the seduction led into a trap.

When the time of reckoning finally arrived, totalitarian societies proved to be anything but hospitable to daring, restless, refractory, stubbornly experimenting modern spirits. Under their new totalitarian managers those societies hastened to impose another routine – incomparably more suffocating and stultifying than anything that had made modern spirits suffer in the 'weak and wobbly' democracies they so detested. Totalitarian powers would not tolerate any experiments, for the very reason that they were experiments, thorns in the flesh of monologic and ruthlessly dictatorial rulers; even less gladly would they suffer visions standing out from the realities they had already brought into being and ran; they would fight experiments and visions tooth and nail, for the original sin of being born from methods and purposes and values other than those proclaimed and made legitimate, and above all administered, by the powers-that-be. The only freedom totalitarian regimes were prepared to offer intellectuals and artists was the freedom to listen, to take note and to obey. Obey or perish; in totalitarian palaces there was room solely for court poets and court painters, ordered to *represent reality of the rulers' choice*, not to create it. (In a witty definition by the Russian dissident writer Voinovich, 'socialist realism' was the art of praising the rulers in terms they could understand.) The right to create reality, as well as to decide what is real enough to be represented, was to remain the sole prerogative of the rulers.

Once the totalitarian tendency found its fulfilment in the fascist or communist totalitarian state, the ideologists of totalitarian society – the kind of society which less than any other form of human cohabitation needs the crutches of ideology – were no longer needed.

> Wherever totalitarian movements seized power, this whole group of sympathizers was shaken off even before the regimes proceeded toward their greatest crimes. Intellectual, spiritual, and artistic initiative is as dangerous to totalitarianism as the gangster initiative of the mob, and both are more dangerous than mere political opposition.[24]

This is how the romance of modern intellectuals with totalitarian power came to an end. Together with the romance, however, something else reached its finishing line: namely, the long story of the war of attrition launched against the *agora* from the side of the *ecclesia*.

One often hears alarms about the invasion or surreptitious colonization of daily life by public powers. As a rule the argument used to justify the alarm is an updated, rehashed version of once well-grounded fears of the state usurping undivided rule over the *agora*. Under present conditions, however, such an argument in any of its many renditions seems less to derive from the diagnosis of the current dangers as to be a recycled product of historical memories. The memories are hard to eradicate; they remain, by and large, the cognitive frames for the perception and representation of the current trends. After all, the successive generations of thinkers learned to view the interface between *agora* and *ecclesia* as the most vulnerable of the front-lines and the one most prone to be rolled back. Earlier generations might have liked what they saw and entertained high hopes for the results of the imminent invasion and the benign occupation that would follow the conquest. In later generations suspicion and vigilance replaced the trust and great expectations. But all generations alike had their sights fixed on one front-line. They might have expected different things, but they hardly differed in one adumbration: that all truly important things will happen at the boundary between *agora* and *ecclesia*, and that the battles fought along that boundary will be decisive for the shape of the human society to come.

With the eyes fixed on the frontier between *ecclesia* and *agora*, less thought was given to the other borderline – that between the *agora* and the *oikos*; the interface which connected/separated the 'private/public' sphere and the 'private'. On the *agora* private interests were expected to adapt to the needs/requirements/pressures of the public. The things expected to happen on the *agora* had a decisively pedagogic/enlightening/drilling flavour: this was primarily a space where the sharp edges of incompatible interests were blunted, contradictory pressures balanced, dreams and desires trimmed and kneaded so that they would not clash with each other and fit a harmonious whole, and the areas of conflagration cooled off so that it would not come to an explosion. The 'public' and the 'private' met in the *agora* on unequal terms – as, respectively, the guide and the guided, the teacher and the pupil, parent and child. The 'public' was the prime acting subject, with the 'private' cast as the object of its action.

And yet it is now that other border, previously taken for granted, which is the site of the busiest traffic and the prime butt of contention. The *agora* is, as before, an invaded territory, but this time the roles have been reversed and the invading troops are gathering on the fault-line with the private – though, unlike in the case of the 'public' represented by the law-giving and law-executing state, this time it is not a regular army with staff headquarters and a unified command, but rather an unruly and variegated crowd of un-uniformed trespassers. No one is there to stop the advance; the regular armies of the 'public' retreated and withdrew, having lost their combat force, the interest in continuing occupation or both. As far as the public power is concerned, the *agora* looks increasingly like a no-man's-land. The battlefield has been all but abandoned and left vacant for any adventurer eager to invade.

This effect can be traced back to the seminal, previously mentioned departure in the history of the modern state: the separation and increasing gap between power and politics. Claus Offe gave a most precise expression to the various aspects of this most fateful of divorces.[25] Among these aspects he names the implosion of the orthodox centres of economic, military and cultural powers once condensed in the nation-state, but now sapped and eroded simultaneously from 'above' and 'below'; the postmodern transformations of social morphology, which led to the progressive decline of the established elites' support and of the overall trust in political institutions, both resulting in the new

volatility, fragmentation and rapid fluctuation of the issues and
foci of public attention; and – last but certainly not least – the
fact that 'political agents have lost the certainty of their roles and
domains because the political economy of postindustrial and
global capitalism no longer provides the clear-cut categorization
of "places within the system of production" in which forms of
collective action (political parties, associations, trade unions) were
once anchored'. The overall outcome of all these closely intertwined transformations is a situation in which 'sovereignties have
become nominal, power anonymous, and its locus empty'. If the
traditional question 'What is to be done?' about the present state
of public affairs in case that state is found unsatisfactory is asked
ever less frequently, and if when asked it tends to be quickly
dismissed on the ground of a TINA (There Is No Alternative)
creed, this is not so much for the lack of ideas as for the absence
of agencies which could conceivably carry them out. The assess-
ment of the feasibility of actions and the practicality of projects is
a function of the relative strength of the agent and its adversary;
and under present circumstances the main question, the question
to be asked most urgently but a question to which no clear
answer is in sight, is the query 'Is anybody capable of doing
whatever needs to be done?'

We may say that, while the traditional agents are no longer
capable of effective action, the truly powerful and resourceful
agents have escaped into hiding and operate beyond the reach of
all established means of political action – let alone the democratic
process of negotiation and control centred on the *agora*. These
new agents celebrate their independence and detachment from the
agora. They have nothing to gain from their presence there, but
everything to gain from their absence. They see no profit in
normative regulation and so do not need the *agora*; but they sense
profit in having their hands untied and so do their best to keep
their distance from the *agora* and to stay out of sight of the
crowds that fill it.

Having cut their ties with the *agora*, the powers that truly
matter have no use for philosophers, educators or preachers. They
do not need to change the world which is their oyster; they feel
quite comfortable in the 'networked', internet-like world without
a controlling desk but with floating responsibilities; and, having
no mission to perform which would require spiritual uplifting of

the masses, cultural crusades or mass conversion, they may only applaud the consistent dismantling of all actual or prospective agencies of collective action aimed at the 'totality'.

All this could only have, and does have, a devastating effect on the status of the intellectuals as it was shaped in the *Sturm and Drang* era of modernity, in the times of nation-building, legitimation-seeking powers, Panopticon and eliciting of obedience through normative regulation.

Claus Offe summarizes the current experience of intellectual elites in the following way:

> on the one hand, nearly all factors of social, economic, and political life are contingent, elective, and gripped by change, while on the other hand the institutional and structural premises over which that contingency runs are simultaneously removed from the horizon of political, indeed of intellectual choice.

They are 'removed from choice' for a simple reason: under the present circumstances (in our terms: with one part of *ecclesia* safely insulated from the *agora* and the remaining part powerless), 'the very attempt to reflect normatively upon or to renew . . . the nature of the co-ordination of the processes' 'is virtually precluded by dint of . . . practical futility and thus . . . essential inadequacy'. As a result, the manner in which various subsystems (however flexible each one of them may be in its own right) 'are related to and affect each other must . . . be considered extraordinarily rigid, fatal, and sealed off from any freedom of choice'.[26]

In other words, the integration and reproduction of the 'global order' once more takes the guise of a spontaneous and self-propelling process. The great novelty of modernity was to present the creation, preservation and continuity of 'order' as a *task* – a purpose unlikely to be fulfilled without goal-conscious, concerted and determined human action. But order-making is not seen as a task any more; on the contrary, all purposeful action aimed at imposing a different order from the one currently in existence is suspect as unduly interfering with the skill and wisdom of the 'invisible hand' (with the emphasis on 'invisible'); a risk-producing endeavour, bound to spoil or throw out of joint no less, perhaps more, than it can repair or improve. And if the continuing existence of totality is no more a task, no task-designers are needed; while the possible impostors of which there is never a shortage, the self-appointed prophets of global change, should be kept at bay. And there is no need for knowledge classes to assume the role of the intellectuals – of spiritual guides intending to make people different from what they now are by teaching them things they would not learn by themselves and teaching them first of all that learning such things is worth their while. There are no big tasks, so there is no use for big ideas.

Memories of *paideia*

It has been said already that in our society Synopticon gradually, yet relentlessly, elbows out the early-modern Panopticon as the prime tool of 'pattern maintenance' and 'tension management', or, simply speaking, the preservation of order; and that we are passing, or have passed already, from the heroic times of spiritual leaders to the times of 'personal examples'.

Umberto Eco performed a vivisection of one of the most popular 'objects of watching' in contemporary Synopticon, the comic-strip Superman: the super-example, the ultimate example of self-assertion in a world which proclaims assertion to be a private business, like all businesses to be conducted by private resources.[27] Eco notes that Superman uses his extraordinary and mysterious power to conserve and preserve intact the ordinary order of things.

> Superman will never park his car in a no parking zone and he'll never be a revolutionary ... This ultra-powerful hero uses his extraordinary gifts to bring about an ideal of absolute passivity, turning down any project without a prior seal of approval for its good sense, thereby becoming a paragon of high moral standards untouched by political concerns.

The TINA message oozing from every successful adventure of Superman and his many mass-produced likenesses or counterfeits, the need to do nothing in particular about the world apart from sticking to the law and observing order, and occasionally helping the uniformed or plain-clothed people who see to it that this is done, may exert a consoling and comforting effect on most watchers, but it sounds rather an apocalyptic message and the prophecy of doom in the ears of whoever might yet aspire, for nostalgic or any other reasons, to the roles and responsibilities once associated with the position of an intellectual.

According to their reactions, Eco divides contemporary cultural theorists and practitioners into 'apocalyptic' and 'integrated'. The essential difference between them is that 'if apocalyptics survive by packaging theories on decadence, the integrated intellectuals rarely theorize. They are more likely to be busy producing and transmitting their own messages in every sphere, on a daily basis'. Apocalyptics are most certainly pessimists; the integrated, on the other hand, are neither pessimists nor optimists (though privately they might be either), but first and foremost they are not *dissenters*. What the apocalyptics bewail is for the integrated intellectuals their natural element.

Why do the apocalyptics bewail what they see as cultural decadence? And why do they see the present-day state of culture as decadent in the first place? The reasons, one would gather from Eco, are primarily theoretical (or, since the integrated seldom theorize, it is rather the apocalyptics' knack of theory-building that makes the difference). The apocalyptics and the integrated, so Eco suggests, entertain different ideas about what culture is and what it is about. One is likely nowadays to grow apocalyptic if one thinks of culture as 'an aristocratic phenomenon', 'the assiduous, solitary and jealous cultivation of an inner life that tempers and opposes the vulgarity of the crowd'. If one believes that, then 'mass culture', aimed at everybody indiscriminately and trimmed down to everybody's taste and capacity for comprehension is not culture at all; it is, rather, the destruction of culture, an 'anti-culture' (not unlike the 'anti-matter' of science fiction). But if one has not accepted first the aristocratic, or any other ennobled and lofty, postulated rather than descriptive, vision of culture, then one would also take without much distress and aggravation the fact that 'the combined efforts of TV, newspapers, radio, cinema, comic-strips, popular novels and *Reader's Digest* have now brought culture within everybody's reach': no brows would be then raised at the sight of the middle-brow or low-brow, yet best-selling 'cultural products', and instead of scribbling another prophecy of doom, culture practitioners would proceed from where they and all the others stand. Busy as they are using the new tools of pumping-up mass offer and mass consumption, they would have little time left for despair and breast-beating.

According to Eco, the difference between apocalypse and integration is, in other words, one between cognitive perspectives or, rather, the presence or absence of preconceived ideals: perhaps between utopia and realism; between measuring reality against certain unfulfilled ideals (like an 'unfinished project of Enlightenment') and taking reality as it comes. What Eco does not say, though, is why there should be two sharply different optics; and particularly, why certain visions of culture should have been dropped, abandoned, made light of or simply forgotten. He does not say either what the fate of that vision might tell us about those who once held it and those who do not hold it now.

Eco makes a point that what the apocalyptics now call, with horror and contempt, 'mass culture', is in fact a phenomenon which precedes by quite a few centuries the coining of the concept; it goes back at least to the invention of printing with wooden blocks (that is, before the epochal Gutenberg's invention of movable type). Chivalrous epics or 'real-life stories' which printing presses made available to ordinary folk with meagre means bore all the marks which are now taken for the symptoms of cultural decadence; they were ephemeral, mawkishly sentimental, they catered for lowly passions, they flattered all the unwholesome prejudices and lusts of their readers, they even brandished what could be seen retrospectively as an equivalent of advertising blurbs. But no record of any outcry among the learned public survives. No one among the elite seemed to mind, no call to resist and repel the danger was heard. Why such equanimity – so uncharacteristic of 'intellectuals' as we came later to know them? I suggest that trying to solve this puzzle would reveal the limitation of Eco's explanation of the difference between the 'apocalyptics' and the 'integrated' of our time. It would make salient 'the missing link' of Eco's analysis: the modern adventure separating pre-modern equanimity and late-modern alarm.

Most of the allegedly descriptive concepts are praxeo-morphic; they cut out, segregate, connect and map the bits and pieces of the world as those bits and pieces lend themselves to the actions of the concept- and map-makers. The 'humble folk', the hewers of wood and drawers of water, the uncouth readers of pulp fiction bought at fairs from itinerant traders, were not the wards of the learned classes of the day; they might have been savages, but not savages waiting for refinement; ignorants, but not ignorants waiting for enlightenment; perhaps idol-worshippers, but not infidels waiting for revelation and conversion. They were not, in short, the objects for the learned classes' current or prospective action. They stayed and were bound to remain outside the *Lebenswelt* of the learned elite securely ensconced within the harder-than-rock walls of Latin. The learned elite bore no responsibility for what they read or did not read, just as it did not feel responsible for what they sowed and how they milked their cows.

At some point, though, popular beliefs became superstitions, popular habits became signs of obscurantism and vulgarity, and the popular life-styles became symptoms of a *lack of culture*. That point is well defined on the historical continuum. It marks a seminal departure not so much in the ways and means of the *hoi polloi*, as in the social placement of knowledge and its bearers. We may plot that point on the historical continuum at the start of modern nation-building and the birth of the modern type of power – the kind of power that struggled 'to reach the parts other powers could not reach'.

Only in this new and essentially unprecedented context (a context which sets apart the modern condition from the Greek political settings, however numerous are the often stressed analogies between the two) did the learned elite become 'spiritual leaders' or missionaries with the task of converting – supervisors, censors, teachers and trainers of the *populus*. Only then did they set about the task of designing a mode of life for others to learn, embrace and follow. This new position and role was not free of incurable antinomies, and Eco is right when he picks up the urge to *oppose* 'the vulgarity of the crowd' as one of the distinguishing traits of the culture-makers' posture – a motive which could not but thwart and sometimes incapacitate the other urge to free the crowd of its vulgarity; the attitude of modern learned classes to what they alternately, depending on the mood, dubbed 'people' or 'the mob', was a mixture of love and hate, of the impulse to come closer and the horror of 'dissolving in the mass'. With all that, though, the learned classes assumed the role of custodians and wardens of the 'uneducated' and 'not yet fully cultured', and held to that role through thick and thin, for the duration of the modern era. That role signalled both rights and responsibilities. What defined the learned elite in the modern era was not the set of unique characteristics of its individual members, but its collective relationship to the rest of the population in-need-of-enlightenment-and-cultivation, and the role they collectively played, hoped to play, wished to play, or considered to be theirs of right, in that relationship.

The assumption of such a vocation was made possible by the order-making ambitions of the modern state, and the vocation was practised within the context of such order-making activity. The assumption remained feasible and seemed relatively uncontentious and secure as long as those ambitions and matching practices lasted; as long as *ecclesia* maintained its acute interest in the *agora* and stayed bent on day-to-day intervention in its proceedings. It could not survive – certainly not in its past shape and not without a major crisis – the retreat or incapacitation of the *ecclesia* in its institutional form of the modern nation-state. By the learned classes brought up to perform the culture-guardians' vocation, that latter development could not but be perceived as a major catastrophe, indeed an apocalyptic nightmare. Suddenly the learned classes found themselves without the reality which rendered their own status and function realistic. They found themselves deprived of the custodial prerogatives which they had grown to see as their birthright; and without their wards, since their past charges were now entrusted to other wardens, looking around for other wardens, or having just been set free, going about their life-businesses apparently without any appointed custodians.

When bewailing cultural decadence, the cultural theorists and practitioners mourn the descent of their modern proselytizing mission. No one seems to need missionaries any more; clerics, churchwardens and vergers for the new cult of pleasurable and entertaining sensations will do nicely. On this point the residents of the edifices of *ecclesia* and the inhabitants of *oikos* seem to be in full agreement, leaving yesterday's missionaries alone with their fond memories and fresh frustrations. The victims of betrayal, too, find their own ranks to be massively deserted and fast depleting. (As Stuart Hall caustically remarked on the fate of the universities, that staunchest and least disputed institutional fortress of the orthodox intellectualists' role, 'The state did not send out the secret police to transform higher education into an entrepreneurial sector. We have done it ourselves . . .'[28]) Temptations to abandon what anyway looks like being irretrievably lost are great, and siren calls sound appealing to many once differently tuned ears.

Pierre Bourdieu has recently quipped that since contemporary men and women of knowledge can no longer count on the immortality of their *oeuvres*, they are after as many appearances on TV screens as possible; in an up-dated version of Berkeley's famous dictum, 'To be is to be seen on TV.' Television, says Bourdieu, has become the intellectualists' equivalent of Narcissus' mirror. The pursuit of eternity has been replaced, in the strategy of men and women of knowledge, by the pursuit of invitations to TV shows; daily work tends to be shaped in such a way as to make the invitations more likely. But the pragmatics of TV shows and of intellectual work differ sharply. That of TV is ruled by ratings and speed; but the mass audience and high velocity are enemies of thought. 'Communication' with the mass audience on TV is instantaneous; but, as Bourdieu points out, it is 'instant because it does not exist. It is no more than an apparition. The exchange of the commonplace is a kind of communication which has no other content than the very fact of communicating.' That pseudo-communication breeds 'fast thinkers', suppliers of intellectual 'fast food' . . .[29]

A widespread, perhaps prevailing view among writers on the historical fate of the intellectuals is that what is currently happening cannot be resisted; and that even if the intellectuals' adventure with the responsibility for the values people live by was not a grave mistake or illusion of grandeur from the start, it is certainly over by now. For consolation (if consolation is needed) a variant of the 'invisible hand' is recalled from exile. That by-definition skilful and benevolent hand is once more expected to pull the strings of the commodity-and-finance market operators, but if the facts make that expectation a bit too incredible, the hand is relocated to the market of ideas and interests called democracy. Thanks to the hand which, in order to do a good job, should stay invisible, the *agora* unattended and left to its own resources (except for hired counsellors), will steer or drift towards all the right solutions to all the genuine problems, together with the values and principles which inform them.

No doubt, this view is an excellent *plaidoyer* for the new posture of disengagement and disinterest, amounting to the renunciation of supra-professional responsibilities, of that urge to 'go beyond the call of duty', which was the trade mark of modern intellectuals. It sums up well the sentiments of the intellectuals as long as they are defined, and define themselves, as the orphans of the now extinct, or disappeared *ecclesia* (one is tempted to say 'ecclesia disparue', or 'ecclesia abscondita'); or as long as the role of the intellectuals in the *agora* is identified with that of the plenipotentiaries, agents or partners of the *ecclesia*, and no other role is contemplated. This view does not allow for the possibility that the marriage between knowledge and *ecclesia* was an event in history rather than made in heaven; and for the possibility that the mission of the intellectuals may survive the divorce.

The question remains, though, that just as much as the 'invisible hand of the market' failed to produce the affluent existence for all, the prospect that the 'invisible hand of democracy' will produce secure individuals in a just society is far from being a foregone conclusion. Recalling Aristotle, Castoriadis points out that mere following of the democratic procedure would not guarantee by itself either the 'State of Law' or the 'State of Rights':

> Majority rule can be justified only if one grants equal value, in the domain of the contingent and the probable, to the *doxai* of free individuals. But if this equality of value among opinions is not to remain a 'counterfactual principle', some sort of pseudotranscendental gadget, then the permanent labour in the institution of society must be to render individuals such that one might reasonably postulate that their opinions all have the same weight in the political domain. Once again, the question of *paideia* proves ineliminable . . .
>
> Such individuals can be formed only in and through a democratic *paideia*, which does not grow up like a plant but instead has to be one of the main objects of society's political concerns.[30]

Society cannot make its individuals happy; all historical attempts (or promises) to do so generated more misery than happiness. But the good society can – and should – make its members free; not only free *negatively*, in the sense of not being coerced into doing what they would rather not do, but in the *positive* sense, that of being able to do something with their freedom, in order to be able to do things . . . And that means primarily the ability to influence the conditions of their own life, to formulate the meaning of 'common good' and to make the institutions of society comply with that meaning. If 'the question of *paideia*' is ineliminable, it is because there is still the unfulfilled democratic project of autonomous individuals constituting an autonomous society.

Individuals cannot be free unless they are free to institute a society which promotes and guards their freedom; unless they institute together an agency capable of achieving just that. And so the task on the agenda is to recapture the *ecclesia* by the *agora*.

This task opens a vast area of action for the knowledge classes. But in order for such action to be undertaken a reorientation is needed: from the *ecclesia* to the *agora*, to that political space where the public and the private meet, where not just the selection from the choices on offer is made, but the range of choices is examined, questioned and renegotiated. And the first step to be taken once the reorientation takes place is rebuilding the *agora* to make it fit for this task. This is not going to be an easy job, considering the present parlous state of the private/public sphere; of a sphere from which 'the public' has recoiled, seeking shelter in politically inaccessible places, and 'the private' is about to redraw in its own image. To make the *agora* fit for autonomous individuals and autonomous society, one needs to arrest, simultaneously, its privatization and its depoliticization. One needs to re-establish the translation of the private into the public. One needs to restart (in the *agora*, not just in philosophy seminars) the interrupted discourse of the common good – which renders individual autonomy both feasible and worth struggling for.

Not an easy job, let me repeat, considering the paradox that, as Offe puts it, 'The new social movements have taken as the object of their critique precisely those institutional arrangements of political rule, material production, and scientific-technical innovation with the help of which the demands of the older movements could be satisfied . . .' As a result, the movements which aspire to fill the vacated private/public space have deprived themselves of the chance to go 'to the roots' of the present trouble and to construct or construe an agency which would make any change in the public sphere plausible. '[T]he ecological, pacifist, feminist, regionalist, and neighbourhood autonomy movements are far from having developed even the outlines of a programme of social transformation with the same degree of consistency and comprehensiveness that characterized the earlier sociopolitical movements.'[31]

Ulrich Beck suggests, aptly, that doubt is the most precious gift thinkers may offer to the people who try desperately to find their way while smarting in the double bind of the inert burden of the TINA strategy at the top and the hazards of the privatized life-politics at the bottom.

> Scepticism, contrary to a widespread error, makes everything possible again: ethics, morality, knowledge, faith, society and criticism, but differently, a few sizes smaller, more tentative, more revisable and more capable of learning and thus more curious, more open to the unsuspected and incommensurate, with a tolerance based on and rooted in the ultimate final certainty of error. After Marx, Engels and Lenin, after Horkheimer and Adorno, perhaps Montaigne ought to be rediscovered as the founding father of the social theory of the new reflexive modernity.[32]

Excursus 1: Ideology in the Postmodern World

Habent sua fata verba, though some words have a fate more bizarre than others. The word 'ideology' sets, however, a record which is difficult to beat. Finding a common denominator to the sharply different historical uses of the term, or a transformative logic productive of its successive avatars, is a notoriously tall order. But there is another difficulty apart from reaching an agreement about the term's semantic load and uses. 'Ideology' is a discursive concept which in different times was put by different people to different uses, but the notion of ideology tries also to grasp certain changing aspects of the world which modern men and women inhabit, and that aspect is itself a focus of continuous reassessment as well as dissent and contest. The link between the historical convolutions of the term and the historical fate of that aspect of human reality is not immediately apparent while the two phenomena referred to by the same term are not easy to set apart and to tell apart.

The essentially contested concept

Etymologically, the word 'ideology' means 'science of ideas'; and it was indeed meant to carry this meaning when it was coined, towards the end of the eighteenth century, by Destutt de Tracy, a founder and a leading member of the French Institut National, and assigned the pivotal place in the project to which the Institute was to dedicate its work. The business of the Institute was to fulfil the ambition of Enlightenment: to advise rulers in their task to legislate a new, rational order of society. And the proposed method to achieve it was to use precise, scientific knowledge of the way ideas are formed in human minds, in order to make sure that only the right kind of ideas, reason-approved ideas, are formed.

The key role which the 'science of ideas' was bound to play in the building of a human world ruled by reason and composed of rationally behaving beings required virtually no further argument. This was thanks to a chain of simple assumptions: human conduct is guided by the ideas people hold; ideas are formed by processing human sensations; this processing, like everything else in nature, is subject to strict laws; those laws can be discovered through systematic observation and experiment; once discovered, they can be used – like other known laws of nature – to improve on reality: in this case, to assure that no misleading sensations are available for processing and that true sensations do not get distorted in the course of processing – and thus only *true* ideas, such ideas as pass the test of reason, are formed and adopted. In the words of Mercier, one of the Institute's leading lights, ideas 'are all that there is', and according to de Tracy himself, 'We exist only through our sensations and our ideas. No things exist except by ideas that we possess of them.'

Itself a strict and precise science, ideology was called to occupy the watchdog position in the world of science. Its brief was to surveil, supervise and correct the works of all other branches of human knowledge – to investigate, regulate and, if necessary, bring into line all human cognitive efforts. But there was another, hidden, agenda which the idea of ideology implied. In practical terms, the centrality of ideology among the sciences meant centrality of the ideologists among the builders and stewards of an enlightened society: by manipulating the human environment, and thus also the sensations likely to be aroused, and by guiding the subsequent processes of idea-formation, the experts of ideology would secure the rule of reason over the whole field of human beliefs and behaviour.

The theory of truth in terms of which the project of ideology was argued was at the same time a theory of error; false beliefs were blamed on wrong sensations prompted by an uncontrolled or wrongly arranged environment – that is, in the last account, on the absence of a programmed education or on an education programmed and conducted contrary to the demands of reason. Accordingly, ideology was to be a wonder-weapon in the battle waged simultaneously on two fronts: against ignorance, and against the wrong kind of education (that is, the wrong kind of teachers).

When Karl Marx wrote his *German Ideology* with the help of his friend Friedrich Engels, he shifted the meaning of 'ideology' in a quite seminal way: the 'ideology' in the title referred to what the self-proclaimed 'ideologists' did, or rather to what they pretended or hoped to be doing: that is, to the very project of prompting proper human actions through the management of the actors' ideas. It was the validity of the strategy they proposed for 'bringing the world in line with reason' that came under scrutiny. Marx and Engels, who had few equals in their devotion to Enlightenment ambitions, had no quarrel with de Tracy and his colleagues as to their *purpose*: there was little question that the world was not up to the standards of Reason and that something needed to be done to change the sorry state of affairs. But they derided and castigated the 'ideologists' for the gross inadequacy and futility of the proposed *means*.

This was the message of *German Ideology*: yes, human conduct needs badly to be changed to bring it more into line with genuine human potential, which, as reason shows, remains sorely underused, if not wasted. But no, it cannot be changed just by correcting the ideas people hold, since wrong ideas are here to stay as long as the world which supplies such ideas itself is wrongly built. The omnipotence of ideas is one of the many illusions which such a world is turning out on a massive scale. Not just the wrong ideas that prevail, but the concept of 'ideology' as the alleged antidote against error, was, in Marx and Engels's view, itself a poisoned fruit of an incorrectly constructed world. And so the 'Ideologists' and other thinkers who shared their hopes stood accused of barking under the wrong tree; or, rather, of starting their voyage to a rationally ordered society from the wrong end. Instead of thinking of changing the world through fighting wrong ideas, they should have put the change of the material world first, since it was and still is the perversely constructed human reality which has given and goes on giving birth to false ideas. The truth of thoughts stands little chance unless the errors of the world are corrected first.

In other words, Marx and Engels rejected the project of 'ideology' on the ground of its being but one more version of *historical idealism*, sharing in the inanity of the idealist philosophy, and like the rest of its varieties 'standing the world on its head', while being itself a reflection of human reality turned upside down . . . The task was to put both the world and its philosophical reflection on their feet again – and in order to get down to the task one needed to expose the naivety of the 'ideologists' and debunk the uselessness of the strategies suggested by the 'ideology' project.

All this, when pondered in retrospect, appears to be a family quarrel inside the Enlightenment camp – a debate over the *best means*, waged by thinkers who agreed on the *ends*, that is on the urgent need of a thorough, Reason-guided reconstruction of human society. Above all, the thinkers on both sides of the philosophical divide agreed on their own role in the fulfilment of that arduous task, which was to be the role of the spokesmen of Reason, of the educators of rational human beings and the enlighteners of all those already charged with the task of legislating the new rational order of society, or bound to replace the present legislators in case they are found unable or unwilling to undertake that task and to see it done.

When, after a prolonged absence from philosophical debate, almost a century long, the concept of ideology resurfaced in the late 1920s, and then turned into one of the major concepts of political discourse and social sciences, it held a somewhat different meaning (and one contrary to its primary, etymological sense): partly continuous, partly discontinuous with the sense carried by its early-nineteenth-century precedents, by that time largely forgotten (*German Ideology*, let us recall, remained an unpublished and unread manuscript). As it happened, it was continuous with Marx and Engels's rendering of 'ideology' as a name for an essentially erroneous way of thinking, though oblivious of the arguments with which Marx and Engels justified their verdict. In particular, the concept of 'ideology' no longer stood for the philosophy of 'historical idealism' as it did for Marx and Engels; neither did it stand for the 'science of ideas', as the founders of the Institut National wished. In a remarkable *volte-face*, 'ideology' came to denote an essentially non-philosophical or pre-philosophical thought, of the type that would fail the essential tests of philosophical reasoning and correct thinking as such; something which philosophy may encounter only in the activity of critique, a kind of common and inferior knowledge which it is called to fight and eventually conquer.

Like its predecessor in both Destutt de Tracy's and Marx and Engels's version, the new concept of ideology emerged in the context of the post-Enlightenment, modern 'truth versus error', 'science versus ignorance/prejudice/superstition' philosophical discourse, and was meant to draw and guard the boundary between correct and incorrect knowledge. Like its predecessor, it expressed the bid by the men of knowledge to serve as the trustees and the arbiters of that boundary. But unlike its predecessor, the idea of 'ideology' in its twentieth-century incarnation was no longer to be viewed as a weapon which the border-guards intended, whether rightly or wrongly, to use when fighting off the past and future trespassers. On the contrary, it moved to the other side of the barricade, changing place with the prejudice and superstition which in its original embodiment 'ideology', that science of ideas, was rightly or wrongly supposed to defeat and destroy and keep off limits for ever after.

The term 'ideology' had thus been moved from the dominion of 'knowledge' to the inferior realm of 'beliefs'. It stood now for the not-yet-uprooted and not-yet-overcome, false, misguided and harmful beliefs, arrogantly resisting the test of knowledge; the beliefs which science had sworn to unmask, disempower and in the end efface from human consciousness on its way to the undivided rule of reason. In this second stage of its history, the theory of 'ideology' intended to deal systematically with the kind of phenomena which had been at the dawn of the modern era set apart and targeted, by Francis Bacon, as the prime obstacles to rational knowledge in his repeated diatribes against the 'idols' of tribe, theatre or the market-place.

The concept of 'ideology' in this new incarnation has been conceived in a Europe emerging from the ravages of the Great War, at a time when new, profound and seemingly unbridgeable political divisions and the thickening cloud of intolerance and politically inspired violence sapped the self-confidence of knowledge elite. Doubt was cast on the certainty of progress and the ultimate victory of scientific reason – by definition non-sectarian, indivisible and universal.

It seemed less and less plausible that the new breed of despots wished or could be enticed to be enlightened, and that therefore one could use the power they wielded to legislate reason into the world. The marriage between knowledge and earthly powers, blessed in the heyday of Enlightenment hopes, came under a back-breaking strain. The seekers after and guardians of truth could not count on the rulers' support with the same sanguine confidence (now seen as naive) which was the mark, the privilege, of *les philosophes*. In its second coming, the concept of ideology emanated from a pessimistic and defensive mood and was handled by fingers singed too painfully ever to move with confidence again.

When confronted with a world so evidently reluctant to follow the itinerary drawn in the Enlightenment scenario, twentieth-century philosophers set themselves the twin tasks of spelling out the criteria which would set apart true, scientifically authorized knowledge from all other opinions, and of locating the causes of the public reluctance or inability, and particularly the reluctance or inability of public rulers, to accept, embrace and put into practice the verdicts of science. The philosophers of the *Wienerkreis* or the school of logical positivism, for instance, ascribed the resilience of false beliefs to the endemic impairment of natural languages, and saw the salvation in the entrenchment of truth in an exact and precise language of science, incommunicado with everyday life and so cleansed of the meaningless, untestable beliefs abounding in the messy language of daily life and partisan politics. Edmund Husserl, the founder of phenomenological philosophy, went further still: he doubted whether science is capable of performing the task, rooted as it is, much as daily life itself, in the 'natural attitude', that breeding-ground of unsound and fickle opinions disguised as true knowledge. Husserl suggested that only the herculean effort of 'phenomenological reduction' – stripping knowledge of the successive layers of error sedimented by the narrow-sighted, locally and temporally limited circumstances in which natural attitude is confined – can allow the philosopher an insight into the non-historical, supra-cultural realm of 'transcendental subjectivity' where all pristine meanings are intentionally constituted and reside in the pure form untainted by shifting public interests and cultural fashions. It went without saying that nothing in the daily pursuits of ordinary people immersed in a 'natural attitude' is likely to prompt them to embark on a phenomenological journey. The pursuit of truth seemed to be no longer the Kantian universal potential of any reasonable person; it was now the job of a special breed of people – of philosophers and philosophers alone; their, the philosophers', badge of distinction, and the sign of their loneliness.

Slowly, by default rather than by design, the legislative ambitions of yore have been abandoned, together with the urge of remaking the world and of direct engagement in the exercise of power. As the twentieth century went by, fewer and fewer major philosophers would willingly repeat Plato's gesture and ask the tyrants of modern Syracuses to make their philosophers' words into political flesh. The few who did just that soon found to their horror that the only job in which the tyrants would be ready to employ them was that of courtiers – the king's messengers, the court poets, sometimes the court jesters, but more likely the court clowns.

And so the *disengagement* has become an ever more pronounced tendency of the times. Its irrevocability, however, its purpose and duration were all subject to dispute. The polar positions between which all other attitudes were plotted have been most perceptively mapped and argued in the notorious exchange between Strauss and Kojève. Both correspondents agreed that the truth cannot be pursued amid the hubbub and confusion typical of daily life and that there is hardly a passable road leading from ordinary mundane experience to the truth accessible to philosophical investigation. If Strauss, however, insisted that this is precisely as things must be and should stay forever, and that for the sake of the truth's integrity the link between philosophical truth and the living world can be under no circumstances restored or established anew, for Kojève the philosophers' retreat was a temporary measure, a manoeuvre performed in order to regroup the troops, replenish the supplies and then try to conquer again with more confidence and a better chance of victory. Neither of the two letter-writers entertained much hope, though, that the powers that be may be effectively used to promote the cause of truth and to pave the way to its rule. Both would accept, even if they would not say so in so many words, that philosophy had better have no truck with such powers; if it is to encounter them, then it should do so solely in the role of prosecutor or judge.

The twentieth-century concept of 'ideology' was born of these worries and preoccupations. It offered a way of accounting for the growing gap between the hopes of Enlightenment and the rising tide of irrationality in the world increasingly fragmented socially and politically; and it suggested another legitimation for the changed role claimed by the enlightened elite. The new concept of 'ideology' fit to serve this double purpose was forged by Karl Mannheim.

The essentially contested reality

Mannheim's concept of 'ideology' was influenced by the idea of 'false consciousness', elaborated within the Marxist tradition by György Lukács to account for the astonishing (and baffling) failure of the Western working classes to rally around the cause of socialism, which according to the Marxist vision of progress was both the rational expression of working-class interests and the fullest implementation of the project of rationally organized society. In line with the Kantian vision of reason, the marriage between the working class and socialism was expected to occur in the natural course of events. In Lukács's account, however, inspired by his reading of Lenin's theory and the practice of the revolutionary avant-garde, grasping the truth was anything but a natural process guided by the universally available, all-too-human faculty of reason. Without the assistance of social scientists able to raise their sights above the level of the narrowly circumscribed day-by-day experience accessible to the workers individually or even collectively, those workers will go on reflecting in their consciousness a counterfeit, falsified reality of capitalism in which the truth of their plight is disguised or denied; and the more rationally (in its legitimized, market meaning) they behave, the deeper they will sink in the abysmal illusion.

Mannheim stretched Lukács's hypotheses to a universal principle. (To be more precise, he 'generalized' Lukács's class-focused cognitive theory by glossing over Lukacsian distinction between 'false' and 'tragic' consciousness.) Each group within society, distinguished and set apart by the particularity of its cognitive perspective, as determined by its class position, national membership or professional practice, is confined within a *partial* reality which leaves the *totality* out of sight. While rationally reflecting upon the truncated reality accessible through their experience, *all* groups tend to form from their own cognitive perspective their own *particular* distortions of the 'objective' (that is, universal for all yet invisible to all) truth.

It was such a distorted knowledge conceived within limited cognitive perspective that was given by Mannheim the name of 'ideology' (semantically parallel to that of Lukács's 'consciousness of class', as distinct from 'class consciousness'). The drama was played in the theatre of cognition, where ideology stood against truth as its major enemy. Since the difference between truth and distortion or falsehood ran parallel to that between totality and partiality, truth has been identified by definition with non-belonging and non-commitment: the non-ideological may be only an unattached knowledge, untied to any of the socially separated cognitive standpoints. True knowledge of social reality must be a non-partial, anti-particularistic knowledge, and so it can be only the work of a category of people able to put themselves in any of the cognitive positions because unattached to any of the particular class, national or religious groupings; of a group which draws its members from all other groups, and therefore is neither confined by, nor owes loyalty to, any one of them; of a category which embodies defiance of all particularity by standing outside all established groups and taking a detached view of any one of them, being thus capable of confronting all beliefs conceived from diverse cognitive perspectives and of exposing the partial, limited, relative character of each one of them. Such people, in Mannheim's view, were members of the *intelligentsia*, who, thanks to their *soi-disant* social exterritoriality and variegated origins are called to play the role of a collective impartial critic of political practices grounded in ideological distortions – but also the role of the promoters of scientific politics, founded on non-relative, objective truth. The tool which would render the proper performance of both roles feasible was to be the *sociology of knowledge*: the systematic exposure of the link between ideologies and socially determined vantage points and group interests.

Despite an apparently total reversal of its original meaning, the concept of ideology in Mannheim's rendition is still fully immersed in the post-Enlightenment discourse of power. Like its predecessors, it is all about the link between knowledge and power, or – more precisely – about the legislative prerogative of the producers and carriers of knowledge. The unity of interests and purpose between the latter and the holders of political power is, however, no more assumed, and so the men of knowledge turn from the servants and counsellors of power-holders into their watchdogs and critics.

It was only the 'positive concept of ideology', the relatively recent invention that gained ground in the last two decades, which proposed a radical departure from the Enlightenment programme of founding true knowledge in the universality of the human condition. One by one, the items of the intellectual agenda in force since the beginning of modern times have been deleted, and the evaluation signs unchanged since the times of Enlightment have been reversed. The 'positive concept of ideology' encapsulates these seminal departures.

In its presently fashionable 'positive' version, ideology stands for the indispensable precondition of all knowledge, including its scientific variety (that is, the kind of knowledge founded in, and endorsed by, the community of scientists). The name of 'ideology' has been assigned to the cognitive frames which allow various bits of human experience to fall into place and form a recognizable, meaningful pattern. The frames are conditions of knowledge, but themselves are not its parts; they are seldom, if ever, reflected upon, spelled out, given a detached, 'outside' look. One may say that such cognitive frames are, essentially, 'monitoring', 'sifting', or perhaps 'slowing-down' devices; they arrest the otherwise unstoppable flow of sensations, holding to those among them which fit into the framed pattern while letting through the rest. By the same token, they preserve the patterned, structured perception of lived reality amidst the accelerating speed of information which threatens to explode all structures and thus to annihilate all meanings.

As the presently favourite narrative goes, having a cognitive frame is as universal as having a language; and yet, again like languages, the fact of having a frame simultaneously unites and divides the human species. All humans carry cognitive frames, but different humans carry different frames. Human encounters and dialogue are therefore processes of continuous, and in fact infinite, translation: between languages, and between cognitive frames. The 'positive concept of ideology' is in the last account founded in linguistic analogy. And just as the presence of a variety of languages is not an impairment of the human condition nor an impediment to human cohabitation, so the plurality of ideologies – of pre-reflexive frames of knowledge – is an attribute of the human world one can live with and is probably bound to live with for ever.

Ideology in its 'positive' incarnation is akin to the Kantian idea of transcendental conditions of knowledge, that is the idea that were not the knowing subject armed beforehand with a sensation-ordering capacity, no cognition could and would conceivably occur. The difference with Kant is, of course, one between exterritorial and extemporal universality and a socially and historically shaped particularity. The transcendental conditions of cognition have been moved one or more steps below the species-wide (or, indeed, the all-knowing subjects') level where Kant located it.

The shift is, however, seminal. Once they include ideology, 'transcendental conditions of knowledge' are not confined to ideas as general as space, time or causality, without which no image of a phenomenon may be put together. On the contrary, they embrace the ideas which make images different and diverse. In Kant's version transcendental conditions are what unite cognitive subjects and what may therefore serve as the foundation for unified knowledge and unified human species, and so also for the fulfilment of Enlightenment's universalizing hopes. Cognitive frames are, on the contrary, divisive. Continuous and unredeemable differentiation and diversification of knowledge, and so also of the lived worlds, are built into the positive notion of ideology, just as the prospect of universality has been built into the Kantian idea of transcendental conditions of all knowledge.

The positive notion of ideology, in other words, makes a virtue out of that feature of cognition which Mannheim would still consider to be its vice. Not only does it signal reconciliation with a plurality of world-views, now considered incurable and indeed indispensable; it also proclaims the new disinterested, neutral attitude of the knowledge class and the intention to renounce the past project to rectify the post-Babel confusion of tongues, to proselytize, to correct, to homogenize and to unify what has been unduly and harmfully split and set in conflict.

What sort of collective experience of the intellectuals is reflected in such a 'positive' idea of ideology? And what sort of intellectual strategy does it imply?

A prominent feature of the contemporary world is the tension between two closely related yet apparently contradictory tendencies, those of globalization and of localization. The intimate link between them has been aptly grasped in Roland Robertson's term of 'glocalization': the two trends stem from the same root and are conceivable and comprehensible only in their togetherness.

Globalization means, among other things, the progressive separation of power from politics. As Manuel Castells pointed out in his recent monumental three-volume study of the 'information society', capital, and particularly financial capital, 'flows', no longer bound by the limitations of space and distance, while politics stays as before local and territorial. The flow is increasingly beyond the reach of political institutions. We may say that power and politics reside in different spaces. Physical, geographical space remains the home of politics; while capital and information inhabit cyberspace, in which physical space is cancelled or neutralized.

It was probably the latter kind of space which Paul Virilio had in mind when he wrote that, while the notorious Francis Fukuyama's declaraction of the end of history is grossly premature, one can speak confidently of the end to *geography*. Space is the sediment of time needed to overcome it, and when the speed of capital and information movement equals that of the electronic signal, the overcoming of distance is practically instantaneous and the space loses its 'materiality', its ability to slow down, arrest, resist or otherwise constrain movement – all the qualities which are normally taken for the distinguishing traits of reality.

'Locality' gets devalued in the process. Capital is exterritorial, no longer bound by state frontiers and the prohibitive costs of travel. So is information; the circumstance symbolically conveyed by equal – 'local' – rates, paid by the receivers of any World Wide Web information whether originated next door or on the other side of the globe. In both respects, locality with its mutuality of face-to-face communication loses its privilege; it has no more advantage over far-away places, once derived from the awkwardness and the high costs of transportation and from the comparative slowness of indirect and mediated, not-face-to-face, communication. A local 'cottage industry' of information has little chance to compete successfully with whatever flows inside cyberspace. Locality is fast expropriated of its once formidable 'holding power'. It loses its significance as the site of a self-contained, and largely self-sufficient, economy or culture.

This is a situation radically different from the past 'hardware' era, when power and knowledge, just like their objects, remained essentially 'local' and earthbound. Mass factory-bound industry, mass barracks-bound army, mass school-bound education held power-holders and power-subjects in the same place and brought them together, face-to-face. Power and knowledge, capital and information were as much rooted, space-dependent and distance-constrained as the labour and military force and the trained, drilled and surveilled populace which they engaged, managed and supervised. Capital tied up in heavy machinery and thick factory walls as well as in the local, closely guarded markets of labour and commodities was no more free to move than the factory hands or prospective conscripts. For better or worse, capital was bound to stay in place, and whatever happened in that place was for its investors, owners and managers, just as it was for all the rest of its residents, a matter of success or defeat, perhaps even of life and death.

Much the same applied to the possessors and guardians of knowledge and values. In the 'hardware' stage of modern times, also, the rational order which intellectuals were meant to assist in constructing and which they were to serve in its day-to-day work was bound to be, and indeed was, 'locally oriented'. The territorial state, a political entity, and the nation, a cultural entity, were bent on converging or overlapping; the two concepts tended to become synonymous. The task of constructing the new politically safeguarded order was identical with the nation-building effort; cultural crusades, the substitution of one unified language for a variety of dialects, the replacement of local customs and calendars with a national timetable of festivities and public holidays were its major vehicles. For all practical purposes, the projects of state citizenship and nationality blended into one, even if theorized separately and entrusted to the care of different sections of the power elite.

For all these reasons, this was the era of engagement between the elite of power and the populace. If the major concerns of political rulers were balancing the books, the provision of collective defence, soliciting obedience to universal rules and the collective insurance of individual welfare, the care to secure the commodity aptitude of local capital and local labour, then such concerns made sense on the assumption that economic and knowledge elites are indeed as territorial as the political power of the state, and like the state are set to engage the population inhabiting the territory under the state sovereignty. Reforging the loose collection of work-able adults into the industrial labour force was the economic elite's form of engagement; reforging the heterogeneous collection of disparate 'locals' into a culturally unified body of one nation with a shared history, acknowledged tradition and enemies was the form of the knowledge elite's engagement. What was legislation and administration for the economic elite and its political sponsors, was ideology and ideological indoctrination for the knowledge class. In both cases, the dependence was mutual. In both cases, one side constituted itself through its engagement with the other. Capital was territorial in as far as it could constitute and reproduce itself only as an employer of local labour. Also the knowledge classes, Mannheim's 'intelligentsia', or at least their 'intellectualist' vanguard, constituted themselves through their educational relationship to 'the people'.

We are now witnessing the end, or at any rate the terminal agony, of that engagement. We are entering a largely 'post-engagement' era. Capital and knowledge have both been emancipated from their local confinement. Geographical location of their holders counts little when ninety-nine per cent of wealth-producing financial transactions are no longer bound to the movement of material commodities, and when circulation of information is by and large enclosed within the cyberspatial web. The holders of neither economic nor cultural power are today place-bound; they have cut the ties harnessing them to the 'populace' at large, which remains as local as it used to be in the heyday of the industrial and nation-building phase of modern times. The holders of power occupy cyberspace, separate from the rest of the population; in terms which still hold firmly for that rest they have become genuinely *exterritorial*. The locals do not play a role in the elites' own self-constitution and self-reproduction, and if some locals happen to be assigned such a role for a time, they are no longer indispensable and irreplaceable to playing that role. No wonder one seldom finds today the concept of 'the people' appearing in intellectual discourse; the sole shelter of that concept is the rhetoric of politics, the last 'local' one among the facets of modern power.

In the light of the latest trends one could be excused for musing whether the mutual engagement between elites and local populations was not merely a relatively brief historical episode.

The world no more essentially contested

The capital operators of our time bear a striking resemblance to pre-modern 'absentee landlords'. Their link with the localities from which they cream off the surplus they produce is, however, still more tenuous than the bond tying the absentee landlords to their distant possessions.

Even when bodily absent and socially or culturally not part of the locality, the landlords of yore were *land*-lords all the same, and hence a certain amount of concern with the preservation of the wealth-producing capacity of the land they held was required, lest the source of their wealth and power should dessicate and vanish. In the case of the absentee landlords of pre-modern times, power came together with – however diluted – obligation, and exploitation went hand in hand with some form of – however fickle and unreliable – solidarity with the plight of the exploited. This is no longer the case; at least, it has not got to be the case, and the combined pressures of the all-powerful global financial markets, stock-exchanges and banks see to it that it won't.

The power of capital is becoming more and more dematerialized, ever more 'irreal' when judged by the meaning reality has for people who are not members of the global elite and stand little chance of joining it. The new ability to avoid, elide and escape has replaced the surveilling/managing/training engagement as the prime asset and chief measure of power. It made redundant all and any engagement – however benign or cruel was the form it might have taken. Most notably, the avoidance capacity has made disposable the once paramount panoptic-style form of engagement through the surveilling, drilling and disciplining effort. The defrays of Panopticon-type control are now written down on the side of unnecessary and unjustifiable, indeed non-rational, losses – to be dodged, or better still eliminated altogether. Synopticon – a do-it-yourself Panopticon, luring the many to gape at the few instead of hiring a few to watch the many – has proved to be a much more effective and economical instrument of control. The remnants of the old-style Panopticon still in operation are not meant for bodily drill or the spiritual conversion of the masses, but for keeping in place those sections of the masses which are not meant to follow the elite in its new taste for mobility.

The learned classes of our time, the producers and the possessors of knowledge, also resemble their pre-modern counterparts: at the time when the latter were securely enclosed inside the impenetrable walls of their Latin fortress which insulated them from the simple folk next door. Indeed, the cyberspace of the World Wide Web is in many respects the present-day equivalent of medieval Latin. It renders the members of the learned classes exterritorial and out of reach for people close to them in physical space, while laying a technological foundation for another, virtual universe, which brings the members of the knowledge classes close to each other. In their capacity of men and women of knowledge, members of the learned classes inhabit cyberspace, in which distances are measured by entirely different yardsticks from those inside ordinary, geographical space; in cyberspace, tracks are laid independently of the routes along which other people move and the road-signs and milestones are arranged in a fashion only perfunctorily and accidentally, if at all, related to ordinary cartography or topography.

Whatever else ideology was, it was also a declaration of intent on the part of its preachers: an intent of engagement with the society to which the preachers belonged and saw themselves as belonging. It was also a bid for responsibility for that society, the expression of readiness to assume or share it. Last, though not at all least, it was a sign of disaffection with the world as it was at the moment, of a critical attitude towards the present state of affairs and the urge to improve on that state or to transform it altogether. All ideologies, including the most conservative among them, were sharp edges pressed against the reality as it happened to exist at the time: they were heresies even if dressed up as orthodoxies, drawing their vigour from some *noch-nicht-gewor-den* ideals. In short, the realization that not everything in social reality is as it should be, that something must be done to correct the present state of affairs and that whatever is to be done must be done in a systematic, consistent fashion, was the main reason to engage in weaving the canvas of ideology. All ideologies were born of non-acceptance of the *status quo*, and above all from disbelief in reality's own capacity for rectification. All ideologies were born as projects to be actively and concertedly implemented – even when they projected the future (which they envisaged) into the past (which they imagined) and portrayed the novelty as a return, and the reform as a restoration.

It is the absence of such projects that gives a certain substance to the diagnoses of the twilight of ideology; the age of ideology may not be yet over, its agony may yet prove not to be terminal, but most certainly its present condition has changed almost beyond recognition the likeness it bore since the inception of modernity. An ideology without a project – some project which by being a project and a plan for action spells out a future different from the present – is an oxymoron, a contradiction in terms.

The 'ideology' failing the eleventh of Marx's Feuerbach theses ('philosophers so far explained the world; the point is, how to change it') can be put next to its modern predecessors only at the expense of losing from sight the decisive, constitutive features of ideological reason. But more than that is at stake. The world-view disseminated, by design or by default, through the messages coming these days from the quarters of the learned elite, is about time devoid of historical dimension – a flat time, or a roundabout, continuously recycled time, a time with a lot of to-ing and fro-ing but with not much change of position, a time of 'more of the same', a time of *plus ça change, plus c'est la même chose*. This is not just the message that lost the sense of its own historicity: this is a message denying history to the world.

Cornelius Castoriadis asserted in one of his last interviews that the trouble with our civilization is that it stopped questioning itself. Indeed, we may say that the proclamation of the demise of 'grand narratives' (or, in case of Richard Rorty, of the retreat from the 'movement politics', one that used to evaluate every step in terms of shortening the distance to an ideal state of affairs, in favour of the resolution of problems at hand, which is the principle of the one-issue-at-a-time 'campaign politics') announces the disengagement of the knowledge classes, the grand refusal of the modern intellectual vocation.

There are two apparently sharply opposed, but in fact converging ways in which the knowledge classes tend to wash their hands of that questioning of society which once was their defining trait.

The 'positive concept' of ideology is one of them. If all knowledge is ideological, if one can confront ideology only from the perspective of another ideology, if *il n'y a pas hors d'idéologie*, no outside standards to measure and compare the validity of different ideologies – then there is no 'problem of ideology' left, nothing the students of ideology need or ought to do apart from describing them *sine ira et studio*. Above all, no taking of a stand is required. Since there is no way in which one could establish a superiority of one world-perception over another, the sole remaining strategy is to take them as they come and go along with the brute fact of their vast and irreducible variety. If no critique of ideology is allowed, then the task of social reflection ends once it has been pointed out that ideology is everywhere and everything is ideological. The idea of active engagement with society loses its justification and urgency.

Ironically, the ostensibly opposite view leads to the same practical conclusions. That other view, never quite absent from modern discourse yet now gaining in force, is that the presence of ideology is the sign of a not yet fully modernized society; ideology is a backward, as well as a harmful variety of knowledge. If it persists, it can be only due to ignorance or a insidious conspiracy of self-appointed reformers of reality. On the occasion of his admission to the French Academy, Jean-François Revel defined ideology as an 'a priori construction, elaborated in spite of, and with contempt for the facts and the laws; it is the opposite of, simultaneously, science and philosophy, religion and morality' (reported in *Le Monde*, 12 June 1998). Why science, philosophy, religion and morality found themselves standing shoulder to shoulder as defenders of facts and laws, we can only guess. But it is a credible supposition that the role of the commander has been assigned in that army to science, which, as Revel points out, tests its assertions against reality (unlike ideology, which, as Revel does not say, tests reality against its assertions). Revel hopes that science will eventually replace ideology. When it happens, Castoriadis's premonition will finally come true: society will stop questioning itself.

The announcement of the 'end of ideology' is on the part of social commentators a declaration of intent more than it is a description of things as they are: no more criticism of the way things are being done, no more judging or censoring the world through confronting its present state with an alternative of a better society. All critical theory and practice is from now on to be fragmented, deregulated, self-referential, singular and episodic as postmodern life itself.

A case is often made, however, for the market/neo-liberal apotheosis of economic results, productivity and competitiveness with its cult of the winner and its promotion of ethical cynicism, to be the present-day equivalent of the great ideologies of yore; an ideology, moreover, which comes closer to uncontested hegemony than any of its predecessors. There is much to be said in favour of this view. The point of similarity between the neo-liberal world-view and a typical 'classic' ideology is that both serve as *a priori* frames for all future discourse, setting what is seen apart from what goes unnoticed, awarding or denying relevance, determining the logic of reasoning and the evaluation of results. What, however, makes the neo-liberal world-view sharply different from other ideologies – indeed, a phenomenon of a separate class – is precisely the absence of questioning; its surrender to what is seen as the implacable and irreversible logic of social reality. The difference between neo-liberal discourse and the classic ideologies of modernity is, one might say, the difference between the mentality of plankton and that of swimmers or sailors.

Pierre Bourdieu (in *Le Monde diplomatique*, March 1998) compared the apparent invincibility of the neo-liberal world-view to that of the 'strong discourse' of Ervin Goffman's asylum: this kind of discourse is notoriously difficult to resist and repel because it has on its side all the most powerful, indomitable earthly forces which have already preselected the 'real' from 'unrealistic' and made the world as it is. The neo-liberal apotheosis of the market confuses *les choses de la logique avec la logique des choses*, while the great ideologies of modern times, with all their controversies, agreed on one point: that the logic of things as they are defies and contradicts what the logic of reason dictates. Ideology used to set reason *against nature*; the neo-liberal discourse disempowers reason through *naturalizing* it.

Antonio Gramsci coined the term 'organic intellectuals' to account for those members of the knowledge class who took it upon themselves to elucidate the genuine, putative or postulated tasks and prospects of large sections of the population, thereby assisting in the elevation of one or another *klasse an sich* into the *klasse für sich*. That elucidation, 'putting the plight of the class into a historical perspective', was the work of ideology; intellectuals became 'organic' through engaging in ideological praxis. Let me remark that the adding of the qualifier 'organic' to the concept of the 'intellectual' renders the resulting combination pleonastic; it is precisely the fact of being 'organic' in the Gramscian sense that makes mere 'men and women of knowledge' into intellectuals.

When developing the *notion of ideology* as the device to change the world, as a lever lifting the classes of class society to the rank of self-conscious historical agents, or more generally as a contraption to reshape and condense heteronomous and heterogenic populations into autonomous and homogenic cultural units, intellectuals did act in an 'organic' role; in that case, however, they acted as 'organic intellectuals' of *themselves*, lifting the knowledge class not just to the *klasse-für-sich* status, but to the rank of a very special class of people with a peculiar missionary vocation, of a meta-class of sorts, the 'class-producing class'. Any notion of ideology allocates a crucial, historic agency to the men of knowledge, proclaiming them responsible for spelling out the values and the purposes fit, adequate and proper to classes, ethnic groups, genders or nations and for making their discoveries historically effective. This crucial underlying assumption of the concept of ideology casts intellectuals in the role of culture creators, teachers as well as the guardians of values; it demands direct engagement with society or its selected sections and, indeed, gives sense to the very idea of 'intellectuals' as women or men of knowledge *with a mission to perform*, as well as underpinning the collective bid of the knowledge class to a position of authority corresponding with that collective vocation.

The question is whether the currently widespread, perhaps

dominant gospel of the 'end of ideology' or the 'demise of grand narratives' (and, overarching them all, of the 'end of history') is the act of surrender on the part of the knowledge class and of withdrawal of the collective bid; or, on the contrary, it can be seen as another, up-dated version of the 'self-organic' strategy and, accordingly, of that ideology which supplies its justification and *raison d'être*.

It seems that if the knowledge class of the late-modern or postmodern era does assume the role of organic intellectuals at all, it is only the role of organic intellectuals of themselves. What most conspicuously marks off the present-day thought of the knowledge classes is its self-referentiality, its acute preoccupation with the conditions of its own professional activity and the increasingly uncommittal stance it takes towards other sectors of society, indeed, its almost total abandonment of the traditional 'synthesizing' role – the unwillingness to see in the rest of society anything more than an aggregate of individuals, coupled with the proclivity to theorize them as solitary, rather than collective, agents. The 'privatization' of the notion of agency in present-day social thought is a case in point – one of many.

It would be naive to blame the current seminal departure on another stage-production of the *trahison des clercs* and seek redress in the orthodox invocation of commitment as duty. The retreat from a public agenda to professional shelters can hardly be explained away by (equally inexplicable as it were) sudden change of heart or a spell of selfish mood. In all probability the causes reach deeper, into the profound transformations in the way power and the ability to act and to act effectively which go with power are distributed and exercised in postmodern society and the way conditions of social life, including that of the knowledge classes, are reproduced.

Analysing the causes of the rapid weakening of links between concerns and preoccupation of the knowledge classes and the public agenda, Geoff Sharp has recently (in *Arena*, 10/1998) pinpointed 'the insulation of the social theoretical "discourse" from the language of everyday life' as paramount among them. Again, this insulation is not just an outcome of contingent choice nor a matter of character fault. It comes in the wake of a radical redeployment of intellectual resources and the change of the way in which intellectual work is conducted. In the terms I propose to use, we may say that the insulation in question may well be the only form which the self-referential ideology of the intellectuals might take, were they to remain under postmodern conditions, as they did throughout modern times, the 'organic intellectuals' of themselves; though, simultaneously, this form demands that the knowledge classes cease to be the 'organic intellectuals' of anybody else.

The more general point, says Sharp,

> is that intellectual practice as such is radically dependent upon technological mediation for its distinctive way of constituting a form of life. Mediated action is its hallmark . . . It holds as well for the mediate manner in which the technosciences take hold of and constitute their objects: that is, by way of an intervening apparatus which allows that object to be represented and understood in ways which are unavailable to more directly sensate knowledge. Finally mediation allows all expressions of intellectual practice to constitute their objects more abstractly: which is to say, constitute them in different and typically more inclusive categories than is characteristic of the relations of mutual presence.

Let me add that, with all their flaunted inclusivity and typicality, the categories in question are not inclusive of the total human beings as they emerge and act in their everyday life. On the contrary, generalizing abstracted aspects of human agents, *pars pro toto*, the categories in question split and divide rather than 'make whole' and stand in the way of human life ever acquiring the totality it strives for. Whatever is the case, though, let us note, after Sharp, 'the unprecedented way in which intellectually related practices are reconstituting the world of postmodernity in their own image: mediately, abstractly and via the textual archive'.

The World Wide Web which the knowledge classes inhabit, which they process and by which they are processed, leaves *Lebenswelt* – the lived world – outside; it admits bits of that world only when properly fragmented and so ready for processing, and returns them to the world outside in duly recycled, abstracted form. Cyberspace, the site of the postmodern intellectual practice, feeds on fragmentation and promotes fragmentation, being simultaneously its product and its major *causa efficiens*.

The ascendance of ideology in the heyday of modernity was,

notoriously, a mixed blessing. But so is its demise. Wise after the fact, we now know the human costs of casting society in ideological straight-jackets, of falling into the temptation of marrying ideological blueprints to the fervour of executive powers – and we are inclined to count them carefully before any new commitment is entered. But we are yet to learn the costs of living without alternatives, without signposts and yardsticks, of 'letting things go' and declaring the consequences to be as inevitable as they are unanticipated. Ulrich Beck's vision of the *Risikogesellschaft* is a glimpse of such living: living from one crisis to another, attempting to cope with one known problem only to provoke an unknown quantity of unknown problems, focusing on the management of local orders while losing from sight their contribution to the global chaos. It is too early to celebrate the end of 'grand narratives' just as it is uncanny, perhaps also unethical, in the light of modern experience, to bewail their passing.

Excursus 2: Tradition and Autonomy in the Postmodern World

Of tradition – that 'message of the past' – we speak when it is no longer clear what the message conveys and how to read it out, when there are so many willing readers that it is easy to get confused and the chorus is so big that one can no longer hear the tune in the cacophony. The concept of tradition is paradoxical, since it speaks of one thing but augurs something else altogether and cannot do otherwise; it denies in practice what it avers in theory. It prompts us to believe that the past *binds* our present; it augurs, however (and triggers), our present and future efforts to *construe* a 'past' by which we need or wish to be bound.

'Tradition' is not synonymous with 'custom' or 'habit', though the terms all too often tend to be confused. In fact, tradition is the very opposite of custom and habit. Customary or habitual behaviour is an unthinking, unreflexive behaviour: one that calls for neither explanation nor excuse – and when pressed to give its own reason is hard put to offer one. The discomfiture that follows the inquiry can be even paralysing, as in the case of the centipede of the famous Rudyard Kipling story, who, when complimented by a sycophant for its exquisite ability to remember which of its hundred legs to put down before and which one after, was no longer able to take a single step. One does not behave habitually *because* one believes that doing so is good and that behaving differently is bad. As a matter of fact, one behaves habitually only as long as one does not imagine, let alone consider, alternative ways of behaving.

'Tradition', on the contrary, refers to a situation of choice: the concept is born as a name for a task; the 'issue' of 'tradition' is brought to attention when one way of conduct is to be chosen among many which are possible, feasible and plausible, known or adumbrated. 'Tradition' is all about thinking, reasoning, justifying – and first and foremost about *choice*.

Eric Hobsbawm introduced into our vocabulary the concept of 'invented tradition': aspiring political leaders of yet unformed communities often invented, as Hobsbawm showed, a common past which, as they imply, holds the community together and obliges it to stick together. They deploy arguments from the past to bind the future, and the fact that there is no past to draw fitting arguments from is not for them an obstacle; after all, what matters is the common present and common future; the sole importance of a common past is that it makes the job of shaping them and keeping on course somewhat easier. 'Invention', though, marks the origin of selected traditions only. There is a sense in which all tradition, at any rate all traditions that coexist in our type of society, must be invented and cannot but be invented.

We live, as Anthony Giddens suggests, in a 'post-traditional society' ('Living in a Post-Traditional Society', in Anthony Giddens, *In Defence of Sociology: Essays, Interpretations & Rejoinders* (Cambridge; Polity Press, 1996)). One should beware, however, of interpreting that poignant phrase as a reference to tradition losing its authority, or our loss of respect for it, or our demand for 'heritage' and 'historical memory' having been exhausted or running low, or the erosion of our belief that old is beautiful and needs to be venerated just for the fact of its being old – though such explications are common in the descriptions of modernity as a way of life programmatically inimical to everything ancient, which treats 'the old', the 'outdated' and the 'obsolete' as synonyms and refuses to accept longevity as an entitlement to authority. The idea of the 'post-traditional society' is better understood as referring not to tradition running out of fashion, but to the *surplus* of traditions: the *excess* of readings of the past vying for acceptance, the absence of a single reading of history likely to command a universal or near-universal trust. As Giddens puts it, 'There is a fundamental sense in which the whole institutional apparatus of modernity, once it has become broken away from tradition, depends upon potentially volatile mechanisms of trust.' I would modify this sequence a bit: it is not so much the mechanisms of trust-allocation as trust itself that tends to become volatile, and there are no mechanisms in sight which could stop it from being volatile, because there are too many competitive traditions for any one of them to secure a long-lasting allegiance and command supreme authority. Or, to put it another way, the 'unfixedness' of trust which results in the weakening of the hold in which any one tradition can keep contemporary society, is intimately related to the essentially *polycentric* character of modern society.

It is not that – being modern – we have become particularly fastidious and fussy or that we have developed a particular liking of picking and choosing. It is, rather, that whether we like it or not we are doomed to choose, to go on choosing and to justify our choices and to be painfully aware that choosing and being pressed to prove ourselves right is our fate, since in a polycentric setting we are continually exposed to more than one image of the good life, more than one personal ideal pattern, more than one proposition how to tell apart the 'should' from the 'should not', and more than one credible story told of the world, past or present, in order to justify trust in some of the alternative propositions always coupled with the rejection of some others.

If we manage to acquire steady habits which we practise for a stretch of time to the detriment of others, then the superficial similarity of such a behavioural pattern to conduct described as the 'observance of tradition' hides a very profound difference between the two. The first may happen solely in a *no-choice* situation in which the very absence of viable alternatives prevents the practised way from being given a second thought, let alone being viewed as a choice. The second is an *outcome* of choice: the profusion of visible and ostensibly available alternatives effectively staves off the possibility of forgetting that what is practised is indeed a choice and could be replaced – at short notice or without notice – with another, perhaps even a quite different, form of life.

By necessity rather than by design, ours is a society of choosers; of such choosers, moreover, as tend to be taught to make a virtue out of this necessity. Certainly our market suppliers show this tendency: they have discovered (and are unlikely to forget) the awesome seductive power of diversity and the allurement of rich and variegated displays. So do the creators and distributors of all sorts of artistic goods, who raise choice to the rank of a value in its own right and see it as one aspect of reality most fit to offer both content and form to the works of art. And so do the members of the blossoming counselling profession, purveyors of the new type of marketable skills which are born of the need to choose and which thrive when the choice gets more profuse, bewildering and off-putting. As one of the distinguished members of that profession advises those who feel lost without the counsel of experts and thus keenly seek their services,

> look at what you can do, starting at any time you choose, by making conscious, *active* choices every time the opportunity comes up. It is what we do with these choices (and many other choices just like them) that will always determine not only how well each day works for us, but how successful we will be at anything we do. (S. Helmsletter, *Choices* (New York: Product Books, p. 104); here quoted after Giddens)

Having made their choices, the choosers may behave in a way strikingly reminiscent of the compulsive behaviour, the kind of conduct often imputed (wrongly) to the people in the grips of tradition. Again, similarity is superficial and misleading. Compulsion is, in Giddens's apt expression, *frozen trust* – but any trust in the society of choosers is easily defrosted, and even when frozen it has the 'use by' warning printed on the wrappings in bold letters. The only true compulsion left in the society of choosers, the only form of repetitive behaviour oblivious of or blind to all other choices, is the compulsion to choose. All other quasi-compulsions are, by Giddens's suggestion, better described as *addictions*.

Addiction is the very opposite of the permanent and fixed investment of trust, it has nothing 'trustworthy' about it: it is by its nature fickle, uncertain of its own wisdom and lacking in confidence, dissatisfied with itself, constantly in need of reassurance, covertly or overtly shame-faced and apologetic. Addiction, says Giddens (after A. W. Schaeff), is 'anything we have to lie about'. Being what it is, addiction is 'the obverse of that integrity which tradition once supplied and which all forms of trust also presume'. Addiction is not just what I have been *forced* to do, it is what I have *chosen* to be forced to do; the awareness of choice, and of the responsibility for what has been chosen, is built into it and cannot be excised. Hence the constant, incurable uncertainty about the wisdom of the choice made, however tightly that choice has been embraced: the proclivity to self-indignation, self-reproach, regret, repentance – all things conspicuously absent from the obedience to tradition ...

This is it: the ultimate difference between compulsive-looking conduct in the society of consumers/choosers and the mythical 'traditional society' with its customs and habits as the sole springs of behaviour is one between chosen strategy and unsolicited fate, or quite simply between choice and no-choice.

'Tradition' in its proper sense (not the sense twisted and manipulated in order to recycle it for the uses of a society which is not its natural home) belongs with the *heteronomous* society. The heteronomous society, as Cornelius Castoriadis kept on repeating, is one which refuses to recognize or resents the human origin of the rules which it calls its members to obey; a society which for this reason imagines itself being shaped and guided by commands not of its own making – commands given by an *external* force. In the last interview he gave before his death ('L'individu privatisé', an interview with Robert Redeker, given in Toulouse on 22 March 1997), Castoriadis pointed out that heteronomous societies (and this means almost all societies recorded in history)

> incorporated in their institutions an idea not to be contested by their members: the idea that their institutions are not human-made, were not created by humans, at least not by the humans who are alive at the moment. These institutions have been made by spirits, by ancestors, by heroes, by Gods; they are not of human making.

'Tradition' in its proper sense implies precisely such a 'built-in' institutional quality: the assumption that there is nothing that people currently alive can do to change the institutions they inherited, and that if oblivious to their impotence they try to meddle with the legacy – then unimaginable disasters will follow, whether brought about by divine punishment or by the laws of nature which neither admit nor bear any violation.

The bid to pass from the heteronomous to an autonomous society (the first step towards societal autonomy, laying down its necessary, though not a sufficient, condition) is made once it has been recognized that the laws of society have no other legs to stand on but the will of the people who declared them; and that whatever is human-made can be also unmade by humans. That bid was first made by the Greeks once they introduced the formula *edoxe te boule kai to demo* – 'it is deemed good by the council and the people' – to precede the laws they required people to obey. Laws preceded with such preambula called for discipline in the name of the common good; but by the very fact that they tried to justify their demands, to 'lay the ground' for the required discipline, they also called for *reflection*, for *responsible reflection* and for *reflective responsibility*: look, these are laws which most of us think are good – but are they indeed as good as we think they are? Is there something we may and need do to make them better? The formula reminds us of the *choice* which has been laid at the foundation of whatever has been authorized to rule our conduct. And it reminds us of the responsibility for making that choice good – a responsibility we cannot shake off and lay at the doorstep of another, external and unreachable, power.

No wonder Castoriadis insists that a *truly autonomous* society (not just a society which pays lip service to the principle of autonomy so understood, not a society which fails to follow up its own bid for autonomy) is a society of *autonomous individuals*. There is no autonomy of society without the autonomy of its individual members. Society may be autonomous, that is self-choosing and self-governing, only if its members are given the right and the resources to choose and never renounce that right nor cede it to someone (or something) else. An autonomous society is a self-constituting society; autonomous individuals are self-constituting individuals. In both cases, self-constitution is a matter of degree, but the degree of self-constitution may rise on both – societal and individual – levels only simultaneously.

But what is a 'self-constituting individual'? We may say that the first step towards self-constitution, its necessary though not sufficient condition, is the recognition that the individual has not been given her or his identity ready-made, but that identity is something to be built by the individuals themselves and taken responsibility for; that, in other words, rather than 'having an identity', the individuals are faced with the long and arduous, never to be finished job of *identification*. Unlike the idea of preordained identity, the project of identification, in Stuart Hall's poignant words,

> does *not* signal that stable core of the self, unfolding from the beginning to end through the vicissitudes of history without change; the bit of the self which remains always-already 'the same', identical to itself across time. Nor . . . is it that collective or true self hiding inside the many other, more superficial or artificially imposed 'selves' which a people with a shared history and ancestry hold in common and which can stabilize, fix or guarantee an unchanging 'oneness' or cultural belongingness underlying all the other superficial differences. It accepts that identities are never unified and, in late modern times, increasingly fragmented and fractured; never singular but multiply constructed across different, often intersecting and antagonistic, discourses, practices and positions. ('Who needs Identity?', in *Questions of Cultural Identity*, ed. Stuart Hall and Paul du Gay (London: Sage, 1997), pp. 3–4)

Replacing the assumption of an 'always-already-the-same' identity with the prospect of a never-ending effort of identification means, in principle, the acceptance of the absence of ready-made and external foundations of the self and of the full and indivisible responsibility for the self yet to be chosen: 'I am what I manage to make of myself.'

This does not mean, of course, that the choice is made in a void and that it starts, or could start in more favourable circumstances, from a zero point. All choice is a choice among what is on offer, and few if any individuals may boast to have succeeded in starting their self-identification *ab nihilo*. Such exceptional individuals are bound to remain few and far between, since while being an *individual task* 'identity' is nevertheless a *social phenomenon*. Identity is what is *socially recognizable* as identity; it is bound to remain but a figment of the individual imagination unless it is communicated to others in socially legible terms – expressed in socially understandable symbols.

The recognition that there is no external foundation or guarantee of identity *does* mean, however, that whatever is eventually chosen is a matter of individually made decision and will remain a feather in the individual's cap or a burden on that individual's conscience. The model I have chosen could be made by someone else, but the responsibility for its choice is mine and mine alone.

Once that recognition, the very first step towards individual autonomy, has been made, 'tradition' may enter the project of identification only in the form of *traditionalism*: that is, of the preference given to 'our common heritage', to the ways and means shared in the past or believed to be shared by a category of people one would wish to identify with: a category which claims those particular ways and means to be their joint collective endowment and legacy. Even if the preference is being justified by an 'old is beautiful' kind of argument, or by 'The true self is the hereditary self' kind of argument, the very fact that arguments are felt to be needed and are made testifies that it has been the individual decision which had brought that preference about in the first place. The beauty of the old is in the eye of the beholder, and being born into a tradition always means in practice, for an autonomous or would-be autonomous individual, being 'born again'. It is the strength of the commitment which makes the preference stand up to the competition.

Hence the second dimension of the paradox endemic to the idea of tradition. Tradition may enter human awareness only ushered by traditionalism; traditionalism, being a recommendation as to which choice is to be made, and therefore implying the presence of choice and the human need to choose, is therefore organically bound to an autonomous society; its presence, in fact, testifies to the autonomy of the society in which it appears. But traditionalism is a symptom of society ashamed of its autonomy – feeling awkward about it and dreaming of escaping it. Just as hypocrisy is a roundabout tribute paid by the lie to the truth, so traditionalism is an oblique, embarrassed and shame-faced tribute paid by heteronomy to autonomy.

Excursus 3: Postmodernity and Moral and Cultural Crises

Few people remember today that the word 'crisis' was coined to mean the time to make decisions . . . Etymologically, the word comes much closer to the term 'criterion' – the principle we apply to make the right decision – than to the family of words associated with 'disaster' or 'catastrophy' in which we tend to locate it today.

It was Hippocrates who picked up the Greek verb Κρινειη (to decide, to determine) to forge a name for the rising tide of the four humours of the body – phlegm, blood, choler and black bile – which, according to his teachings, is the proper time for the healer to decide what turn the condition of the patient is most likely to take and determine the right therapy to assist him on the way to recovery. It is the time of κρισις – that is of flow, not of ebb, which is best for making the decisions. The vision of how the human body works has, since Hippocrates, changed beyond recognition, but the old sense of the term 'crisis' as the moment when the turn of events is decided, survives – though this is mostly in a medical context. Elsewhere, where it moves as a metaphor, and particularly in daily speech the word brings to mind quite the opposite situation – a state of touch-and-go, of indetermination and indecision, of ignorance about where things are moving and of the impotence to push them the way one would wish them to move . . . One is tempted to say that nowadays the very idea of crisis (as we once knew it but have since forgotten) is in deep crisis. But were we to say that, we would not use the term 'crisis' in the sense Hippocrates wished to give it.

To put it a bit more precisely, we still think today of crisis as a moment of decisive change for better or worse; but no longer as the time when sensible decisions can be taken self-assuredly to secure a turn for the better. In the state of crisis we do not know where things are moving; in the state of crisis things get out of hand; we do not control the flow of events; we can try, desperately, to find the way out of the predicament, but all our efforts will be little more than a story of trials and errors, experimenting in the dark, hoping that something, ultimately, may come out of it. Whatever wave rises in the time of crisis, it is not the part of the tide of confidence and self-assurance. More likely, confidence is at its lowest ebb, while feelings of uncertainty and helplessness and the intuition of inadequacy of mental and/or material tools of action reach their highest flow.

In his once very influential study of the 'legitimation crisis' Jürgen Habermas suggested that the perception of a certain state of affairs as a 'crisis' is a matter of theory. To speak of crisis, one needs first a theory – an image of a normal, unproblematic state of affairs; 'crisis' comes when that normal, usual and familiar state crumbles, things fall out of joint, randomness appears where regularity should rule and events are no longer routine and predictable; we felt on top of things before, but now we feel more as if we are drifting in an unknown direction. In other words, we call a 'crisis' a situation in which events defy whatever has passed for normality and routine actions no longer bring the results we became used to in the past.

Logically speaking, Habermas's reasoning is impeccable. But the twisted roads of our awareness do not necessarily follow logical signposts. To unravel those roads it would be perhaps better to reverse the suggested order of discovery, and accord the idea of 'crisis' conceptual priority over the perception of 'normality'. Indeed, it is through the extraordinary that we recognize what the 'ordinary' means; as Martin Heidegger explained a long time ago, it is only when something 'goes wrong' that we posit the idea of the right and proper and give it a closer look; it is only when the hammer has been broken and we feverishly look for a replacement that we start asking questions about the 'essence' of the hammer, the traits which an object must possess in order to be a hammer. We reach for theory when things preciously at our fingertips get out of hand.

In defiance of logic, but in tune with the way our cognitive faculties work, the perception of crisis *precedes* the awareness of the norm. And so, contrary to Habermas, it is the perception of a crisis that prompts the search for a theory of the 'normal', which posits the image of 'normality' – and not the other way round. Without that perception of crisis we could go on, perhaps indefinitely, without reflecting and theorizing, without giving 'normality' a second thought; habits and routine would do perfectly, and they need not be spelled out to hold us in their grip.

Normality is at its strongest and best entrenched when it is not noticed; when daily labours do not congeal in the mind of the labourers into the vision of the norm. One can sharpen this assertion still further and say that whenever the idea of a norm or a rule surfaces in consciousness, it can and should be seen as an oblique testimony to events not tightly enough overlapping with habitual expectations; of the discrepancy between the blatant 'is' and the tacit 'ought'. When we speak of crisis in its modern sense of incomprehension and uncertainty, the message conveyed sometimes overtly, but more often implicitly, is that the tools we have become used to handling to good effect without thinking now feel awkward in our hands and do not seem to work; and so we feel the need to find out what were the conditions that used to make them effective in the past, and what is to be done to either restore those conditions or change the tools.

However frequent and widespread the use of the term 'crisis' has become in our times, the state of mind it stands for was and is still more frequent. The feelings that things 'go wrong', differ from what was expected, and the resulting bafflement as to how to go on, are frequent, common, perhaps a universal accompaniment of the human existential experience. All human being-in-the-world is reflexive; it always entails recapitulation and overhauling, it cannot last long without self-critique.

That this must be the case, we realize already when we heed Ortega y Gasset's discussion of the impact of generations (in *Esquema de las crisis*, 1942). If it is true that none of us invents the world anew nor collects knowledge of it from scratch, but owes most of their contents to ready-made artefacts of communal effort, then it is also true that successive generations enter that effort at different points and so in building up their own *Lebenswelte* deploy different sets of artefacts. This much is pretty clear and trivial; what is less often taken into account, though, is the fact that at each moment in history several generations live together, interact, exchange services, and so face the task of co-ordinating their actions and communicating with each other. Already for this reason society is perpetually in a 'critical state', and the older generations, people who have been around longer and have had more time to develop habits and expectations, tend to be the first to perceive the present state of affairs as a state of 'crisis'. 'Society' is an imagined entity anyway, but it is imagined in many different, sometimes sharply different, forms which are not readily translatable. For this reason alone, leaving out of account the resulting plurality, frictions and tensions when leaving the canvas of a 'social system' is a gravely confusing mistake.

Let me sharpen the point yet further: *crisis*, in as far as the notion refers to the invalidation of customary ways and means and the resulting lack of certainty as to how to go on, *is the normal state of human society*. In a paradoxical way we can say that there is nothing critical about society being in crisis. 'Being in crisis' is the ordinary, and perhaps the sole conceivable, fashion of self-constitution (Castoriadis) or auto-poïesis (Luhmann), of self-reproduction and renewal, and every moment in the life of society is one of self-constitution, re-production and self-renewal.

All this stands to reason; moreover, what has been said so far hardly contains a single new, let alone startling, idea – since for at least a few decades now the fact that society exists through constant disequilibration rather than through a perpetual return to the equilibrated state is taken by social scientists far and wide to be the starting point of all sensible theorizing. If this is the case, though, then the fact that the public alarm and panic over crisis is unevenly distributed over time and that concerns with crisis surface intermittently and with varying intensity, calls for explanation. What needs to be explained in particular is the unusually high intensity of the present-day public concern with the 'crisis of the world order', 'crisis of values', 'crisis of culture', 'crisis of the arts' and other innumerable crises discovered daily in ever new areas of the human world.

The obvious and simple (seeming obvious *because* being simple) response to the above query would be to point to the sheer volume of unprecedented and unfamiliar ideas, which play havoc with expectations gestated and born at times when things changed at a much slower pace. It is said that though the world was always a-changing, never before had the changes been so plentiful and so profound; and that the rapid increase in the quantity and the depth of changes makes the perpetual human task of self-orientation that much more difficult.

A slightly less obvious, but also relatively simple response would be to point out that never before have the seminal, generation-constituting events and transformations kept ageing, fading out and succeeding each other at such a high speed, and that consequently the time spans enclosing separate generations are now shorter than ever – a few years rather than a few dozens of years; and so the number of distinct generations, each holding its own different experiences and anticipations but cohabiting and interacting inside a common social space, has grown enormously. That fact explains in part the astonishing polyphony (some would say cacophony) of the public scene and the resulting difficulty in communicating and reaching agreement despite all the indubitable progress in the technology of translation.

Both responses convey a similar idea of crises being somewhat deeper and more frequently felt, but still carrying essentially the same meaning as before. Perhaps, however, these responses do not go far enough; perhaps the present worry signals a change in the very meaning of 'crisis'. Perhaps we use an old term to express a new kind of anxiety. Perhaps what we call 'crisis' today differs in kind, not just in degree or frequency, from what we used to name 'crisis' half a century, or more, ago.

This, indeed, may be the case. There is an added meaning lurking in the present alarm. What we call 'crisis' today is not just the state in which forces of conflicting nature clash; the future is in the balance and life is about to acquire a new, but imprevisible shape – but first and foremost a state in which *no emergent shape is likely to solidify and survive for long*. In other words, not the state of *indecision*, but of *the impossibility of decision*. The fears which flicker beneath all that 'crisis' talk are akin to the horrors of the passengers who do not just feel the aircraft to quaver and waver but have also discovered that the pilot's cabin of their aircraft is empty. When we speak today of the world-order crisis, or the value crisis, or the crisis of the arts or culture, we do not mean that all these things are at the moment undecided, but that they are *undecidable* – that there is no way in which a sensible, let alone binding, choice could be made, and that even if such a way were found, there would be no agencies capable or at least willing to carry the decision through.

The world appears to us as a monstrously obese, gargantuan version of the Internet: here as there, everybody adds to the universal scramble but no one seems to visualize the consequences, let alone to control them. Here as there, a game goes on without an umpire and without legible rules which could be drawn upon to arbitrate the results. Here as there, each player plays a game of her or his own but no one is sure what sort of a game, if any, their moves amount to. The world is no longer the benchmark of 'reality' against which to measure the soundness of the players' moves; the world itself is one of the players, like all players keeping the cards close to the chest, holding a sleeve full of tricks, bluffing and – given the chance – cheating. Or, like the Web, the world is not just out of control, it is *uncontrollable*.

To put the same proposition in a different way: it now seems that gaining control over the course of events, or at least spotting in time the winning horse and so gaining control over the consequences of one's own moves, is not a matter of acquiring some presently missing knowledge. Today confusion is not the outcome of subjective neglect or error, rectifiable through more strenuous effort and better logic. The frightening feature of the contemporary world is that the more knowledgeable the actions tend to be, the more they add to the overall chaos. To use the felicitous term coined by Anthony Giddens, ours is a *manufactured* uncertainty. Uncertainty is not something we *repair*, but something we *create*, and create ever anew and in bigger quantities, and create it *through our efforts to repair it*.

Perhaps it was always like this, or perhaps it was like this for a very long time. But if it was like this in the lifetime of our grandfathers, they most certainly did not know it. To employ the phrase used by George Steiner on a different occasion, their ignorance was their privilege. Thanks to their ignorance, they could believe that whatever confusion they happened to fall into was but temporary; and they believed that they knew well what to do in order to make it disappear; and they believed that gaining more knowledge and more skill was the way to achieving just that. Those beliefs might have been false and in the end misleading, but thanks to holding such beliefs no despair, however deep, was bottomless; there was always a reasonable hope that climbing out of it was within human reach, if not just around the next corner. And with that hope foremost on everybody's mind, climbing could go on with rising vigour even if the crest was nowhere in sight and not getting nearer either.

As it was only to be expected, to eyes so trained crises appeared to be an evil, but an evil both transient and amendable; momentary hitches, ulcers or thorns not yet removed from the basically healthy body; temporary malfunctions of an essentially neat and tidy mechanism. Past crises could be written off as successive chapters in the long history of human ignorance and silliness. But with history being the chronicle of successive victories of science over prejudice and reason over superstition, one could also anticipate that this history of stupidity would eventually grind to a halt, that there would be ever fewer crises in the future, while full knowledge, once achieved, would certainly mean no crises at all.

We do not have any more the benefit of such benign and soothing beliefs. And for the loss of our ancestors' youthful naivety we pay in the currency of anxiety, of a kind which our not-so-distant ancestors had seldom, if at all, experienced.

Think, for instance, of the recent substitution of the term 'risk' for another term, that of 'danger', which for a long time sufficed to denote our fears and apprehensions. 'Dangers' differ from 'risks' in that they can be more or less exactly located and that one can, therefore, take measures to avert them or at least resist them. But, above all, dangers come and go; they are accidental and external to what we do; they are disturbances in the otherwise smooth pursuit of our objectives, coming from outside and unrelated to what we are after. Risks are an entirely different matter: they are endemic features of our own actions; they are present in and arise from whatever we do; they may be perhaps reduced in size, but never extinguished completely. From an 'either – or' situation we have passed to the 'and – and' or 'yes, but' condition, the condition of permanent trade-off, when gains never come unless accompanied by losses, when we must choose not between good and bad solutions, but between greater and lesser evils. First and foremost, we may try to calculate the risk involved in our undertakings – but no more than in probability terms, which means that we can never be quite sure what the outcome of our actions will in fact be and whether the precautions we take will not in the end bring more harm than benefit.

Ulrich Beck gained his well-deserved fame for coining the term *Risikogesellschaft*; but what follows from his incisive and minute description of that kind of society is that the human condition is one of *Risikoleben* – a life in which no step is likely to be unambiguously 'a step in the right direction', and so the uncertainty about the correctness or propriety of our undertakings will never, even retrospectively, be dispersed. Many old popular sayings refer to that kind of life – adages about 'groping in the dark', 'living to regret it' or 'playing fast and loose'; popular wisdom condemned such a kind of life, regretted the lot of its carriers and implied the need to avoid it. It also assumed that such a life was a wrong choice which *could*, and so *ought to*, be avoided. But what follows from Beck's analysis is that *Risikoleben* is not a choice of the adventurous or the error of the foolhardy; it is our common fate – whether we like it or not, whether we praise its pleasures and joys or condemn its discomforts and traps.

The replacement of the idea of 'danger' by that of 'risk' portrays faithfully (and allows one to grasp better) the fateful change in the meaning of 'crisis'. 'Being in crisis' is no longer seen as a regrettable reversal of fortune or a misadventure, but an irremovable attribute of the human condition. We live constantly in a 'touch and go' situation; we take risks whatever we do; and while our decisions may be in some respects better or worse, they would hardly ever be flawless, or better in *all* respects that count.

What follows from all that, if you think of it, is that the concept of 'crisis' has become all but redundant . . . The word signifies, after all, the permanent condition of things; an indispensable attribute of whatever follows it. Phrases coined with the word 'crisis' are therefore as a rule pleonastic, along the lines of 'butter made of milk' or 'liquid water'. For instance, the phrases 'cultural crisis' or 'crisis of the arts' do not distinguish a particular and peculiar form of culture from all the rest, or a special moment in the life of the arts from the rest of their history. They are in fact analytic statements, unpacking the nature of culture or the arts, or better still are their oblique definitions.

Whether it was always like that but we are only now coming

to see it clearly, or whether the kind of culture and artistic scene from which we extrapolate today our notions of culture and the arts as such are truly novel and unlike their predecessors, is a moot question; to my mind, though, instead of engaging in a debate which is notoriously difficult to resolve because of the inevitable interference between 'the facts of the matter' and the intellectual frames which mould 'the matter' into 'the facts', it is better to concentrate on tracing the consequences, which our new *perception* of 'crisis' might have for our orthodox notions of values, culture, arts and whatever else we now see as existing-through-crisis.

Let us look first at the notion of the 'value crisis'. Here Habermas's idea of the perception of crisis being a derivative or a projection of the theory of the area allegedly in crisis may indeed come in handy.

Theory, as it were, is a way of seeing as much as of averting the eyes; it focuses the sight on some aspects of reality by blurring the rest. The perception of 'value crisis' is an artefact of the overtly or implicitly fundamentalist concept of ethics. According to such a concept moral standards may be observed in society solely on the condition that people are systematically put in the situation of 'no choice'; either through manipulating the environment of their actions so that it renders immoral conduct unrealistic or too costly to contemplate, or by indoctrinating people with unquestioning respect for one moral code and aversion to all alternative precepts. The perception of 'value crisis' is an artefact of such a fundamentalist concept of ethics in a double sense.

First, it prompts one to believe that the sheer abundance of competing values, both chosen and choosable, is by itself tantamount to an unhealthy or even morbid, ungodly or unnatural state of affairs; such an abundance is by itself the sign of failure or the 'moralizing project' while, according to the spirit and the letter of that project, its own failure spells the end of the sole morality which the project recognizes as being morality – and thus of morality as such. From the fundamentalist point of view the plurality of values, the diversity of choices, is by itself an evil; the frequently added argument that it is evil *because* it holds the likelihood of wrong choices is but a rationalization of what is in its essence a gut feeling; it is but a lip service paid to the ruling spirit of rational debate.

Second, the active promotion of morality-through-ethical-legislation breeds not so much moral responsibility, as obedience to the stronger and conformity to the rule; all the emphasis is on the unquestionable submission to whatever one is told to do, on compliance with authority, while little attention is drawn to the substance and the quality of the command. It does not matter what one is called to do; what does matter is the power and the power-supported legitimacy of the authority that is calling on one to do so. Contrary to the intention and most certainly to the promise, the cultivation of morality by unconditional surrender to the rule, whatever the rule might be, results in the selfsame moral nihilism which the promoters of the one-and-only ethical code set out to prevent. Nothing relies on the moral subject's own reflection – the link between the code and the conduct ought to be, ideally, unmediated, to exclude the chance of deviance. It all hangs instead on the monopoly of the legislating power, since the chance of humans behaving morally is deemed to depend on effacing, not developing, their proclivity and ability to make autonomous (and so in principle unpredictable) judgements and choices. The moment that monopoly is shaken and the authorities multiply, human individuals are faced with the necessity of their own choices according to their own power of moral judgement – that is, to resources they are not believed to possess or are suspected of using wrongly, and therefore have been given little chance to develop. This is what is meant by the 'crisis of values' and no wonder it is viewed with alarm.

The 'crisis of values' so understood is seen as a major threat to (indeed, the very opposite of) morality, mostly because in that theory of morality and the practice of its cultivation the idea of the moral subject's own autonomous responsibility is missing if not openly denied or disparaged. Explicitly or obliquely, that theory defines moral subjects by their conformity to the rule, not by responsible choice of conduct, while the practice of ethical education and enforcement sees to it that individuals live down to that definition.

There is, however, another way of looking at the nature of morality, one in which the responsibility of the autonomous actor is accorded pride of place. In such a perspective, the abundance of competing values does not appear to be the sign of 'crisis'; and if it is a crisis, then far from sounding a death knell to morality it augurs conditions favourable to those individuals facing up to the fact of their inalienable responsibility for moral choices. Such a 'crisis' is not the mark of a land inhospitable to moral selves; on the contrary, it signals an atmosphere auspicious to their birth and maturation – a situation which more than any other prompts the individuals to take up responsibility for their responsibility . . .

If the multiplicity of values requiring judgement and choice is a sign of a 'value crisis', then we need to accept that such a crisis is a natural home of morality: only in that home are freedom, autonomy, responsibility, judgement – all of which loom large among the indispensable features of the moral self – allowed to grow and mature. The multiplicity of values by itself does not guarantee that moral selves will indeed grow and mature. But without it, they stand little chance of doing so. What we often call the 'crisis of values' shows itself under closer scrutiny to be the 'normal state' or the human moral condition.

Let us consider now, also briefly, the notion of 'cultural crisis'. In public discourse as well as in numerous scholarly commentaries that notion has come to signify the alarm and anxiety triggered by an apparent lack of normative cohesion; by the illegibility or ambiguity of precepts meant to regulate or to assist the selection of preferred forms, meanings and behavioural patterns; by the apparent absence of agreement as to what is important and worthy of pursuit; by the fact that the disparate signals coming to the individual from that mysterious imagined space called 'society' do not amount to a coherent totality, do not combine into a system; and by the fact that for every norm promoted by certain authorities some different, often contradictory exhortations are audible, voiced from other, no less authoritative sources. In other words, the concept of the 'cultural crisis' has come to refer to the state of normative ambiguity, ambivalence, inconsistency, unclarity, indeterminacy; and to the perception of such a state as off-putting and in one way or another threatening to the well-being of society as a whole and the successful life of its members.

Again, it is difficult, perhaps impossible, to decide whether this is a matter of a drastic and recent change in the state of the world or just a matter of a belated discovery and admission of the nature of things – true for a long time, yet previously unnoticed or denied. We have grown used to the idea of 'culture' as a system . of mutually coherent and complementary norms, topped with the 'dominant value syndrome', which, like the mythical ether, impregnate, penetrate and saturate all 'specific', category- and situation-bound, norms from the top to the bottom of the social system. That idea also assumed the essential 'functionality' of culture; according to that idea, culture served the task of pattern-maintenance, tension-management and – more generally – the self-identity, continuity and monotonous self-reproduction of society in its given shape. Codifying that two-centuries-long view, Talcott Parsons introduced the concept of culture into his theory primarily as a device to explain why voluntary actions, despite being voluntary and apparently individually chosen, would still fall into regular patterns and display repetitiveness and regularity.

Bluntly speaking, the idea of culture came to be associated with constraints, with cutting down the number of conceivable options, with the limitation of the freedom of choice. With such an idea in mind, any observed case of incoherence between cultural norms had to be taken as evidence of 'malfunctioning', and explained away as but a temporary irritant; the disturbance was seen to be temporary, since culture, like the society it was expected to serve, was assumed to possess an inbuilt tendency to systemness and self-equilibration. The cases of malfunctioning could be easily explained away by the phenomenon of 'cultural lag', the inertia of by-now obsolete relics of bygone social settings, or by 'cultural clash', the interference of otherwise cohesive, but mutually incompatible cultural systems.

Whether or not such a conception of cultural phenomena was plausible at the time when it dominated social theory, it certainly appears unsustainable in the framework of the late-modern or postmodern mentality. When we speak of culture today, what comes to mind is not an image of a coherent and cohesive, self-enclosed and self-sustained totality with clearly articulated and closely interlocked parts, but a picture of a vast matrix of possibilities, in which uncountable and not at all co-ordinated combinations and permutations may be, and indeed are, made. Or better still, to visualize the change in perception we can use Lotman's allegory of the two ways in which creative energy may be distributed. The creative energy, Castoriadis's *vis formandi* or Luhmann's power or *autopoïesis*, may flow like that spring-water which descends towards the riverbed, becoming a powerful stream which – if given enough time – would sweep aside or carry away everything that bars its way, eroding, crushing and dissolving even the most solid of rocks. But it may be also scattered over the vast expanses of a minefield, of which one can say with certainty that explosions will occur time and again, here and there, but that there is no way to know where and when. The image of the riverbed is akin to the modern-orthodox cultural imagery; the image of the minefield has an obvious affinity with the present-day thinking of culture.

In this – our – thinking, culture is seen mostly as a process of a continuous and essentially undirected change, militating against all structure, and particularly against solid and constraining structures – instead of assisting at their birth and helping them in the task of survival. With the realm of culture not being viewed as divided between self-enclosed, internally harmonious systems, it is difficult to interpret the plentiful incidences of cultural ambivalence and normative pressures at cross-purposes as the product of the 'clash of cultures' and more generally as an impact of an alien body, a foreign influence. Lack of coherence and co-ordination, the spontaneity of change, the scattering of innovations – all these combine into the culture's way of life, and ambivalence cannot but be continually turned out in large quantities as the by-product, perhaps even – unknowingly – the *main* product of culture's own activity. Fertility, vibrancy, exuberance, the very life of culture depends on that production. What is more, it is thanks to this existential mode, to this perpetual 'malfunctioning' (as the orthodox anthropologist would say), that culture supports the cause of human freedom, instead of servicing, as it was supposed to do, social orders self-reproducing with the help of the constraints put upon that freedom and exterminating human inherent variety and spontaneity of self-creation.

As before in the case of morality, so in the case of culture we need to conclude that if its usual meaning of indetermination and uncertainty is to be retained, 'crisis' cannot be used as the opposite of 'normality'. Similar conclusions may be drawn from a closer analysis of other brands of 'crises'. These conclusions open up a theoretical task that in crucial respects is the very opposite of the tasks the social theory struggled traditionally to fulfil. To put it in a nutshell, the task is no longer to explain the crisis away, digging up from their shelter the peculiar factors responsible for producing extraordinary states in otherwise regular and normatively regulated systems. On the contrary, the task is to build a theory of human-being-in-the-world which would not cast incoherence and non-functionality as undecidably extra-ordinary events, which would incorporate in its description of human existence those phenomena that are inexplicable in utilitarian terms – and therefore would have no need of a special 'theory of crisis'.

alone dispute it, contest it or actively seek it. The other is that the
state is encouraged thereby to assume that once freedom is not
interfered with, the contents of the common good have been
exhausted and the state owes its subjects nothing – nor does it
bear respsonsibility for the damage done to all its subjects by the
selfish, short-sighted or inept way in which freedoms are exercised
by some among them. Civil society, in other words, has its
splendours and its less prepossessing proclivities. These two are
much more difficult to separate than state and society proved to
be. The political indifference and apathy of the citizens and the
state retreating on its obligation to promote the common good
are civil society's unpleasant, yet legitimate children.

This is not idle talk about what might happen, if . . . The two
unwelcome tendencies show themselves all over the place, vividly
enough to arouse the concern of political philosophers, but, more
importantly still, to undermine the trust invested in the state and
to cause widespread anxiety about the deepening fissures in the
texture of society.

Seven French intellectuals, Régis Debray, Max Gallo and Mona
Ozouf among them, have noted recently (see their joint statement
under the poignant title 'Républicains, refusons la nation à deux
étages!', published in *Le Monde* of 20 October 1998) some
dangerous signs of a progressive deformation of the 'really existing' liberal democracy, stemming from growing insecurity experienced by a large and increasing part of its citizens.

> If the Republic, which once entered a compact with its popular
> classes founded on peace and security, shows itself unable to
> guarantee them, and worse still, gives the impression that all care
> for some publicly installed order is in its nature reactionary – then
> the temptation is great to turn to self-defence.

Once the state recognizes the priority and superiority of the
laws of the market over the laws of the *polis*, the citizen is
transmuted into the consumer, and a consumer 'demands more
and more protection while accepting less and less the need to
participate' in the running of the state. The overall result is the
present 'fluid conditions of generalized anomie and rejection of
the rules' in all their versions. Between the ideal of liberal democracy and its really existing version the distance is growing, rather

than diminishing. We have a long way to go before we may hope to reach a society in which 'the individuals recognize their autonomy together with the bonds of solidarity which unite them'. As things stand at the moment, with the state refusing its responsibility for the security of all and every one, 'The laws of the strong triumph at the expense of the weak'; the really existing version of liberal democracy seems to gestate a 'society of two gears, a two-tier nation'.

There are signs that we are currently in the throes of what can best be called the second – this time a secular – reformation.

The second reformation and the emergence of modular man

The first, religious, reformation broke and took apart one iron cage to allow the congregation of believers to put together self-made cages of their own choice. Having privatized the business of spiritual salvation, it made each individual into a priest while loosening the grip in which the institutionalized priesthood kept them all. Salvation was the first public good to be privatized in modern times, while repentance and redemption were the first ritualized, synchronized and co-ordinated activities to be deregulated. After those first acts of privatization and deregulation it was up to the individual faithful to follow the road to salvation.

The current, secular reformation dismantles what the first reformation shunned or failed to take apart: the iron cage as such, of any shape or colour – the supra-individual patterns and sanctions of individual choices; or, in other words, the controlling vision of the preferred, let alone one and only, 'road to salvation', whatever the form the eternal dream of redemption may take in the times of a life focused on itself, rather than on its impact on eternity. The lodestar of the first reformation was the individual freedom to enter and traverse the road leading to eternal bliss through his or her own life-work; the catchword of the second reformation is 'human rights', that is the right of every individual to use her or his freedom of choice to decide what the bliss she or he wants ought to be like and to select or design her or his own track which may (or may not, as it happens) lead to it. The second reformation is about to finish the job which the first reformation started but stopped short of fulfilling, and by so doing to make salient the hidden potential of its predecessor. That hidden potential is the emergence and prevalence of what Ernest Gellner called 'the modular man'.

To describe that new type of human being Gellner picked his metaphor from the furniture industry: the difference between the old and the new types of human beings, he says, is like the difference between a complete, one-piece wardrobe, and a modular one. The old-style wardrobes and other pieces of furniture used to be given final shape from the start, made once for all, precluding all further change in size, shape or style. They could be exquisitely or sloppily designed, well made or botched, but whatever the case, the design was there to stay. If the user's needs grew beyond the aesthetic or utilitarian qualities of past purchases, there was but one choice: to replace the wardrobe with another – bigger, or better suited to the changing taste. Not so modular furniture: one can obtain it in bits and pieces, to which one may add further bits later. One can also go on endlessly rearranging the parts to compose ever different wholes to keep up with the changing circumstances and fancy. Except for the size of the room, there is no limit to such adding and rearranging. But that means that the process of adding and rearranging is never really finished; there is no point at which one could say with certainty that the piece of modular furniture has reached its final state.

Much the same could be said of the 'modular man', the most remarkable product of modern society. Just as modular furniture has no single predesigned 'proper' shape, but an infinitely expandable set of possible shapes, the modular man has no preordained profile and assignation. He is not Robert Musil's *Mann ohne Eigenschaften*; he is rather a being with *too many* features and aspects, so that most of them can only be held for a time, ready to be put in or taken away as needs arise. The modular man is a creature with *mobile, disposable and exchangeable qualities*; he is someone reminiscent of the 'protean man', that celebrated ideal of renaissance philosophers. To put it in a nutshell: the modular man is, first and foremost, *a man without essence*. Unlike modular furniture, the modular man is, however, doing the assembling and disassembling job himself. He is a modular man, but also *a self-modelling man*. If a modular wardrobe is made to be a set of *possibilities* to choose from, the modular man lives as a set of *tasks* to be performed.

This circumstance, as Gellner points out, has tremendous importance for the nature of liberal-democratic, or civil society.

> Modular man is capable of combining into effective associations and institutions, *without* these being total, many-stranded, under-written by ritual and made stable through being linked to a whole inside set of relationships, all of these being tied in with each other and so immobilized. He can combine into specific-purpose, *ad-hoc*, limited association, without binding himself by some blood ritual. He can leave an association when he comes to disagree with its policy, without being open to an accusation of high treason . . .
>
> The associations of modular man can be effective without being rigid.[2]

And so the bonds with which modular men (and women) tie themselves to other modular men (and women) are *not rigid*, and they are *ad hoc*. This has remarkable effects: it makes possible a society which is simultaneously 'well integrated' – and sewn together many times over in all sorts of directions – and yet not forced into a stiff shape, monotony and homogeneity by either a coercive tyranny, ubiquitous tribal surveillance or the dead hand of the self-reproducing ritual. Parallel to the advent of modular men and women is the emergence of what Manuel Castells calls the 'network society', better called, in my view, a 'multi-network' society; a kind of society which is neither *segmental*, like its remote pre-modern ancestors, nor *class-divided*, like its immediate modern predecessor, and which, unlike them, is able to live with its own underdetermination, ambivalence and contradictions – absorb them, recycle and even recast into resources for action.

The emergence of modular men and women puts paid to the centuries of the rulers' temptation and the philosophers' urge to impose a fixed set of commandments and norms as the only way to keep the 'natural man' out of mischief and thus the only way of holding society together. Modular men and women can do quite well without such a fixed code of rules – and yet steer clear of the Hobbesian nightmare of a life which is bound to be nasty, brutish and short. With men and women become modular, the tyranny of coercive powers and the dumb pressure of ritual are redundant. Besides, were it ever tried, tyranny would find no 'total individuals' in which a 'total power' could be anchored. In the multi-network society of modular men and women the business of integration and control has been deregulated and privatized.

But, as it happens, you win some, you lose some . . . The non-rigid and *ad hoc* bonds characteristic of multi-network societies and their modular members, have also their less prepossessing aspects. Such bonds are imbued with uncertainty and risk. Life supported by such bonds alone is conducted most of the time, perhaps all of the time, on crossroads. Whatever track is chosen, there are risks involved – of the road ending in a quagmire or leading towards places less attractive than other sites to which some other overlooked or abandoned roads might have led. Whatever the case, one cannot help suspecting that no final and unambiguous judgement on the advantages or handicaps of the track chosen and followed will ever be obtained, and so the pain of hesitation and the suspicion of making or having made a wrong move will precede and follow every step, now and in the future. One is also inclined to guess that judgements, when they come, will be many and different, perhaps even contradictory. Being left to one's own choices is liberating and gratifying. It is at the same time stressful and, more often than not, painful. To quote Gellner once more, the price of 'modularization' is 'a kind of fragmentation which leaves each activity unsustained by the others, cold and calculated by its own clearly formulated end, rather than part of a warm, integrated, "total" culture. Such "alienation" and "disenchantment" is a price which some consider too high.'[3]

Instead of 'alienation' we should better speak these days of 'unsettlement' or 'unhomeliness'. Indeed, 'alienation' presupposed a total world and a total person which could be estranged from each other, but neither does the multi-networked society offer much chance to be experienced as a totality nor do its modularized members have many occasions to develop the self-consciousness of total persons. For the 'modularized' residents of the 'multi-network' society, 'belonging' becomes a major problem; it is their daily concern in spite of (or rather because of) seldom finding a satisfactory solution, and hardly ever finding a solution which could be reasonably expected to be durable, let alone lasting forever. As Niklas Luhmann famously put it, we are all, everywhere and always, 'partly displaced'. To none of the groups which we enter do we belong 'fully': there are parts of our modular persons which 'stick out' and cannot be absorbed nor accommodated by any single group, but which connect and interact with other modules. Each act of self-ascription is therefore subject to contradictory, centripetal and centrifugal, pressures.

All forms of togetherness are in effect vulnerable and fragile, while the modules remain poorly integrated. In no group do we feel 'fully at home'; in whatever group we happen to be at a time, being there feels more like an overnight stay in a hotel or a night-out in a restaurant than sitting at the dining table in the family home. Even this allegory, however, worrying as it is, does not really convey explicitly what is implicitly missing, because the only family homes known to many a postmodern man or woman are also increasingly hotel-like: places of temporary sojourn no one expects to last forever.

The condition of 'modularity' is therefore one of *Unsicherheit* – the triple bane of uncertainty, insecurity and lack of safety. The impression of *Unsicherheit* tends to be projected, with good reason, upon the outside world with its many criss-crossing and uncoordinated networks, its poorly signed roads and floating signposts. But it is the modularity itself – the absence of bolts, clamps and rivets fastening the modules into a permanent shape – which is a constant source of tension. The tensions tend to coalesce into a longing for great simplification, for a straight-forward, unambiguous, one-to-one link between wishes and opportunities, actions and their consequences – for the *Eindeutig-keit* of the world and the self and the perfect union of the two. That longing is encapsulated in the idea of 'belonging'; an idea, to be sure, which itself resists being anchored, an idea bound to remain diffuse and unspecified, since there is little in daily life to accommodate it securely or at least to display its tangible model.

Tribe, nation and republic

The fullest embodiment of the idea of belonging is the tribe – the form of togetherness which dominated the greater part of human history. Indeed, belonging in the tribe is total and all-embracing;

it makes all alternatives to itself invisible and therefore non-existent, rather than merely denigrating them and fighting them back. The tribal mode of belonging provides what can be only called the *compleat mappa mundi* – the totality of knowledge about the world and one's place within it. One is born a member of the tribe and one dies in the same capacity, putting on in the meantime and taking off again a series of strictly defined and non-negotiable identities in a strictly defined and non-negotiable succession. Nothing is required of the tribesman but to conform to that succession and to perform according to the prescription attached to each successive identity. What it involves can be learned matter-of-factly just by looking around at other tribesmen and requires no special schooling. Things in life may turn out good or bad, but hardly ever are they ambiguous and cause confusion, for the simple reason that the *Lebenswelt* does not include the possibility of life outside the tribe, and so it is free of existential choices. Indeed, *il n'y a pas hors de tribu.*

Modernity augurs the end of totalities as complete as the tribes, and also, therefore, of the kind of *Lebenswelt* as coherent as that of the tribesman. Modern social totalities lack the tribe's cohesion for the reason of being a combination of two, and so endemically incomplete, totalities – 'republic' and 'nation'. Each has the appetite to ingest or subordinate the other, but the other is of use to the first only as long as it retains its own distinctiveness. The appetite therefore as a rule stops short of fulfilment. In the rare cases when the complete merger of the two had been attempted, as in Communist Russia and Nazi Germany, the product proved to be still-born or self-destructive. The two best-known monster hybrids were, by historical standards, short-lived, and in all probability non-viable and death-bound from birth. The Fascist and Communist experiments apart, modern societies tend to be products of uneasy coexistence of two distinct formations guided by separate sets of principles. Most of the time there is a compromise between the two, but the cohabitation is interlaced with overt or subterranean conflict; the possibility of clash cannot be put to rest for good nor excised from the complex structure called modern society. Time and again after a long period of peaceful coexistence it once more flares into the open for one reason or another; it does so, for instance, today in Europe, where the eminently expandable republics rush into the European Union while the eminently unstretchable nations stay behind and lean over backwards to hold the escaping republics back.

There is, in short, a *Haßliebe* relation between republic and nation. They need each other, but they find it hard to cohabit in peace and infuriatingly difficult to negotiate and reconcile their differences. They attract each other and repel at the same time, with the results similar to that obtained in Miller and Dollard's famous experiment with rats: behaving incoherently whenever torn between the two opposite pulls of 'adience' and 'abience' – attraction and repulsion.

Apart from operating on the same ground and aspiring to be the principal adhesive which binds and holds together the same population, republic and nation differ from each other in virtually every other respect. Each one, being doomed to the company of the other, must also deploy other means than those used matter-of-factly by the tribe living as it was in a luxury not available to either of them – the luxury of being alone in the field.

Being the sole life-setting with solitary death as its only alternative, the tribe could do without ideology, indoctrination and propaganda – something the nation cannot live without. If tribes needed no 'tribalism', the nation needs 'nationalism', that curious, not to say incongruous, creed which simultaneously proclaims that essence precedes existence and that existence precedes essence; that is, that nationhood is and is not a matter of choice at the same time. The nation of nationalism has been given before its members may come to any deciding, but it is also a value its members are to cherish, cultivate, enhance and adorn through their daily choices. The tribe was a reality, not a value; if the nation of the nationalist creed wants to be a reality, it must become a value.

Membership of the nation calls for daily effort. As Ernest Renan put it once, the nation is a daily plebiscite – the totality which has to be daily renewed by the vote of allegiance. The sweetness of belonging which the nation holds out does not come free; it has to be earned. The belonging on offer is sweet because, in the case of the nation, is stands a chance of being secure; but this security is a matter of accomplishment, not a foregone conclusion. It requires holding the ranks, and it takes concerted action.

If this demand alone was at stake, there would be nothing to set the nation apart from the multitude of other associations or voluntary unions and it would be unclear why the loyalty to nation should be given precedence over all other loyalties; nor why it ought to be followed, unlike other commitments, in a 'no-questions-asked', 'my country – right or wrong' fashion. To claim, unlike other associations, the sole or supreme loyalty superseding all other commitments, the nation must explicitly postulate to be what the tribe used to be without telling this in so many words, perhaps even without knowing: the matter of blood and soil, but more crucially (we live in times conscious of their contingency, after all) the matter of shared history.

That all historical narrative is selective is by now a banal statement. What is, however, less immediately understood and often deliberately beclouded or ferociously denied is that it is the narrative itself that 'makes' history. As Hannah Arendt and Paul Ricoeur pointed out in their own separate and different ways,[4] it is historical narrative which cuts 'events' out of the flow of life and then reforges disorderly, truly 'noumenal' and contingent events into a meaningful series, ready to be interpretatively absorbed and memorized. Arendt compared the work of the historian, who transforms the raw material 'of sheer happenings' into a story capable of being told, grasped and contained, to the work of the poet who transfigures 'grief into lamentation' and 'lamentation into praise'. Nationalism is such an operation of selection and transfiguration performed collectively on the past. Ernest Renan's another famous phrase is his depiction of the nation as an agreement to remember certain things from the past and to forget some others. (I would sharpen the point a bit: nationalism prescribes that all the things not agreed to be remembered should be forgotten.)

The republican idea seldom stoops to quarrel with its nationalist associate/adversary about which things are to be retained in memory and which are to be cast into the dustbin of oblivion. It does more than to question the selection: it denies the virtue, the authority and the need of historical remembrance, just as it devalues the past itself. The republican idea in its pure form (which found its arguably most vivid expression in the headiest days of the French Revolution) is precisely about the *dethronement of past history* (remember Marx, the French Revolution's spiritual heir, dismissing all the past as just 'prehistory' and announcing that history was yet to begin) and about the 'new beginning'. In her lecture[5] delivered on the occasion of accepting the Marc Bloch Prize, Mona Ozouf pointed out that at least at the time of the Revolution republicans thought themselves to be capable of deliberate reconstruction of the totality of social and political order – and believed that nothing that belonged to the past may possibly be of service to that reconstruction. 'History supplies neither precedent nor support, while duration has nothing to say about value.'

Nationalism proclaimed the nation itself, the living legacy of long and tortuous history, to be *a good in its own right* – and not just one good among many others, but the *supreme* good, one that dwarfs and subordinates all other goods. Revolutionary republicans, on the other hand, postulated the republic as *the factory of common good* – and as the *sole* factory capable of producing it. The good society of the republicans was all in the future, not yet attained, and not likely to arrive other than through the work of the republic. This said, however, the idea of the republic entangled itself from the start in a deep contradiction which was to haunt it throughout most of modern history.

The idea of the 'new beginning' (in fact, not a single beginning, but an unending series of new beginnings) and the stout refusal to be bound by the legacy of history just in the recognition of its longevity – left the human capacity to criticize, to reason and to judge as the sole resource available to the republic in its production of the common good. It made the triad of freedoms – of speech, expression and association – into the *conditio sine qua non* of republican life. On the other hand, though, the introduction of the common good was put on the top of the list of republican values; universal happiness was proclaimed to be the supreme purpose of the republic. People were to be free to pursue happiness and to negotiate the ways of making that happiness universal; but at some point the cause of universal happiness and the cause of individual liberties were bound to clash, and one or the other forced to let go. Questions of the type 'Which is better – to let people read bad books or to keep them illiterate?' were bound to arise, to which there was no foolproof answer. The life of the republic was to be an uneasy balance between two sets of principles expected to co-operate but all too prone to struggle, and was destined to navigate for ever between two equally preposterous or downright disastrous extremes.

The conflict inside the pattern of the republic is always there, and the danger of striking a wrong kind of compromise or of venturing too far in making room for one principle and unduly constraining the other is always lurking in the wings. And yet the two principles are like two legs – the republic would not walk straight without either. Only together do they make the republic what it is – an institution which casts the liberty of its citizens not just as negative freedom from constraints but as an *enabling power*, as freedom to participate; an institution which tries, always inconclusively yet with undiminishing zeal and vigour, to strike a balance between *the individual's liberty from interference* and *the citizen's right to interfere*. That right of the citizens to interfere, to participate in the making of laws that outline the order binding them all, is the republican answer to the nation's blood, soil and historical legacy – the specifically republican mortar which cements individuals into a community, the *republican* community. Cornelius Castoriadis baptizes this type of community the 'autonomous society', and defines it in the following way:

> What will be the collective identity, the 'we' of an autonomous society? We are the ones who make our own laws, we are an autonomous collectivity made up of autonomous individuals. And we are able to look at ourselves, recognize ourselves, and call ourselves back into question in and through our works.[6]

Liberal democracy and the republic

In itself and by itself, the pursuit of the common good gives no guarantee that the citizens (or rather, in this case, the would-be citizens) will indeed be able to engage in that 'looking at themselves' and 'calling themselves into question', casting a critical eye over and passing judgements on the laws that govern them all. But without such a pursuit the call to the would-be citizens to do just that would sound all but empty. This is where republicanism and liberalism part ways; while liberalism is inclined to alight from the republican train at the station named *laissez faire* – 'Let us be and let others be' – the train of the republic runs further, towards reforging the freedom of the individuals into a self-monitoring community and so deploying individual liberty in the communal search of the common good. Having refused to travel that next stretch of the road, liberalism is left with an aggregate of free yet lonely individuals, free to act yet having no say in the setting in which they act, no inkling of the purpose to which their freedom to act may be put, and above all no interest in seeing to it that others are also free to act and in talking to them about the uses of everybody's freedom. In such an aggregate of lonely, all-free yet all-impotent and all-indifferent individuals, contradictions immediately crop up between freedom and equality, between individual and society, between private and public welfare – the kind of contradictions which liberalism is notoriously unable to handle, but also the kind of contradiction which only liberalism itself, as long as it remains reluctant to endorse the republican principle, brings into being.

This is why, as Castoriadis observes, 'the nation emerges like a rabbit out of the hat' of 'contemporary theories and "political philosophies"' – in as far, I would add, as most of these theories and philosophies remain enchanted by the kind of liberalism which is prepared to close its eyes to the atomizing consequences of personal liberty not complemented by the citizens' dedication to the pursuit of the common good and their ability to act as that dedication prompts them. The nationalism which liberal practice, albeit unintentionally, ignites and incites, emerges as a promise to remedy liberalism's own failings. In order to keep nationalism at bay, liberal society would have had to accommodate the principle of ethics and justice as a common good rather than a private affair; in other words, it would have had to lift itself to the level of the republic.

By itself, liberalism does not therefore solve the conflict between the nation and the republic, let alone decide the litigation in favour of the republic. There is in liberal democracy a place for both; one can go as far as defining the liberal-democratic setting as the area where nationalism and the republican idea are in constant competition. They meet head to head, offering radically different solutions to essentially the same problem of reconciling individual freedom and communal security, a problem endemic to modern society.

As mentioned before, the solution offered by nationalism to this problem is 'My country, right or wrong.' The solution offered by the republican idea, if expressed with similar epigrammatic brevity, would be something like 'This being my country, I must make sure that it is keen to be right and eager to eschew the wrong', or – even more demanding – 'It is my country in as far as it is right – but not if it refuses to repair the wrong it has done.'

Nationalism requires signing a blank cheque and striking off past deeds from the crime register. The main virtue it expects its followers, the patriots, to display, is loyalty; while the feature declared to be the main vice – indeed, the mortal sin deserving the most severe of punishments – is the wide range of disloyal or not sufficiently loyal conduct, stretching from open dissent to mere tepidity. One activity the members of the nation are not expected to indulge in under any circumstances is an inquiry into the *ratio* of what they are expected to be loyal to and the moral status of the demand that values and norms should be obeyed with no questions asked about their virtue. To paraphrase Hegel's famous adage, we may say that nationalism defines freedom as 'knowing one's duty'.

The republican idea, on the contrary, puts critical inquiry in the heart of community membership; citizens belong to the republic through the active concern with the values promoted or neglected by their polity. The declaration of citizen's allegiance could be expressed in the following words of Castoriadis: 'I have a positive (and even egoistical) interest to live in a society that is closer to that of the *Symposium* than to that of *The Godfather* or of *Dallas*.'[7]

If assignment to nationhood is unconditional and making it conditional is an act of treason, the republic is judged and evaluated by the degree of freedom it offers and secures for its citizens in setting the conditions of membership. Renan's 'daily plebiscite' may or may not grasp the reality of the nation, and more than once was it criticized as such by nationalist preachers; but the 'daily plebiscite' most certainly reflects both the reality of the republic and the substance of the republican idea.

A parting of the ways

Throughout the history of the modern state, the 'catchment area' of nation and republic tended to overlap. This circumstance was a constant source of potential conflict, but also offered a chance of mutual correction, of each partner/competitor protecting the other from the dire consequences of going to the extreme, and assuaging or balancing off the adverse effects each partner on its own might have on the plight of the individuals. The republic offers an avenue of escape *into freedom* when the loving yet insidious and domineering embrace of the nation becomes too tight for comfort. The nation offers escape *from freedom*: the warmth of belonging and the cosiness of the 'no-need-to-choose' situation when public space feels too cold and impersonal for self-assurance, and the responsibilities that republican life demands seem too onerous to carry.

It is all changing now, though. The republic is, so to speak, 'emigrating' from the nation-state which for a few recent centuries it shared with the nation. Not that contemporary states tend to become less democratic, and hence less in line with the essentials of the republican model; but democracy as practised within the state, however faithfully observing its procedure, is becoming increasingly toothless and impotent to guard or adjust the conditions vital for the life of the citizens. Having lost much of their past sovereignty and no longer able to balance the books on their own or to lend authority to the type of social order of their choice, contemporary states fail to meet the other necessary condition of a viable republic: the ability of the citizens to negotiate and jointly decide 'the public good', and so to shape a society which they would be prepared to call their own and to which they would gladly give their oath of unswerving allegiance.

It is because the republic in the nation-state is fast losing most of its welfare-defining and welfare-promoting potency, that the territory of the nation-state is turning increasingly into the private estate of the nation. The republic has little power left to ensure the long-term security of the nation and so to cure or mitigate its 'besieged fortress' complex and to defuse or reduce its pugnacity and intolerance. The nation no longer seems to be securely settled, its future no longer seems assured and in safe keeping – and so the failure of the republic ushers in the times of born-again, vigorous, rampant and unbridled nationalism.

The most decisive parameters of the human condition are now shaped in the areas the institutions of the nation-state cannot reach. The powers which preside over preservation and change of those conditions are increasingly globalized, while the instruments of the citizen's control and influence, however potent they might be, remain locally confined.

Globalization of capital, finances and information means first and foremost their exemption from local, and above all nation-state, control and administration. In the space in which they operate there are no institutions reminiscent of the vehicles which the republican state has developed for citizen participation and effective political action. And where there are no republican institutions, there is no 'citizenship' either. The concept of 'global powers' captures the emerging, but already tough, resilient and apparently indomitable reality, while the concept of 'global citizenship' thus far stays empty, representing a postulate at best, but in most contexts not much more than wishful thinking. Being buffeted by the powerful tides, drawn by stormy winds blowing from distant places and arriving without warning, is a condition exactly opposite to that of citizenship. The sudden upheavals and downfalls in collective fortunes today acquire an eerie likeness to natural catastrophes, though even this comparison looks increasingly like an understatement: as it happens, we have these days better means to anticipate the imminent earthquake or approaching hurricane than to predict the next stock-exchange crash or collapse and the evaporation of apparently secure places of mass employment.

In a recent essay[8] Jacques Attali explained the phenomenal popularity of the film *Titanic* by the remarkable resonance the viewers felt to exist between that parabolic case of human conceit floundering upon the iceberg which, due to the captain's arrogance and his staff's docility, was not (nor could be) taken seriously enough and spotted in time – and their own present-day plight.

> *Titanic* is us, our triumphalist, self-congratulating, blind, hypocritical society, merciless towards its poor – a society in which everything is predicted except the means of predicting . . . [W]e all guess

that there is an iceberg waiting for us, hidden somewhere in the misty future, which we will hit and then go down to the sounds of music.

There are, Attali suggests, not one but several icebergs ahead, each one rougher and more treacherous than the last. There is the financial iceberg of unbridled currency speculation, profits shooting sky-high and shamelessly overvalued stocks. There is the nuclear iceberg, with about thirty countries, each of them embroiled in its own network of contentions and animosities, expected to be capable of launching a nuclear attack twenty years from now. There is the ecological iceberg, with the volume of carbon dioxide in the atmosphere and the global temperatures unstoppably rising and the dozens of atomic installations which – as all the experts agree – must sooner or later explode, causing a catastrophe of global proportions. Last but not least, there is the social iceberg, with three billions of men and women expected to be made redundant – devoid of economic function – during the life-span of the present generation. The difference between each one of these icebergs and the iceberg which sank the *Titanic*, Attali bitterly comments, is that when its turn to hit the ship comes, there will be no one left to make the film of the event or to write epic or lyrical verses about the mayhem that ensued.

All these icebergs (and perhaps certain others which thus far we cannot even name) float outside the territorial waters of any electoral constituency of any of the 'world's greats'; no wonder, therefore, that people operating political controls are placid or lukewarm about the magnitude of danger. But there is a still more potent reason for doing nothing than equanimity arising from lack of interest: 'The politicians are no more in command of the ship launched to sail at full speed.' Even if they wished, there would be little for them to do.

The political economy of uncertainty

But do they wish to act? And with the republic's weapons broken, confiscated by global powers or decommissioned by the state surrendering to global pressures, where are the forces able to force them into action?

In democracies there is no coercive power determined to keep dissent at bay. In the present-day liberal-democratic state there are no concentration camps nor censorship offices, while prisons, swelling as they are, have no cells reserved for political opponents or heretics. Freedom of thought, expression and association has reached unheard-of proportions and comes closer than ever before to being truly unbound. The paradox, though, is that this unprecedented liberty comes at a time when there is little use to which it can be put, and little chance of reforging freedom from constraint into liberty to act.

Pierre Bourdieu has reminded us recently of the old and universally binding rule: '[T]he capacity for future projections is the condition of all behaviour considered to be rational ... [T]o conceive of a revolutionary project, that is to have a well thought-out intention to transform the present in reference to a projected future, a modicum of hold on the present is needed.'[9]

The snag is, though, that the 'hold on the present' is one feature conspicuously missing from the condition of contemporary men and women. None of the most important levers and safeguards of their current situation comes under their jurisdiction, let alone control, practised singly or severally. Some levers have been already hit by the mysterious forces variously dubbed 'recession', 'rationalization', 'fall in market demand' or 'downsizing'. But the blows reverberate far beyond their direct targets, and it is not just those who have overnight been demoted, degraded, deprived of their dignity or/and their livelihood who have been hit. Every blow carries a message for all those who have been (for a time) spared, and prompts them to assess their own future by the severity of the likely sentence, not by the (unknown) length of its temporary suspension. The message is simple: everyone is *potentially* redundant or replaceable, and so everyone is vulnerable and any social position, however elevated and powerful it may seem now, is in the longer run precarious; even the privileges are fragile and under threat.

Blows may be targeted, but the devastation they cause is not. The fear they generate is diffused and ambient. As Bourdieu puts it, that fear 'haunts consciousness and the subconscious'. To climb the heights one must have one's feet firmly on the ground. But it is the ground itself which feels ever more shaky, unstable, infirm, undependable – no solid rock underneath on which one can rest the feet to jump. The trust, that indispensable condition of all rational planning and confident action, is floating, vainly seeking ground firm enough to use it as a catapult. The state of precariousness, Bourdieu observes, 'renders all the future uncertain, and so forbids all rational anticipation – and in particular disallows that minimum of hope in the future which one needs to rebel, and especially to rebel collectively, against even the least tolerable present.'

It is common nowadays to deplore the growing nihilism and cynicism of contemporary men and women, the short-sightedness or absence of their life-projects, the mundaneness and selfishness of their desires, their inclination to slice life into episodes, each to be squeezed to the last drop with no concern for the consequences. All these charges have ample evidence to support them. What most moral preachers fulminating against moral decadence fail to mention, though, is that the reprehensible tendency they condemn draws its strength from the fact of being a rational response to the world in which one is compelled to treat the future as a threat, rather than as shelter or promised land. What most critics fail to discuss as well is that this world, like any other human world, has been human-made, and that far from being a product of inscrutable and invincible laws of Nature or sinful yet irredeemable human nature, it is, to no small extent, a product of what can only be called *the political economy of uncertainty*.

The political economy of uncertainty is the set of 'rules to end all rules' imposed by extraterritorial financial, capital and trade powers upon local political authorities. Its principles have found full expression in the ill-famed Multilateral Agreement on Investment – in the constraints it imposed on governments' freedom to constrain capital's freedom of movement, as well as in the clandestine way in which it was negotiated and the secrecy in which it was kept by common consent of political and economic powers – until discovered and brought into light by a group of investigative journalists.[10] The principles are simple, since they are mostly negative; they are not meant to establish a new order, only to take apart the extant ones; and to prevent state governments of the day from replacing the dismantled regulations with new ones. The political economy of uncertainty boils down essentially to the prohibition of politically established and guaranteed rules and regulations, and the disarming of the defensive institutions and associations which stood in the way of the capital and finances becoming truly *sans frontières*. The overall outcome of both measures is the state of permanent and ubiquitous uncertainty, which is to replace the rule of coercive law and legitimating formulae as the ground for obedience (or, rather, warranty for the lack of resistance) to the new, this time supra-state and global, powers.

The political economy of uncertainty is good for business. It makes bulky, unwieldy and costly instruments of discipline redundant, replacing them not so much with the self-control of the trained, drilled and disciplined objects, as with the inability of privatized and endemically insecure individuals to act in a concerted way; an inability made all the more profound by their disbelief that any such action may be effective and that private grievances may be recast into collective issues, let alone into the shared projects of an alternative order of things.

The political economy of uncertainty puts paid to the cumbersome and capital-intensive discipline drill, and particularly its coercive arm and the agencies of indoctrination. As far as eliciting passive submission to the rules of the game or to a game without rules is concerned, endemic uncertainty from the bottom to the top of the social ladder is a neat and cheap, yet highly efficient substitute for normative regulation, censorship and surveillance. Apart from the excluded and redundant margins who are much too certain of their exclusion and redundancy to be receptive to the policies of uncertainty, panopticons in either the old and heavy, or the updated, high-tech and lightweight versions, are not needed. Freedom alone, in its market rendition, can be relied upon completely to elicit all human conduct needed to keep the global economy going.

On the road to the uncontested rule of the political economy of uncertainty, republican institutions go by the board as its first victims. Indeed, everything which the idea of the republic stood for jars stridently with the aims or effects of the policies of uncertainty. When trying to explain what it took to be a republican, as he was, the great French historian Marc Bloch settled for the conviction that the form of power should (and could!) be the matter of mature deliberation of the citizens; that it cannot and shall not be imposed upon individuals without their having a say in its choice. Bloch, writing in times of high modernity and sensitive to the wounds which the modern weapons of imposition used to inflict, named the insidious communal drill penetrating the most intimate disposition of human subjects, and the equally modern inclination to charge the examination of merits and vices of the group one belongs to as sacrilegious, as the main threats to republican faith and practice.[11] Were Bloch to compose his plaidoyer for the republic half a century later, he would probably focus on other enemies: the first and foremost among them being the ambient fear emanating from existential uncertainty and condensing into fear of action – and then the new political opacity and impenetrability of the world, the mystery clouding the places where the blows originate and sedimented as disbelief in resistance to fate and mistrust of any suggestion of an alternative way of life.

The cause of equality in the uncertain world

Freed from political reins and local constraints, the fast globalizing and increasingly exterritorial economy is known to produce ever deepening wealth-and-income gaps between the better-off and the worse-off sections of the world population, and inside every single society. It is also known for laying off the ever wider chunks of the population as not just living in poverty, misery and destitution, but also permanently evicted from whatever has been socially recognized as economically rational and socially useful work, and so made economically and socially *redundant*'.[12]

According to the most recent report of the United Nations' Development project (as reported in *Le Monde*, 10 September 1998), while global consumption of goods and services was in 1997 twice as big as in 1975 and multiplied since 1950 by a factor of six – one billion people 'cannot satisfy even their elementary needs'. Among 4.5 billions of the residents of the 'developing' countries, three in every five are deprived of access to basic infrastructures: a third has no access to drinkable water, a quarter has no accommodation worthy of the name, one-fifth has no use of sanitary and medical services. One in five children spends less than five years in any form of schooling; a similar proportion is permanently undernourished. In 70–80 of the 100 or so 'developing' countries the average income per head of population is today lower than ten or even thirty years ago. 120 million people live on less than one dollar a day.

At the same time, in the USA, by far the richest country of the world and the homeland of the world's wealthiest people, 16.5 per cent of the population live in poverty; one-fifth of adult men and women can neither read nor write, while 13 per cent have a life expectancy shorter than 60 years.

On the other hand, the three richest men on the globe have private assets bigger than the combined national product of the forty-eight poorest countries; the fortune of the fifteen richest persons exceeds the total product of the whole of sub-Saharan Africa. According to the report, less than 4 per cent of the personal wealth of the 225 richest people would suffice to offer all the poor of the world access to elementary medical and educational amenities as well as adequate nutrition.

The effects of this undoubtedly most worrying of contemporary tendencies have been and are widely studied and discussed, though for reasons which ought by now to be well understood, little except a few *ad hoc*, fragmentary and irresolute measures have been undertaken to roll back the effects, let alone to arrest the tendency. The ongoing story of concern and inaction has been told and retold many times over, with no visible benefit thus far. It is not my intention to repeat the story once more, but to question the cognitive frame and the value-set in which it is as a rule contained; a frame and a set which bar the full comprehension of the gravity of the situation and so also the search for its feasible alternatives.

The cognitive frame in which the discussion of growing poverty is commonly placed is purely economic (in the dominant sense of 'economy' as primarily the aggregate of money-mediated transactions) – that of the distribution of wealth and income and the access to paid employment. The value-set which informs the choice of relevant data and their interpretation is most often that of pity, compassion and solicitude for the lot of the poor. Occasionally, concern with the safety of the social order is also expressed, though – rightly – seldom in full voice, since few sober minds would sense in the plight of the contemporary poor and destitute a tangible threat of rebellion. Neither the cognitive frame nor the value-set is wrong in itself. More precisely, they are not wrong in what they imply, but in what they gloss over in silence and leave out of sight.

One fact they suppress is the role played by the new poor in the reproduction and reinforcement of the kind of global order which is the cause of their destitution and of the ambient fear making the lives of all the rest miserable; another is the extent to which that global order depends on that destitution and that ambient fear for its own self-perpetuation. Karl Marx said once, in the times of up-and-coming, savage and yet-untamed capitalism, still too illiterate to decipher the writing on the wall – that the workers cannot liberate themselves without liberating the rest of society. It could be said now, in the times of capitalism triumphant and no longer heeding the writing on any wall (nor the walls themselves, for that matter), that the rest of human society cannot be liberated from its ambient fear[13] and impotence unless its poorest part is liberated from its penury. Lifting the poor from their poverty is not just a matter of charity, conscience and ethical duty, but an indispensable (though only preliminary) condition of rebuilding a republic of free citizens out of the wasteland of the global market.

To put it in a nutshell: the presence of the large army of the poor and the widely publicized egregiousness of their condition is a countervailing factor of great importance to the extant order. Its importance lies in off-setting the otherwise repellent and revolting effects of life lived in the shadow of perpetual uncertainty. The more destitute and dehumanized the poor of the world and the poor in the next street are shown and seen to be, the better they play their role in a drama which they did not script or audition for.

Once upon a time people were induced to endure meekly their lot, however harsh it might be, by being shown vividly painted pictures of hell ready to ingest everyone guilty of rebellion. Like all things other-wordly and eternal, the nether-world meant to achieve a similar effect has been now brought to earth, placed firmly within the confines of earthly life and presented in a form ready for instant consumption. The poor are the Other of the frightened consumers – the Other who, for once, is fully and truly their hell. In one vital respect the poor are what the non-poor rest would dearly like to be (though they would not dare to try) – free from uncertainty. But the uncertainty they received in exchange comes in the shape of disease-, crime- and drug-infested mean streets (if they happen to live in Washington DC) or a slow death from malnutrition (if they inhabit the Sudan). The lesson one learns when hearing about the poor is that certainty is most certainly to be feared more than the detested uncertainty; and that the punishment for rebellion against the discomforts of daily uncertainty is swift and merciless.

The sight of the poor keeps the non-poor at bay. It thereby perpetuates their life of uncertainty. It prompts them to tolerate or bear resignedly the unstoppable 'flexibilization' of the world. The sight incarcerates their imagination and handcuffs their arms. They do not dare to imagine a different world; they are much to chary to try to change this one. And as long as this is the case, the chances of an autonomous, self-constituting society, of republic and citizenship, are – to say the least – slim and dim.

This is a good enough reason for the political economy of uncertainty to include, as one of its indispensable ingredients, the casting of 'the problem of the poor' as, alternatively, the issue of law-and-order or the object of humanitarian concern – but nothing else and no more than that. When the first representation is used, the popular condemnation of the poor – depraved rather than deprived – comes as close as conceivable to the burning of popular fear in effigy. When the second representation is deployed, the wrath against cruelty and callousness of the vagaries of fate can be safely channelled into innocuous carnivals of charity, and the shame of impassivity can evaporate in short-lived explosions of human solidarity.

Day by day, though, the world's poor and the country's poor do their silent work in undermining the confidence and resolution of all those still in work and on a regular income. The link between the poverty of the poor and the surrender of the non-poor has nothing irrational about it. The sight of the destitute is a timely reminder to all sober and sensible beings that even the prosperous life is insecure, and that today's success is not a guarantee against tomorrow's fall. There is a well-founded feeling that the world is increasingly overcrowded; that the sole choice open to countries' governments is, at best, one between widespread poverty with high unemployment, as in most European countries, and widespread poverty with a little less unemployment, as in the USA. Scholarly research confirms the feeling: there is less and less paid work around. This time around unemployment looks more sinister than ever before. It does not seem a product of a cyclical 'economic depression', no more than a temporary condensation of misery, to be dissipated and wiped out by the next economic boom.

As Jean-Paul Maréchal argues,[14] during the times of 'heavy industrialization' the need to construct a huge industrial infrastructure and to build bulky machinery saw to it that more jobs were regularly created than old ones were destroyed as a result of the annihilation of traditional crafts and skills; but this is evidently no more the case. Until the 1970s there was still a positive relation between growth of productivity and the size of employment; since then the relation grows more negative by the year. An important threshold seems to have been crossed in the 1970s – but on an otherwise continuous line of development running for at least a century. We learn, for instance, from comparative research conducted and collated by Olivier Marchands[15] that in France the volume of work available in 1991 was just 57 per cent of that on offer in 1891: 34.1 billion hours instead of 60 billion. During that period, the GNP multiplied by ten, hourly productivity by eighteen, while the total number of people at work increased in a hundred years from only 19 million to about 22 million. Roughly similar trends have been recorded in all countries which began industrialization in the nineteenth century. The figures speak volumes about the reasons to feel insecure even in the most stable and regular of jobs.

The shrinking volume of employment is not, though, the sole reason to feel insecure. Such jobs as still can be had are no longer fortified against the unpredictable hazards of the future; work is today, one may say, a daily rehearsal for redundancy. The 'political economy of insecurity' saw to it that the orthodox defences have been dismantled and the troops manning them disbanded. Labour has become 'flexible', which in unadorned speech means that it is now easy for the employer to fire employees at will and without compensation, and that solidary – and effective – trade union action in defence of the wrongly dismissed looks increasingly like a pipe-dream. 'Flexibility' also means the denial of security: the growing number of available jobs are part-time or fixed-term, most contracts are 'rolling' or 'renewable' with a frequency high enough to prevent the rights to relative stability from acquiring force. 'Flexibility' means too that the old life strategy of investing time and effort in specialist skills in the hope of a steady inflow of interest makes ever less sense – and so the once most common rational choice of people wishing for a life of security is no longer available.

Livelihood, that rock on which all life projects and aspirations must rest to be feasible, to make sense and to muster the energy they need to be fulfilled (or, at least, tried to be fulfilled), has become wobbly, erratic and unreliable. What the advocates of 'welfare to work' programmes leave out of account is that the function of livelihood is not just to provide day-to-day sustenance for the employees and their dependants, but – no less importantly – to offer the existential security without which neither freedom nor will of self-assertion is conceivable and which is the starting-point of all autonomy. Work in its present shape cannot offer such security even if it manages time and again to cover the costs of staying alive. The road from welfare to work leads from security to insecurity, or from lesser to greater insecurity. That road being what it is, prompting as many people as possible to take it chimes well with the principles of the political economy of insecurity.

Let me repeat: the endemic instability of the life-worlds of the overwhelming majority of contemporary men and women is the ultimate cause of the present-day crisis of the republic – and so of the fading and wilting of the 'good society' as a purpose and motive of collective action in general, and of resistance against the progressive erosion of the private/public space, the sole space where human solidarities and the recognition of common causes may sprout and come to fruition. Insecurity breeds more insecurity; insecurity self-perpetuates. It tends to twist into a Gordian knot which cannot be untied, but can only be cut.

The problem is to find a spot where the knife of political action can be applied to the greatest effect. Perhaps, as well, to find the courage and imagination equal to that of Alexander the Great . . .

The case for a basic income

It was Thomas Paine who first advanced the idea of a 'basic income' independent of the work done and sold. His idea was, typically, born well before its time; the next century was to entrench labour in its form of a commodity sold and bought. Not only was employment to become the sole legitimate entitlement to income, but work was to be identified with sellable activity, conditional on the presence of buyers eager to pay for it; market demand was to be given the sole right to distinguish 'work' from 'non-work'. Another century was needed to expose the limitation and dire insufficiency of that arrangement, and to reveal the threats to ethical standards, social solidarity and the tissue of human relations which it held in store.

Two centuries after Thomas Paine the idea of detaching essential livelihood from employment has been broached time and again all over Europe: in France by Jacques Duboin in the 1930s and later by his followers; in Belgium by the Charles-Fourier Circle in the 1980s; in recent years, by the Greens in Germany, in Holland and Spain, and in Ireland by no less an authority than the National Conference of Bishops.[16] The idea crops up again and again under different names and in slightly different renditions. For instance, Yoland Bresson and René Passet write of 'revenu d'existence', Philippe Van Parijs of 'universal allocation', Jean-Marc Ferry of 'citizenship income', Jean-Paul Maréchal of 'the second cheque' (see the articles by Euzéby, Maréchal and Bresson in *Manière de voir*, 41/1998).

All sorts of arguments have been advanced in support of the idea. The argument from necessity (a 'no alternative' type of argument: there is just not enough paid work around to secure the survival of all) loomed in the background, rather than moving to the forefront of the debate. Other arguments took pride of place. Some arguments invoked historical justice: the present-day wealth of the West is the joint legacy of generations and ought to benefit all descendants. Other arguments referred to the basic equity of human rights: it is true that everybody has the right to do with his or her life what he or she considers to be best, and the duty to earn the means of making the choice real – but the right to stay alive which precedes and conditions all choice is the inalienable property of all human beings, not something to be earned. Most common arguments, though, have been thus far pragmatic rather than philosophical – pointing to the benefits which societies are bound to derive from enabling people to secure a livelihood without submitting to the definition of work imposed by the labour market. There are many areas which are crucial for the life lived together, for the quality of life and human relations, which require a lot of time and effort but which stay unattended or are poorly attended because of the pressures arising from submitting human entitlements to the verdicts of the labour market. Such areas are, for instance, care for the old, young, invalid and infirm; responsibilities arising from the need to keep the community alive and communal life decent; keeping the environment clean and the landscape pleasing; voluntary work for the sake of shared welfare; or just putting heads together to deliberate about ways of improving the common lot. All these areas and many others (also such as are simply unimaginable under present circumstances, but which are bound to be discovered or invented under more propitious conditions) are laid fallow and quickly turn into wasteland as long as most attempts to cultivate them bump into the vexing question of money to be paid for the work to be done – and so are wound up before they get started. A basic income, such arguments suggest, would release time, labour, thought and will needed to take proper care of the presently neglected areas – to the evident benefit of the quality of life of all involved.

The argument from the need to preserve or restore the basic conditions of republican life and citizenship, however, has not figured prominently in the debate about basic income – not at all as centrally as it deserves. I have no intention to question any of the arguments advanced thus far; they are all valid and all deserve to be considered seriously. And once they are seriously considered, they would certainly be found convincing and appealing. Yet the decisive argument in favour of the unconditional social guarantee of a basic livelihood can be found not in the moral duty towards the handicapped and destitute (however redeeming for the ethical health of society the fulfilment of that duty undoubtedly is), not in philosophical renditions of equity or justice (however important it is to arouse and keep awake human consciences on that point), and not in benefits for the quality of life in common (however crucial they are for the general well-being and for the survival of human bonds), but in its *political* significance, or its importance for the polity: its crucial role in the restoration of the lost private/public space, and in filling the now empty private/public space. In other words, in its being a *conditio sine qua non* of the rebirth of fully fledged citizenship and republic, both being conceivable solely in the company of self-confident people, people free from existential fear – secure people.

The most comprehensive case for the introduction of a basic income thus far has been made by Claus Offe (with Ulrich Mückenberger and Ilona Ostner) in 1991.[17] The authors precede their proposal with the following rationale: 'In this chapter we wish to defend the thesis that a basic income guaranteed by the state is a social policy necessity; that, given the present and foreseeable employment crisis, its introduction fulfils the obligations of a social state; and that, even under these circumstances, such a basic guarantee for all citizens can be realized and also financed.'

The authors, in other words, (1) introduce their proposal as a *social policy* measure. They point out that in view of the shrinking offer of work the orthodox methods of meeting social policy objectives won't do – but (2) they simultaneously assume, though rather tacitly, that there is the political will and force to implement those objectives – by other means if need be. And then (3) they calculate the costs of the measures they propose, with the intention of showing that the costs are affordable; they hope thereby to stave off and disavow what they assume to be the major objections which mean such measures are slow to be accepted by the extant political authorities, or recognized as the right programme to promote by significant political forces. One can hardly exaggerate the merits of the proposal of Offe *et al.*; but the arguments used to convince the reader of its urgency seem questionable on all three accounts (assuming, that is, that the arguments were not, for tactical reasons, deliberately slanted *ad usum Delphini* – given form likely to be telling, understandable and acceptable to the politicians, at least to the politicians in search of a working solution to what they earnestly take to be a problem).

First, the import of the proposal is grossly played down if the basic income is presented as a 'social policy measure'. Such a presentation suggests that the reason to resort to the basic income for all is to resolve 'the problem of the poor' – to lift the poor from their poverty. This, no doubt, is an important argument in favour of a basic income; but if nothing more is said, it casts the proposed measure as another 'crisis management' expedient, another 'one-issue' and 'focused' policy, fully in keeping with the 'problem-resolution' rather than vision-guided strategy of current politics. But basic income is more – much more – than a way to tackle the problem of one category of population while leaving the rest unaffected. On the one hand, its chances of implementation are considerably diminished if it is conceived as the matter of interest only of the poor themselves and aimed at their and no one else's benefit. On the other hand, were basic income to be indeed introduced, it wouldn't change the lot of the poor alone. It would reintroduce ethical standards to the life of society, substituting the principle of sharing for that of competitiveness. It would establish the principle of rights grounded in the enabling quality of being a citizen, rather than in claims grounded in the circumstance of 'needing it most', and hence subject to a divisive and disqualifying 'means test'. And it would change radically the nature of polity; it would transform it from an agency of law and order and a crisis-management fire brigade into a common weal and the arena where individual and group interests are reforged into public issues of concern to all citizens alike. Instead of merely toning down divisions and preventing conflicts from inflammation, the polity might even become the seedbed of solidarity. Last but not least, having liberated its citizens from uncertainty surrounding their survival pursuits, the polity may set them free to pursue their republican rights and duties.

Second, it is not altogether evident that the political class of the day is motivated by the wish, or prompted by necessity 'to fulfil the obligations of the social state', and it is not obvious therefore that the appeal to such motives or 'necessities' (nothing is 'necessary' in politics unless political forces make it so) may cut much ice (why such assumptions are doubtful, I tried to explain at length in my *Work, Consumerism and the New Poor*). The welfare state was a product of a unique historical conjuncture and there is nothing to keep it afloat once the 'overdetermination' generated by that situation ceases to be. With the state no longer bent on the recommodification of capital and labour, and with productivity and profitability finally emancipated from employment, the welfare state has lost a large part of its sociopolitical utility, and particularly that part which underpinned the cross-spectrum consensus. The support of the welfare state was for a long time a non-party issue, genuinely 'beyond left and right'. What is beyond left and right nowadays is no longer the need to keep the 'reserve army of labour' in readiness for return to active service; neither is it the ethical task, chiming well with the above objective – that of improving the lot of the poor. The new across-the-board consensus, to use Löic Wacquant's pithy phrase, is not about making the plight of the poor easier, but about getting rid of the poor; deleting them or making them vanish from the agenda of public concern. This is what the idea 'from welfare to work' (in its British version) or 'from welfare to workfare' (in its clumsier American rendition) is ultimately about. To prove that such policy results in less poverty is a tall order. What it is hoped to result in is a fast-shrinking number of 'people on the dole' and perhaps even a gradual evaporation of the morally painful issue of the 'dependent poor'. The poor are unlikely to get any richer; shifting funds from social wages to subsidies for the employers is, basically, a purely actuarial operation, but one with potential political benefits: it may remove the issue of persisting poverty from the inventory of public concerns (particularly ethical worries) and render more difficult to detect the enormous social costs of the kind of modernization which is set in motion and guided by the price of shares and interests of shareholders.

Third, all arguments in terms of 'affordability' willy-nilly imply the acceptance of the 'social state' as, essentially, the transfer of money from those who earn it to those who don't. That acceptance inevitably relies on a long chain of other tacit assumptions: the identification of work with paid work and social gain with market value are the most seminal among them. Instead of bringing those assumptions into the open in order to expose their arbitrariness (doing it is a necessary condition of 'basic income' success), it obliquely reconfirms their validity while refraining from meeting them point-blank. By the same token arguing in terms of 'affordability' makes the chances of the 'basic income' weaker rather than stronger. Besides, once more the true significance of the proposed reform is played down. If, despite such a handicap, basic income is indeed accepted, the fact of having been introduced under the auspices of the accountant-style calculation will burden it with a potentially terminal blemish tremendously difficult to erase and will thus store up trouble for the future. The policy of a basic income will be condemned to a life of haggling and log-rolling; far from becoming the foundation of new security, it will be another factor of uncertainty. If judged from the republican perspective, the introduction of a basic income as, essentially, another form of redistribution, acceptable on the grounds of its financial feasibility and welcomed and advertised as a precautionary measure against the misspending of the tax-payer's money, is a wasted opportunity to renegotiate the meaning of the polity and of citizenship.

I am defending here the thoroughly thought-through and closely argued Offe/Mückenberger/Ostner proposal against the threats of selling it too cheaply or offering it to the wrong buyer ... As to its substance, it goes a long way towards the composition of a public agenda capable of resurrecting or rejuvenating the fading institutions of republic and citizenship; even more importantly, it offers the potential of cutting the roots of the major contemporary afflications which cause the republic and citizenship to fade, and to shed much of their allure, in the first place. If made into law, the 'basic income' or the *decoupling of the individual income entitlement from actual income-earning capacity* would probably not succeed in eradicating all aspects of existential insecurity (certainly not immediately and in one go), but it does look like the most radical means to remove its currently principal source.

Offe and his collaborators have elaborated their project in great detail, and each of the specific propositions deserves thorough discussion. The authors would agree that many a practical facet of their proposal would benefit from further debate and not everything is foolproof. They would probably accept as well that the odds against the introduction of a basic income may prove to be yet more powerful than the objections they single out to contest – the absence of political motivations or doubts about book-balancing, however daunting such objections may become once the proposal is finally put on the public agenda.

For instance, the idea of Offe *et al.* of guaranteed income entitlement (as well as my previous discussion of that idea in *Work, Consumerism and the New Poor*) was subjected to thorough critical scrutiny in a recent issue of the *Arena Journal*.[18] Trevor Hogan pointed out that the case as presented in the original proposal as well as in my comments was far from complete; in fact, the crucial measure it requires had not been mentioned at all. In Hogan's view, the proposal in its present shape is oblivious to the fact that ours is a consumer society, and to the way in which consumers go on and will go on being produced by it.

The logic of consumer capitalism is to unleash the pursuit of heterogeneous ends and to induce all and sundry to seek individual gratification of infinite desires. Moral communities, and collectivities of any kind, are perennially undermined by a consumerist social order. Schemes to add income and drop the work ethic neither stop the middle class struggling for positional goods nor prevent their fear of falling from their uneasily attained state of grace as good consumers into the fiery pit of the damned.

This, Hogan suggests, won't be changed just by the universal income entitlement. The consumer society will go on doing what follows from its nature – beef up desires and expectations, and topping up ever new commodities on offer with the added value of *positional* goods, coveted not so much for their own sake as for the distinction they promise to bestow upon their consumers; the consumer race is unlikely to stop, and so there will be ever new poor and deprived, ever new 'flawed consumers'. To arrest the race more is needed than offering everyone the chance to participate in it. Hogan recalls that 'most premodern societies place great emphasis on the disciplining of desire and collective restraint on pursuit of material riches'; he points out that, unless some limits are put on presently unbridled desires, the notion of finitude is reintroduced into the life-agenda and societies undertake once more to promote and guard collective restraint, little will be accomplished by even the most radical redistributive measures.

There are no measures which solve all the problems in one fell swoop, and Hogan's critique is correct when he points out that a basic income by itself would leave quite a few unprepossessing side-effects of consumer society unaffected. Indeed, the issue of scarcity and the ultimate finitude of earth resources is unlikely to be resolved; which does not mean, however, that the chances of its resolution won't be improved.

To start with, universal income entitlement will lower the stakes of the consumer game, as gaining entry will no more be an issue of survival. The consumer society in its present form strives to monopolize control over survival; for the denizens of that society, gaining entry to the commodity market and the purchase and consumption of commodities is the sole way to stay alive. This circumstance adds enormously to the attraction of the consumer game; it also invests it with formidable gravity which no one already inside it or knocking on its gate has much chance of questioning. Consumerism is about more choice, but consumerism as such – being a matter of life and death – does not appear to be a choice. Once the issue of life and death is resolved outside of and independently from the market, consumerism may be reduced to its genuine proportions: it may be seen as a matter of a chosen life-style, not an existential necessity. Once the optical illusion of inevitability and 'no alternative', the consumer society's most reliable defence, dissipates – the life-of-consumption-and-even-greater-and-more-fulsome-consumption may turn into one value among others, one life-style among many alternative ones. Having lost the air of no-choice fate, it may be compared with what has now become its realistic alternatives – analysed for its relative merits and vices, embraced or discarded. The possibility of opting out of the consumer game may then become more than marginally realistic – not just for the outcasts-by-decree and vagabonds-by-choice. It is only once the burden of the 'To be or not to be' question is removed, that the consumer game, its worth and desirability, may become a matter of public deliberation and practical choice.

'Basic income' is not intended to be a measure aimed against freedom of choice. Were its effectiveness to be paid for with collective (let alone legislated and *coercive*) constraint imposed on individual choice, such a price would destroy its potential benefits – in as far as they consist, after all, in laying the foundation for a fully fledged autonomous society. The purpose of the republic (if the republic has any substantive purpose) is not an imposition of a preconceived model of the 'good life', but enabling its citizens to discuss freely the models of life they prefer and to practise them; the republic is about widening, not trimming the choices; about enhancing, not limiting individual liberties. The decoupling of income entitlements from paid work and from the labour market may serve the republic in only one way, but a crucial way: *by removing the awesome fly of insecurity from the sweet ointment of freedom*. If something is to be limited, it is the risks involved in practising freedom. But this limitation of risks and damages is precisely the most crucial objective of a basic income. When (if) this objective is reached, men and women no longer afraid to use their freedom may find the time, will and courage to construct ever more humane meanings of their humanity, to consider and select forms of life which are both satisfying and rational.

The focal point of Geoff Sharp's critique, like that of Trevor Hogan, is the destructive impact of consumerism, which is in his view bound to nip in the bud the effects of universal income entitlement, and in particular resist the replacement of the market-oriented work ethic with the impulse of workmanship. That impulse, in Sharp's view, could thrive and guide human productive effort only under conditions of *reciprocity*. True, says Sharp, that 'however suppressed our memories of reciprocity may be, as a form of life, it clearly persists in family life, in friendship, and even in conversation'. But – and this is a huge 'but' – 'as a form of life, reciprocity has never before faced the threat of being totally undermined in the name of progress and normality' – like it is facing today, by courtesy of the eroding pressures of consumerism. Nothing less is therefore required than the 'willed constitution of new practices'.

> Ideally it would call for a capacity to understand how commodity exchange is so structured that it promotes individualism and greed, renders faceless the other in exchange, and invests the things in exchange with an aura of value in and of themselves. A more insightful ethical consciousness of what one was turning away from would be a necessary background for any community of presence and reciprocity.

No doubt Sharp's point is valid. The consumers of the consumer society could learn a lot from Marcel Mauss's reconstruction of a long bygone kind of society in which the *gift*, far from being a (dying-out) exception practised in the few remaining seams of a society sewn to wrap up an altogether different kind of human relation, was the main form all exchange took. But a suggestion that they should start their long and tortuous self-reform by studying Mauss rather than by establishing social conditions for genuine choice (including the possibility of renouncing the life of perpetual consumer choice) is equal to putting the cart before the horse. To read Marcel Mauss as more than a collector of ethnographic curiosities one needs first to be entrenched in life securely enough to dare to swim, if need be, against the current, and to persist in swimming as long as it takes for other swimmers to join in the effort and so, by joint labour of their arms, to turn the current the other way.

As things stand now, it could be surmised that something like nineteen out of every twenty inhabitants of the earth would be on balance better off if reciprocity and commodity exchange changed places – the latter becoming as marginal, or nearly as marginal, as the gift is today. Nothing much follows, however, from numbers, as long as it is but ciphers that make them. Ciphers must stop being ciphers first to make truly rational choices – that is choices which include in the range of alternatives also the meaning of rationality itself; and of images of the good life by which the rationality of choices is to be measured. Lifting the ciphers to the level of rational beings so understood, or at least a more modest task of taking a preliminary step towards it, is precisely the (no doubt distant and only obliquely attainable) objective of the 'basic income' idea.

Recalling universalism from exile

One drawback encumbers the prospects of Offe's proposal perhaps more than any other voiced or concealed objection: under current conditions it is difficult to find an agency potent enough to put the idea through – even if the idea's practical feasibility has been recognized and its immediate as well as far-reaching objectives acknowledged as valid and urgent. As pointed out so many times already, the truly potent powers of today are essentially exterritorial, while the sites of political action remain local – and so the action is unable to reach the quarters where the limits of sovereignty are drawn and the essential premises of political endeavours are – by design or by default – decided.

This separation of power from politics is often referred to under the name of 'globalization'. As I have pointed out elsewhere (in *Globalization: the Human Consequences*), the term 'globalization' has settled in the current discourse in the place occupied throughout the modern era by the term 'universalization' – and it did so mainly because 'globalization' refers to *what is happening to us*, rather than – as 'universalization' did – to *what we need, or ought, or intend to do*. 'Globalization' signals a *sui generis* naturalization of the course world affairs are taking: their staying essentially out of bounds and out of control, acquiring a quasi-elemental, unplanned, unanticipated, spontaneous and contingent character. Just as the user of the World Wide Web can only select from the choices on offer and can hardly influence the rules by which the Internet operates or the range of choices available under these rules – so the individual nation-states cast in the globalized environment have to play the game by its rules and risk severe retribution, or at best total ineffectiveness of their undertakings, if the rules are ignored.

To cut a long argument short, it suffices to say that while the state is the sole legislating agency technically able to undertake the introduction of a basic wage (within its sovereign territory, of course), it is simultaneously singularly incapable of doing this on its own. We can easily guess what would happen if it did try to go alone and will have no difficulty with finding a profusion of facts to back our guesses. A lot may be learned from an American example: once welfare ceased to be a federal issue, the 'negative competition' between the states took off, each state trying to outdo its neighbours in niggardliness, in cutting down welfare services and making access to them more onerous and humiliating – each state being scared of turning into a 'welfare magnet' if it happened to be more generous in its provisions. With the state borders as porous as they are, border controls reduced, and – inside the European Union at least – people allowed to seek domicile and employment in any country of their choice, the same effect might be expected on an international scale, were any of the European states attempting to legislate for its residents life conditions more secure and so more attractive than in the neighbouring countries. Only concerted action, at the continental or even supra-continental level as yet not sufficiently institutionalized for the purpose, could stave off the real threat of the *soi-disant* 'basic income magnet'.

What follows is that once the power that presides over the growing 'flexibility' of life conditions, and so the ever more profound *Unsicherheit* saturating the whole course of human lives, have become *de facto* global (or at least supra-state), the preliminary condition of an effective action aimed to mitigate the level of insecurity and uncertainty is raising politics to a level as genuinely international as that on which the present-day powers operate. Politics must catch up with power which has cut itself free to roam in the politically uncontrolled space – and for that purpose it must develop instruments allowing it to reach the spaces through which those powers 'flow' (to deploy Manuel Castells' term). Nothing less is needed than an international republican institution on a scale commensurate with the scale of transnational powers' operation. Or, as Alain Gresh put it recently in an article commemorating the 150th anniversary of the *Communist Manifesto*[19] – what is needed is a 'new internationalism'.

There are few signs to suggest that anything like a new internationalist spirit is indeed emerging. The outbursts of supra-national solidarity are notoriously carnival-like, sporadic and short-lived. The media coined the telling-it-all term 'aid fatigue' to denote the persistent tendency of international solidarity to wear off and evaporate in a matter of days rather than weeks. As Gresh points out, Bosnia was not a late-twentieth-century replay of the Spanish Civil War; while in the face of the ongoing wars of attrition in Algeria and dozens of other gory civil wars or government-orchestrated massacres of 'aliens', unwelcome tribal or ethnic minorities and infidels, only half-hearted noises are made in conference rooms, but virtually no action is taken on the ground. There are noble exceptions like Amnesty International or Greenpeace, but on the whole the few idealist efforts to break through the wall of indifference muster at best a token or perfunctory support from some state governments (but subterra-nean or overt hostility from quite a few others), and virtually no popular movement to back the attitude they selflessly promote and exemplify. The activists of Médecins sans Frontières bitterly complained that their initiative, cast by the media as 'humanitar-ian action', has been cynically exploited by the powers-that-be to justify their own inactivity in, for instance, Bosnia or Rwanda, and to clear 'by proxy' the consciences of their subjects.

The parochial spirit (*l'esprit de clocher*, as the French call it) rules supreme. The spokesmen of already exterritorial, 'flowing' capital and finances seem to have been the only ones thus far who have raised their voices against it, but their indignation is highly selective. They remonstrate against trade barriers or the control of capital movement and against putting the interests of local populations above those of world-wide competitiveness, free trade and productivity. But they do not mind at all the ongoing fragmentation of political sovereignties, and why should they? The smaller (and so weaker) are the political units, the less chance they have to put up effective resistance against the global finances' brand of 'internationalism' and countervail it with a collective action of their own. And they keep silent about misdirected, xenophobic 'on the ground' responses to their global operations. They do not (neither do they need to) foment such responses deliberately, but they can only rejoice when the anger caused by the growing helplessness of governments and communities to vindicate individual grievances is channelled (and defused in the process) into enmity towards the local 'aliens' – foreign and immigrant workers. And so the public debates about the ways and means to alleviate the sorry state of local affairs focus on the 'foreigners in our midst', on the best methods of spotting them, rounding them up and deporting them to 'where they've come from', while coming nowhere near the true source of trouble.

As exemplified in the popular and popularized rendition of intellectually fashionable communitarianism, the reactions of those under the threat of losing their identity to homogeneous and homogenizing global forces strengthen, if anything, the effects of the pressure. As Phil Cohen pithily put it,[20] 'In such recent writing, the homes from home offered by political ideologies, or religions, popular cultures or new ethnicities have come to seem more like orphanages, prisons or mad houses than sites of potential liberation.'

More often than not, the communal values, ostensibly the stake of the struggle, boil down, as Benjamin R. Barber observed,[21] to the squeezing of Latin rhythms and reggae into the sounds of pop music audible in the *barrios* of Los Angeles, eating Big Macs awash with beer in France and made of Bulgarian beef in Eastern Europe, or demanding that Mickey Mouse in Disneyland-Paris speaks French; concessions which the world-wide traders would not just accept without resistance, but applaud whole-heartedly. One needs to modify the seeds according to the quality of the soil, if the purpose is to gather the same crop everywhere. The global power of the MTV, McDonalds or Disney empires emerges from the 'community-friendly' adjustments reinvigorated and yet more intractable than before.

Knowingly or unknowingly, the separatists of all hues and

colours enter an unholy alliance with the forces of ruthless globalization. It is easier to overwhelm one by one four or five small and weak 'sovereign states' than to throw on its knees a single bigger and stronger state. And so the separatists, and particularly the perpetrators of ethnic cleansing (the measure meant to render the separation lasting and possibly irreversible) can count on the tacit support of the powers-that-be; they may confidently disregard the lip-service paid by those powers and their public relations spokesmen to the noble and lofty principles of humanity and to human rights. What the separatists, after all, accomplish if successful, adds to the political fragmentation of the world on which the dominion of exterritorial powers, their freedom from political control, ultimately rests. The smaller and weaker the many local would-be republics, the more remote are the prospects of a global one.

Fans of ethnic cleansing and tribal purity are extreme cases of the bid for security going haywire. But the advocacy of tightening asylum laws, closing borders to 'economic migrants' and stricter control of aliens already inside the gates represent the same tendency towards rechannelling the energy generated by real threats to security into outlets which, while letting off pent-up steam, prove in the end to be tributaries of the same torrents which erode the foundations of secure livelihood. More often than not, this tendency is aided and abetted by the easily understandable inclination of the political classes to divert the deepest cause of anxiety, that is the experience of individual insecurity, to the popular concern with threats to collective identity. There is quite a convincing pragmatic reason for such a diversion to be politically attractive. It has been said already that since the roots of *individual* insecurity are thrust in anonymous, remote or inaccessible places, it is not immediately clear what the local, visible powers could do to rectify the present afflictions; but there seems to be an obvious, straightforward answer to the other trouble, that related to the *collective* identity – local state powers may still be used to intimidate and turn back the migrants, to put the asylum-seekers under the magnifying glass, to round up and deport the unwelcome aliens. Governments cannot honestly promise their citizens a secure existence and a certain future, but they may for the time being unload at least part of the accumulated anxiety (and even profit from it electorally) by demonstrat-

ing their energy and determination in the war against foreign
job-seekers and other alien gate-crashers, the intruders into once
clean and quiet, orderly and familiar, native backyards.

And so in the language of vote-seeking politicians, the widespread and complex sentiments of existential insecurity are translated as much simpler concerns with law and order (that is with
bodily safety and the safety of private homes and possessions),
while the problem of law and order is in its turn blended with the
problematic presence of ethnic, race or religious minorities – and,
more generally, of alien styles of life.

In Germany Manfred Kanther, the interior minister in Helmut
Kohl's government, in anticipation of the September elections
declared 1998 to be 'the year of security', promising in one go
war against crime and stern measures to curb immigration. Kohl's
opponents, the Social Democrats, neither were nor wished to be
seen lagging far behind. And so Gerhard Glogowski, the Social
Democratic interior minister of Lower Saxony, loudly demanded
the restoration of German border controls since German borders
were in his view poorly and inadequately controlled by the
partners of the Schengen agreement. On both sides of the German
political spectrum, the war on crime merged with anti-foreigner
(particularly anti-immigrant) rhetoric.

On these, as on numerous other occasions, the common security arrangements of the European Union are called into question
and tribute is paid to the memory of nation-state-administered
security. Political leaders of the member states reproach each
other for serving as a sort of 'magnet for foreigners' due to their
manifestation of an unforgivably tepid or sloppy attitude to the
two-faced threat of foreign influx and rising crime; they exhort
each other to strengthen resolve and to flex their muscles in
fighting back that double jeopardy.

Once set in motion, the parochial sentiments tend to gather in
force rather than run out of impetus. Entangled in a mutual
reinforcement loop, the electorate seeking the culprits of their
undiminishing anxiety, and the politicians seeking the ways of
convincing the electorate of their usefulness, produce together all
the proofs which the parochial sentiments may need to corrobor-
ate and, if anything, to exacerbate them. The need for global
action tends to disappear from public view, and the persisting
anxiety, which the free-floating global powers give rise to in every

growing quantity and in more vicious varieties, does not spell its
re-entry into the public agenda. Once that anxiety has been
diverted into the demand to lock the doors and shut the windows,
to install a computer checking system at the border posts, electronic surveillance in prisons, vigilante patrols in the streets and
burglar alarms in the homes, the chances of getting to the roots
of insecurity and control the forces that feed it are all but
evaporating. Attention focused on the 'defence of community'
makes the global flow of power freer than ever before. The less
constrained that flow is, the deeper becomes the feeling of insecurity. The more overwhelming is the sense of insecurity, the more
intense grows the 'parochial spirit'. The more obsessive becomes
the defence of community prompted by that spirit, the freer is the
flow of global powers . . . And so on.

All in all, the public agenda sters clear of the area where the
threats to public interest and individual well-being lie. Even the
movements which try to tackle the public issues evidently born
of global trends find it exceedingly difficult to break through the
magic circle of unbridled globalization and tribal sentiments
which untie the hands of global forces; for instance, the ecological movement, potentially an effective brake on at least some of
the most hideous effects of global deregulation, degenerates all
too often into the 'not in my backyard' policy, sapping in effect
the selfsame global solidarity which it could – and should –
reinforce. The political forces which could attack global insecurity at its source come nowhere near the level of institutionaliza-
tion reached by those economic (capital, financial, trade) forces
which are the source of global insecurity. There is nothing to
match the resourcefulness, the resolve and the effectiveness of the
International Monetary Fund, the World Bank and the increasingly tight network of the world-wide investing-and-clearing
banking system.

By their very nature, neither tribes nor nations (in fact, none of
the extant models of community) are fit to be stretched to global
dimensions. On the planetary scale they have been, and must
remain, the factors of division and separation. The hope that one
can build a planet-wide solidary effort to impose political control
on the global sources of uncertainty through battening down the
national hatches and fortifying communal fortresses – is as mistaken as it is widespread. (I have argued this point in more detail

in the chapter 'On Communitarianism and Human Freedom, or How to Square a Circle', in *Postmodernity and its Discontents*.) Communitarianism is a blatantly wrong answer to the evidently genuine questions. As a remedy against the blight of the endemic insecurity which it is meant to cure, communitarianism is more than a failure; an ever greater part of that blight is today of the *iatrogenic* kind – a result of imprudent treatment with potentially lethal side-effects.

The popular conceptualization of present-day insecurity in terms of 'identity troubles' is a potent case of mistaken diagnosis and potentially harmful prescription. Like so many other (once fashionable, now half-forgotten) sociological models, it mistakes the topic for the resource – it takes the phenomenon clamouring to be explained to be the explanation. Pouring anxiety into the mould of identity concerns is itself an outcome of a long and convoluted series of factors – a symptom, not the cause of the affliction. The popular fascination with the issue of identity, aided, abetted and whipped up by politicians sniffing political (electoral) capital, as well as by the folk (one is tempted to say *volkisch*), mass-consumption, bowdlerized renditions of communitarian philosophy, may be a *sui generis* rational response to contemporary conditions; it may even 'make sense'. But it mislocates its own causes and in its therapeutic conclusions misses them by a wide margin. Militant assertion of group (local, territorial, limited) identity will do next to nothing to remove the source of insecurity which prompted it. It will never be satisfied and will not make the causes of restlessness disappear. Inviting inevitable frustration, it will, if anything, provide more reasons for its own continuing pugnacity.

Multiculturalism – or cultural polyvalence?

Alain Touraine has proposed recently a distinction between the two commonly confused visions/programmes of 'multicultural' and 'multicommunitarian' society.[22]

The first applies to a society tolerant towards cultural difference, to the free flow of cultural propositions and liberty of cultural choices; a society prepared to negotiate continuously the mobile borderline between acceptable differences of life-style and punishable crimes. It belongs to the republican tradition, though it only became feasible once the vision of the homogenizing, 'modernizing' mission, once closely related to the republican idea, had been abandoned. 'Multiculturalism' means, in a nutshell, the separation of citizenship from the cultural assignment and self-ascription of the citizens; making the latter an essentially private matter which in no way affects public rights. It also implies an assumption that cultural distinctiveness does not handicap, let alone disqualify, the citizen from participating in common public life. What multi-culturalism does not assume, though (as 'multi-communitarianism' does and must do), is that keeping cultural differences intact and barring free cultural exchange between communities is a value that ought to be cherished and politically defended; neither does it assume that a meaningful cross-cultural debate about the validity of different cultural solutions and their relative merits or shortcomings is harmful or dangerous – and should be for that reason avoided or even disallowed. In other words, multiculturalism is consistent in its allegiance to freedom as the foremost value: to be genuine, freedom of cultural choice must include the right to opt out from 'a culture' as much as it entails the right to opt in (the demand which 'multicommunitarianism' is up in arms against).

The second vision/programme proclaims the preservation of extant group-bound cultural differences to be a value in its own right. Not only does it deny the existence of an 'objective foundation' on which a critique of cultural choice may rest (this point could be easily granted without risking a conflict with the value of individual freedom), but it asserts in addition that all critique of a cultural choice conducted 'from outside', and so all cross-cultural discussion of cultural values, is both a travesty and an abomination – and that if such a discussion does take place, its conclusions are invalid (on technical grounds, so to speak – whatever may be their substance). 'Multicommunitarianism', in other words, eliminates *a priori* the possibility of sensible and mutually beneficial cross-cultural communication and exchange. It elevates the 'cultural purity' of the group to the rank of supreme value and views all manifestation of culture's absorptive capacity as pollution. It wants cultures to self-enclose inside their respective communal defences (visualized after the pattern of the ghetto).

In the ultimate account, 'multicommunitarianism' cannot, without falling into contradiction, recognize the citizen as the principal public agent (or perhaps even as, simply, a public agent). Community is the only legitimate public agency. The realm of law meant to regulate the cohabitation of communities is viewed as an aggregate of community-oriented privileges. (Will Kymlicka, for instance, argues in fact for inequality of public rights – when demanding that smaller or weaker communities ought to be compensated for their competitive disadvantage.[23] What he takes for granted while making this suggestion is precisely the point which still needs to be proved, being so far just an ideological postulate of the leaders or elders of ethnic or religious minorities: namely, that 'cultural community' is the natural frame for making the sums of relative deprivations for the sake of their collective rectification.)

For reasons which Touraine himself flawlessly spelled out without, however, drawing the necesary conclusion, 'multiculturalism' does not seem to be the most felicitous of terms; it virtually invites confusion, lending itself to mutually contradictory, in fact incompatible, uses. Its separation from its multicommunitarian counterpart, which Touraine rightly demands, would never be radical or foolproof; all attempts to make it so will only go on adding fuel to the interminable, and on the whole unproductive, *querelle* between liberalism and communitarianism. It is better, therefore, to dispose of the term 'multiculturalism' and speak of the *polycultural society* instead.

'Multiculturalism' is a misleading term because it suggests not just cultural *variety*, but variety of *cultures*. More exactly, it suggests cultural systems or totalities – each more or less complete and self-sustained, each to some degree self-contained and 'integrated' – so that all its ingredients, like cultural norms, values and precepts, are interdependent. The term conjures up a vision of relatively enclosed cultural worlds living next to each other – somehow after the patterns of politically or administratively separated areas; one can leave one culture in order to settle in another; one can move to and fro 'between' cultures; one can even speak and listen across the border; but it can be decided with a good deal of precision where one stands at a given moment and in what direction one moves. The term suggests as well, though somewhat more obliquely unless the point is deliberately made salient, that cultures are 'natural' totalities, that being in and of a particular culture is the verdict of fate, not an outcome of choice; that one belongs to this rather than that culture matter-of-factly, through being 'born into' it. Finally, 'multiculturalism' implies tacitly that being enclosed in a cultural totality is the natural and so presumably healthy way of being-in-the-world, while all other states – sitting 'across cultures', drawing simultaneously 'from different cultures' or just not being worried by the 'cultural ambivalence' of one's stand – are all abnormal, 'hybridinal' and potentially monstrous, morbid and unfit to live. All these entities and the suggestions and implications which entail them are products of a cognitive frame – and it is this frame, the legacy of 'systemic thinking' once dominant in sociological thought, which is singularly unfit to grasp the distinctively postmodern experience – whatever might have been its merits in the past.

The reason for such unfitness is not, as is sometimes suggested, the increased 'heterogeneity' or 'impurity' of contemporary cultures. The very term 'heterogeneity' makes sense only as a marked opposition of the more common case of 'homogeneous' culture, a kind of entity which presumes that certain norms, values and tokens 'belong together' more naturally than others, that the 'purity' of compounds is the feature of the ingredients, rather than of the way in which they have been classified.

There is an ideological intent behind every vision of a 'homogeneous culture', and the idea of cultural heterogeneity pays resounding tribute to that ideology. That ideology was hardly ever made salient, let alone questioned under conditions sharply different from ours – when it reflected the modern *practice* of power-assisted homogenization. That ideology was at home in the world of nation-building, cultural crusades, implantation of uniform standards over the variety of life-styles, forceful assimilation and pursuit of cultural harmony. Since then, however, the world has changed sufficiently to deprive that ideology of its hold in political practice, and so to undermine its claim on reality. It is now exceedingly difficult to represent any society as a collection of integrated, cohesive and coherent, let alone 'pure' cultures. For the sake of coming to grips with the reality of contemporary culture, it is therefore high time to refrain from using (once pragmatically useful, now cognitively misleading) concepts like cultural homogeneity and heterogeneity, multiculturalism or cross-cultural communication and translation.

Living together in the world of differences

Far from being a peculiar pastime of a narrow set of specialists, 'translation' is woven into the texture of daily life and practised daily and hourly by us all. We are all translators; *translation is the common feature in all forms of life*, as it is part and parcel of the 'informatics society' modality of being-in-the-world. Translation is present in every communicative encounter, every dialogue. This must be so since polyvocality cannot be eliminated from the way we exist, which is equal to saying that the meaning-establishing boundaries go on being drawn in a scattered, uncoordinated fashion in the absence of a supreme cartographic office and an officially binding version of the Ordnance Survey maps. In the matrix of possible meanings called by Bakhtin the 'logosphere', the multitude of potential permutations, associations and divisions is for all practical purposes infinite, and there is no necessity for those permutations to overlap in the case of their various users; on the contrary, there is a high probability that such an overlapping will never occur.

The discrepancies between the permutations which meet in the act of dialogue tend to be located on different levels of generality – starting from such as are grounded in the idiosyncrasy of individual biography, through various peculiarities likely to be shared by people ascribed to the same class, gender, locality etc. – and all the way to such differences as are presumed to be related to the limited communication between 'communities of meaning', commongly referred to as 'different cultures'. They present, accordingly, translation problems of various degrees of generality – though the individual reader may be excused if, coming across a text with a strange and impenetrable meaning, she fails to note which part of her incomprehension is a matter of personal life itinerary, which a matter of difference in class or gender practices, and which is due to what the theorists of translation would call 'cultural distance' between ethnic, religious or linguistic settings.

The very concept of the 'multi-layered' nature of translation problems is an analytical derivative, already a product of the labour of translation; it derives from the effort to intellectually assimilate the experience of incomprehension – an effort which itself is framed by practices specific to the professionals – the specialists in translation. More than that: what the specialists would articulate as a case of communicative malfunction, as a translation failure, as wrong translation or a specimen of downright incomprehension, need not necessarily be experienced as such by the layperson. On the whole, in most daily encounters, in most modalities of being together, we manage to understand each other in the Wittgensteinian sense of understanding – of 'knowing how to go on' – to cope with the task of sorting out right, adequate or passable responses to each other's moves, even though an analyst would find that understanding wanting, incomplete or illusionary – the illusion being caused by habitualized and mutually tolerated routines of avoidance, rather than the sharing of meanings.

In this common ability to reach effective communication without recourse to already shared meanings and agreed interpretation the possibility of universalism is vested. Universality is not the enemy of difference; it does not require 'cultural homogeneity', nor does it need 'cultural purity' and particularly the kind of practices which that ideological term refers to. The pursuit of universality does not involve the smothering of cultural polyvalence or the pressure to reach cultural consensus. Universality means no more, yet no less either, than the across-the-species ability to communicate and reach mutual understanding – in the sense, I repeat, of 'knowing how to go on', but also knowing how to go on in the face of others who may go on – have the right to go on – differently.

Such universality reaching beyond the confines of sovereign or quasi-sovereign communities is a *conditio sine qua non* of a republic reaching beyond the confines of sovereign or quasi-sovereign states; and the republic doing just that is the sole alternative to blind, elemental, erratic, uncontrolled, divisive and polarizing forces of globalization. To paraphrase the youthfully hopeful schoolboy who was to grow into Karl Marx, only nocturnal moths consider the domestic lamp a satisfactory substitute for the universal sun. The tighter are the shutters, the easier it is to miss the sunrise. Besides, the sun may not keep for ever from setting on even the most powerful of empires, but it most certainly never sets on the human planet.

Notes

Chapter 1   In Search of Public Space

1   Decca Aitkenhead, 'These women have found their cause, but they're not sure what it is', *The Guardian*, 24 April 1998.
2   See Geoffrey Gibbs, 'Demonstrators warn MPs: Get a move on and pass new laws', and Michael White, 'Tighter controls promised as riot over child killer is condemned', *The Guardian*, 27 April 1998. The reaction of governmental agencies to the public outcry fell into line with the priorities and policies which by now have become all but routine. The official projections published on 29 January 1998 anticipate that twenty new prisons will be built in Great Britain at a cost of £2bn and the size of the prison population will rise by 50 per cent in the next seven years, reaching 92,000 by the year 2005.

'The pace of growth in this field is higher than in any other branch of the British economy . . . In three weeks alone, leading to the publication of the projection, the number of people in jails grew by more than a thousand. Two new private prisons have been recently opened, and five more are expected to enter service before the end of the century – but the director general of the Prison Service thinks that the projections err on the conservative side and in fact a further 24 prisons will be needed if the present trends of growth in prison population continue at the present pace.' (See Alan Travis, 'Prison numbers to rise by 50pc', in *The Guardian* of 29 January 1998.)

'However impressive the prison-building boom may be in Britain, it is a small fry indeed if compared with the USA, where deregulation of security, certainty and safety went further than in any other country of the Western world. There, the total number of persons in prison, on parole or probation in 1995 reached 5.4 million and goes on growing at an annual rate of 8 per cent. Since Clinton became president, 213 new state prisons have been built, supplemented by the booming private prison industry. Loïc Wacquant calculates that 'the bulging prison population takes off at least 2 percentage points from the American unemployment statistics'. (See 'L'imprisonnement des "classes dangereux" aux Etats-Unis', *Le Monde diplomatique*, July 1998.)

3   See Jean-Paul Fitoussi, 'Europe: le commencement d'une aventure', *Le Monde*, 29 August 1997.

4   On the connection between speed of movement, structural stability and effectiveness of power, see the remarkable study of N. M. Lee, 'Two speeds: how are real stabilities possible?', in *Organised Worlds*, ed. R. Chia (London: Routledge, 1998).

5   See Hans Peter Martin and Harald Schumann, *The Global Trap* (London: Zed Books, 1997). Also Larry Elliott, 'The weightless revolution', *The Guardian*, 10 November 1997.

6   Kenneth J. Gergen, 'The self: death by technology', in *The Question of Identity*, ed. James Davison Hunter (University of Virginia Press, 1998), pp. 12, 14.

7   Kenneth J. Gergen, *The Saturated Self: Dilemmas of Identity in Contemporary Life* (New York: Basic Books, 1991), p. 150.

8   Harvie Ferguson, 'Glamour and the end of irony', in *The Question of Identity*, ed. Hunter, pp. 8–9.

9   John Seel, 'Reading the post-modern self', in *The Question of Identity*, ed. Hunter, pp. 39–40.

10 Alan Friedman, 'Without structural changes, experts cautious on economic growth', *International Herald Tribune*, 2–3 May 1998.

11 Søren Ambrose, 'Challenging the IMF, intellectually and politically', *International Herald Tribune*, 29 April 1996.

12 Michael Camdessus in interview with Babette Stern, 'Nous avons changé de siècle', *Le Monde*, 24 April 1998.

13 I have argued this point extensively in *Globalization: The Human Consequences* (Cambridge: Polity Press, 1998).

14 Pierre Bourdieu, 'L'essence du néolibéralisme', *Le Monde diplomatique*, March 1998.

15 Interview with Margaret Thatcher, *Woman's Own*, 31 October 1988.

16 'Travelling "The Hard Road to Renewal"', a continuing conver-

sation with Stuart Hall', held in December 1996 in the Open University; in *Arena Journal*, 8/1997.

17   See John Carroll, *Ego and Soul: The Modern West in Search of Meaning* (London: HarperCollins, 1998), p. 1.

18   See Cornelius Castoriadis, 'Pouvoir, politique, autonomie', *Le Monde Morcelé* (Paris: Seuil, 1990), p. 129.

19   Robert Johnson, *Death Work* (Pacific Grove: Brooks/Cole, 1999), p. 153.

20   See Albert Camus, 'Reflections on the guillotine', in *Resistance, Rebellion and Death* (New York: Knopf, 1969).

21   Eric Hobsbawn, 'The nation and globalization', *Constellations*, 1/1998, p. 4–5.

22   See Bernard Cassen, 'La nation contre le nationalisme', *Le Monde diplomatique*, March 1998, p. 9. Cassen quotes also Emmanuel Todd's *L'Illusion économique; Essai sur la stagnation des sociétés développées* (Paris: Gallimard, 1998) to the effect that 'in collective beliefs, "the long term" has no sense any more'. Lives of persons, societies and economies are all inscribed in the 'short term' perspective.

23   Carroll, *Ego and Soul*, pp. 92 and 94.

24   Theodor Adorno, *Minima Moralia: Reflections from Damaged Life*, trans. E. F. N. Jephcott (London: Verso, 1991), p. 65.

25   Decca Aitkenhead, 'Fat is always a feminist issue', *The Guardian*, 23 January 1998.

26   Ronald Hitzler, 'Mobilisierte Bürger', *Ästhetik und Kommunikation*, 85/6 (1996). Quoted here in Mark Ritter's translation, after Ulrich Beck, *Democracy without Enemies* (Cambridge: Polity Press, 1998), p. 134.

27   See Manuel Castells, *The Information Age: Economy, Society and Culture*, 3 vols (Oxford: Blackwell, 1998).

28   On the occasion of the nation-wide outcry caused by Gita Sereny's story of Mary Bell – an outcry promptly endorsed by the Prime Minister of the country – Nicholas Timmins of the *Financial Times* (as reported by Patrice de Beer (*Le Monde*, 8 May 1998) acidly commented that horror, hysteria, hypocrisy and the politics of lynching become symptoms of 'cool Britannia'; the values of remorse, rehabilitation, freedom of expression and of research do not seem to count for much.

29   Phil Cohen, 'Labouring under Whiteness', in *Displacing Whiteness*, ed. Ronald Frenkenberg (Durham, NC: Duke University Press, 1997), p. 268.

30   See *La Justice et le Mal*, ed. Antoine Garapon and Denis Salad (Paris: Odile Jacob, 1997), pp. 11, 192, 208.

31 A Danish People's Party was set up promptly, eager to profit from such sentiments. Its hugely popular leader, Pia Kjaersgaard, who describes herself as '50-year-old middle-class housewife and mother of two grown children', angrily objected to the charges of racism, but then pointed out that 'the Muslims are a problem . . . You must not show a negative attitude towards our traditions and that is the case, I think, for the Muslims. They don't like me.' The People's Party just missed an electoral victory, but the parliament composed of its opponents immediately got down to stealing Kjaersgaard's thunder and proving that other parties are no less 'tough on the unwelcome aliens'.

32 See Beck, *Democracy without Enemies*, pp. 147–8.

33 See Milan Kundera, *The Book of Laughter and Forgetting*, here quoted in the English translation by Aaron Asher (London: Faber & Faber, 1996), pp. 86–7.

Chapter 2   In Search of Agency

1 See Ken Hirschkop, 'Fear and democracy: an essay on Bakhtin's theory of carnival', *Associations*, vol. 1 (1997), pp. 209–34. This quotation comes from Mikhail Bakhtin's *The Art of François Rabelais and the Popular Culture of Middle Ages and Renaissance* (Moscow, 1965), published in English translation under the title *Rabelais and his World* (Boston: MIT Press, 1968).

2 Theodor W. Adorno, *Negative Dialectics*, trans. E. B. Ashton (London: Routledge, 1973), p. 167.

3 Theodor W. Adorno, *Minima Moralia: Reflection from Damaged Life*, trans. E. F. N. Jephcott (London: Verso, 1991), pp. 65–6.

4 See interview in *Le Nouvel Observateur*, 18 March 1992.

5 See Alain Ehrenberg, *L'Individu incertain* (Paris: Calman-Lévy, 1995), section entitled 'La Télévision, terminal relationnel', and particularly chapter 4, 'Le spectacle de réalité'.

6 John Carroll, *Ego and Soul: The Modern West in Search of Meaning* (London: HarperCollins, 1998), pp. 146, 100–1, 142.

7 See Thomas Mathiesen, 'The viewer society: Michel Foucault's "Panopticon" revisited', *Theoretical Criminology*, 1997, pp. 215–34.

8 Theodor W. Adorno and Max Horkheimer, *Dialectics of Enlightenment*, trans. John Cumming (London: Verso, 1979), p. 123.

9 Ibid., p. 216.

10 See Cornelius Castoriadis, 'L'individu privatisé', *Le Monde diplomatique*, February 1998, p. 23.

11 Cornelius Castoriadis, 'Democracy as procedure and democracy as regime', *Constellations*, 1/1997, p. 4.

12   See Hans Jonas, 'The burden and blessing of mortality', *Hastings Center Report*, 1/1992. Quoted after Carlo Foppa, 'L'ontologie de Hans Jonas à la lumière de la théorie de l'évolution', in *Nature et descendance: Hans Jonas et le principe 'Responsabilité'* (Geneva: Labor et Fides, 1993), pp. 55–8.

13   See 'Le délabrement de l'Occident', Cornelius Castoriadis in interview with Olivier Mongin, Joël Roman and and Ramin Jahanbegloo, originally published in *Esprit*, December 1991. Quoted from the version republished in Cornelius Castoriadis, *La Montée de l'insignificance* (Paris: Seuil, 1996), p. 65.

14   Castoriadis, 'Democracy as procedure', pp. 4–5.

15   Cornelius Castoriadis, 'Pouvoir, politique, autonomie' (first published in 1988), in *Le Monde morcelé* (Paris: Seuil, 1990), p. 130.

16   Cornelius Castoriadis, 'Fait et à faire', *Revue Européenne des Sciences Sociales*, December 1989. Here quoted after David Ames Curtis's translation 'Done and to be done', in *The Castoriadis Reader* (Oxford: Blackwell, 1997), p. 400.

17   Hannah Arendt, *The Origins of Totalitarianism* (London: André Deutsch, 1973), pp. 430, 472.

18   Ortega y Gasset, *The Revolt of the Masses* (first Spanish edition 1930) (London: Unwin, 1972), p. 14.

19   Edward Timms, 'Treason of the intellectuals? Benda, Benn and Brecht', in *Visions and Blueprints: Avant-garde Culture and Radical Politics in Early Twentieth-century Europe* (Manchester University Press, 1988), pp. 18–19.

20   Arendt, *The Origins of Totalitarianism*, p. 328.

21   See Peter Reichel, *Der Schöne Schein des Dritten Reiches* (Frankfurt: Carl Hanser Verlag, 1991), chapter 1.

22   See Renato Poggioli, *Theory of the Avant-Garde* (Cambridge, Mass: Harvard University Press, 1968), pp. 60–77.

23   Raymond Williams, 'The politics of the avant-garde', in *Visions and Blueprints*, p. 11.

24   Ibid., pp. 338–9.

25   See particularly his splendid summary of the main propositions in the preface to Claus Offe, *Modernity and the State: East, West* (Cambridge: Polity Press, 1996), pp. vii–x.

26   See Claus Offe, 'The utopia of the zero option', trans. John Torpey, *Praxis International*, 7/1987. Here quoted after *Modernity and the State*, pp. 12, 22.

27   Umberto Eco, 'Apocalyptic and integrated intellectuals', trans. Jenny Condie, in *Apocalypse Postponed*, ed. Robert Lumley (Bloomington: Indiana University Press, 1994), pp. 18ff.

28 'Travelling the "Hard Road to Renewal": a continuing conversation with Stuart Hall', *Arena Journal*, 8/1997, p. 47.
29 See Pierre Bourdieu, *Sur la télévision* (Paris: Raison d'Agir, 1966), pp. 11, 31.
30 Castoriadis, 'Democracy as procedure', pp. 11ff.
31 Offe, 'The utopia of the zero option', p. 20.
32 Ulrich Beck, 'The renaissance of politics in reflexive modernity: politicians must make a response', trans. Mark Ritter, in *Democracy without Enemies* (Cambridge: Polity Press, 1998), pp. 113–14.

Chapter 3 In Search of Vision

1 Ernest Gellner, *Conditions of Liberty: Civil Society and its Rivals* (London: Penguin Books, 1996), p. 80.
2 Ibid., pp. 98–100.
3 Ibid., p. 104.
4 See Hannah Arendt, 'Truth and Politics', in *Between Past and Future* (London: Penguin, 1968); Paul Ricoeur, *Time and Narrative*, vol. 1 (University of Chicago Press, 1983).
5 Mona Ozouf, 'L'idée républicaine et l'interprétation du passé national', *Le Monde*, 19 June 1998.
6 Cornelius Castoriadis, 'Dilapidation of the West', trans. David Ames Curtis, *Thesis Eleven*, 41/1995, p. 108.
7 Cornelius Castoriadis, 'Democracy as procedure and democracy as regime', trans. David Ames Curtis, *Constellations*, 1/1997, p. 6.
8 Jacques Attali, 'Le "Titanic", le mondial et nous', *Le Monde*, 3 July 1998.
9 Pierre Bourdieu, 'La précarité est aujourd'hui partout', in *Contre-feux: Propos pour servir à la résistance contre l'invasion néo-libérale* (Paris: Liber-Raisons d'Agir, 1998), pp. 97, 96.
10 See Pierre Bourdieu, 'Le néo-libéralisme, utopie (en voie de réalisation) d'une exploitation sans limites', in *Contre-feux*, p. 110.
11 Here referred after the quotation in Mona Ozouf, 'L'idée républicaine'.
12 See my *Work, Consumerism and the New Poor* (Milton Keynes: Open University Press, 1998) and *Globalization: The Human Consequences* (Cambridge: Polity Press, 1998).
13 The term coined by Marcus Doel and David Clarke: see *Street Wars: Space, Politics and the City* (Manchester University Press, 1995), also my *Postmodernity and its Discontents* (Cambridge: Polity Press, 1997), chapter 2.
14 See Jean-Paul Maréchal, 'Demain, l'économie solidaire', *Le Monde diplomatique*, April 1998, p. 19.

15 See Olivier Marchands, 'Une comparaison international des temps de travail', *Futuribles*, May–June 1992.

16 See Chantal Euzéby, 'Pistes pour une révolution tranquille du travail', *Le Monde diplomatique*, April 1998.

17 See Claus Offe, with Ulrich Mückenberger and Ilona Ostner, 'Das Staatlich garantierte Grundeinkommen – ein Sozialpolitisches Gebot der Stunde', in *Wege ins Reich der Freiheit: Festschrift für André Gorz zum 65. Geburtstag*, ed. H. L. Krämer and Claus Leggewie (Berlin, 1991). Here quoted from Charles Turner's translation, in Claus Offe, *Modernity and the State: East, West* (Cambridge: Polity Press, 1996), pp. 201–24.

18 See Trevor Hogan, 'Dead Indians, flawed consumers and snowballs in hell', and Geoff Sharp, 'After the poor: a future with the past', *Arena Journal*, 10/98.

19 See Alain Gresh, 'Les aléas de l'internationalisme', *Le Monde diplomatique*, May 1998.

20 Phil Cohen, 'Welcome to the Diasporama', *New Ethnicities*, 3/1998, p. 9.

21 See Benjamin R. Barber, 'Culture MacWorld contre démocratie', *Le Monde diplomatique*, August 1998.

22 Alain Touraine, 'Faux et vrais problèmes', in *Une Société fragmentée? Le multiculturalisme en débat* (Paris: La Découverte, 1997).

23 See Will Kymlicka, *Liberalism, Community and Culture* (Oxford: Clarendon Press, 1989), and *Multicultural Citizenship* (Oxford: Clarendon Press, 1995). See also the perceptive discussion of some of his major theses in Joseph Heath, 'Culture: choice or circumstance', *Constellations*, 2/1998.

Index